MW00991310

THE CLASSICS OF GOLF

Edition of

A HISTORY OF GOLF
IN BRITAIN
PART II

Bernard Darwin
Henry Cotton
Henry Longhurst
Leonard Crawley
Enid Wilson
Lord Brabazon of Tara

Foreword by Herbert Warren Wind

Afterword by Robert Green

For publication in the United States only—
Copyright, Ailsa, Inc., 1990.
ISBN: 0-940889-30-7

Foreword

A few years after the close of the Second World War, the leaders of golf in Great Britain decided that, with the game again flourishing around the globe, it was an appropriate time to publish a definitive book on the game. Eight of the best golf minds in the land joined in writing "A History of Golf in Britain", a large and handsomely illustrated volume that was published by Cassell and Company in 1952. The book was divided into two sections, Part I: The Game, and Part II: The Players. Bernard Darwin, the finest of all golf writers, provided the opening chapter, Then and Now, in which he looked back at the game he was introduced to in England in the middle 1880s as a boy of eight. It is an amazing piece. Darwin rolls out his magic carpet and transports the reader back over the years as surely as Dickens or Trollope, his favorite novelists. The rest of Part I is made up of four lengthy and rather remarkable chapters. The first of these, The History of the Rules of Golf, is a long and scholarly investigation by Dr. Harold Gardiner-Hill, who had become the chairman of the Rules Committee of the Royal & Ancient Golf Club of St. Andrews in 1949. It is a brilliant performance, and golfers who have a deep interest in the rules will admire and enjoy it. The Classics of Golf decided, however, that Dr. Gardiner-Hill's disquisition is probably a bit too special for most readers, and it felt the same way about the three substantial chapters by Sir Guy Campbell that comprise the remainder of Part I: The Early History of British Golf; The Development of Implements—Clubs and Balls; and Links and Courses. A gifted golf-course architect, Sir Guy Campbell (1885–1960) undoubtedly knew more about the evolution of the linksland courses than any person of his time. Ultimately, The Classics of Golf elected to bypass Part I and to bring out a book that is limited to Part II of "A History of Golf in Britain". It has taken the liberty of using Darwin's Then and Now as an Opening Word and of converting the final chapter by Lord Brabazon of Tara into a Closing Word.

The articles that make up Part II are not as lengthy or ambitious as those in Part I, and they have a comparatively modern point of view. The first chapter, Styles and Methods, is an instruction article, but it is a lot more than that, partly because it was written by Henry Cotton, a three-time winner of the British Open, and partly because Cotton was one golf professional who really did his own writing. Born in 1907, he grew up at a time when British golf was undergoing a sharp decline. Beginning in 1924, American golfers carried off the British Open ten straight years. Accordingly, when Cotton stopped this streak with his exciting victory at Sandwich in 1934, he was looked upon as the savior of British golf. In 1937, he defeated a strong field that included the members of the visiting American Ryder Cup team in winning the championship again, at Carnoustie. After the Second World War, he took the British Open for a third time with an inspired performance at Muirfield in 1948. It takes a great player to stay at the top as long as Cotton did.

Near the outset of his career, Cotton did a very intelligent thing. He went to the United States in 1928 to see how we went about playing golf in this country and to study the technique and the practice routines of our best players. He didn't miss much, this shrewd and careful observer. He noted, for example, that many American golf clubs had made provision for a practice tee where a serious player could work on his game by hitting out buckets of balls. Many of our clubs also had a practice green, another new concept that had spread around the country because American golfers realized the significant role that good putting played in low scoring. Some clubs even had practice bunkers to help the members become more adept in playing sand shots. Cotton noticed that a number of our top professionals and amateurs used one basic swing on all their shots from tee to green. Horton Smith, the tall young pro from Missouri, was a good example of a player who had this approach. He had grooved a three-quarter, inside-out swing and drew the ball from right to left on all his shots. However, in 1929, when the new large ball was adopted in the United States, many of the leading American golfers went all out to develop power games, and, in their obsession with distance, they tended to ignore the dangers of the shut-faced swing.

On his return to Britain, Cotton slowly arrived at a very interesting and impressive style of his own. He incorporated in it many features of modern American technique, but he made sure to make his swing a highly individual Henry Cotton production and not just a synthesis of American ideas. He used the two-knuckle left-hand grip. Through hard work and diligent practice, he built up a pair of powerful hands, and they played a key role in his beautifully balanced, handsome swing, a relatively short one on which he barely raised his left heel off the ground on the backswing. He consciously cocked his hands on the backswing, and he hit hard through the ball with his hands and wrists. He was both exeedingly long and exceedingly straight, and he could play wonderful golf in all kinds of weather. If he had a weakness, it was a certain tentativeness on the greens. Cotton thought that the camera was a godsend to golf instruction, and he supplemented this article with some excellent stop-action photographs to illustrate his method of playing the basic golf shots.

The next man on the tee is Darwin, returning to handle a long and complicated chapter, "1848–1914. From Gutty to Rubber-Core". For American golfers, the era of the gutta-percha ball is pretty dulll stuff, and golf becomes dramatic only with the emergence of Walter Hagen and Bobby Jones after the close of the First World War. By that time, the rubber-cored ball, which made its appearance in 1901, had been considerably improved, and golf had come to resemble in its basic respects the game we know today. At the same time, Bernard Darwin's skill as an observer should never be underrated. As a young man growing up in the last quarter of the nineteenth century, he learned that the golfers he got to know as a boy and a young man regarded the invention of the gutta-percha ball in 1848 as the change that made golf an unsurpassed modern game. Darwin feels that way himself. Mid-nineteenth century St. Andrews is a very real place for him. With the arrival of the railway from Edinburgh in 1852, it had come to surpass Musselburgh as the center of golf. There is no doubt in Darwin's mind that Young Tom Morris was not just an outstanding golfer but a really great player. After all, Young Tom had carried off the 1870 Open with a total of 149 for thirty-six holes over the twelve-hole course at Prestwick. That was the equivalent of playing two eighteen-hole *rounds in an average of 74½ strokes at a time when 80 was considered a terrific score. Darwin frequently queried older people in the game about how good a golfer Young Tom really was. In this piece he states, "It convinces me that Leslie Balfour-Melville gave me the right answer when once I asked him, tiresomely enough, how Tommy compared with Harry Vardon. After a moment's thought he said, 'I can't imagine anyone playing better than Tommy did.'"*

Darwin had a special affection for the amateur stars—John Ball, John Laidlay, Horace Hutchinson, Harold Hilton, Freddie Tait, Jack Graham, and Robert Maxwell. He got to know these men well. He considered them first-rate fellows, and the fondness he had for them comes right off the page. Here is part of his evergreen portrait of Jack Graham of Hoylake: "Jack Graham was beyond any doubt the finest amateur who never won a championship, and a far, far better player than many who did. His failure to do so was partly a matter of temperament—he hated to disappoint year after year the high hopes of his friends; partly perhaps the result of working hard at his business in Liverpool and so being quite unaccustomed to a week of continuous golf. The golf that he enjoyed and excelled in was the round on a summer's evening, when he would come back from Liverpool, exchange his town coat for an ancient tweed, take out four or five clubs and some odd balls and run round Hoylake in about an hour and a half with a chosen friend. Then he was wholly magnificent and the scores he could do, and constantly did, in such circumstances were terrific."

Darwin never tired of chronicling the deeds of J. H. Taylor, James Braid, and Harry Vardon, the three professional golfers who made up the Great Triumvirate which ruled British golf from 1894 through 1914. Taylor and Braid each won the British Open five times, and Vardon won it six. In this long chapter, he writes with his customary enthusiasm about the standard of their golf and their personal qualities. If Darwin's prose has an unusual vividness, it is largely because he really understood what he was writing about. In describing the 1914 British Open at Prestwick, the championship in which the era of the Great Triumvirate came to a sensational conclusion, he remarks, "At the end of the first two rounds, it seemed that one out of two of them must fulfill his ambition: Vardon led with 150 and Taylor was second with 152. Being then on the Championship Committee, I was present when the draw was made for the last day's play and can testify to our emotions when the names of Taylor and Vardon came out of the hat together. With the knowledge of what a Prestwick crowd could be, how big, how unruly, how difficult to control as they swirled around the Cardinal and the famous loop, how inevitably they would follow this one couple, there was an immediate and universally felt temptation to put the names back and take another dip into the lucky bag. It could not be done: much agony would have been saved if it could have been, but we should have lost the historic remark of the Scottish miner, who being appealed to make room for the players to pass exclaimed, 'Players be ——! I've come to see.'"

The period between the end of the First World War and the out break of the Second World War produced some of the most memorable champions of all time, and their feats were all the more exalted since golf had become a great interna-

tional game. Ordinarily, one supposes, the committee that decided who should write which chapters for "A History of Golf in Britain" would have chosen Darwin to handle the period of the 1920s and 1930s. He probably knew it better than anyone else. During the Second World war, though, Darwin had written a book called "Golf Between Two Wars" which ranks among his very best work. I would guess that this may have been the reason that, rather than ask Darwin to go over the same ground again, the committee asked him to do "1818–1914. From Gutty to Rubber-Core", and gave the plum assignment to Henry Longhurst. Still a comparatively young man, Longhurst had made a name for himself by his golf writing for the London Sunday Times *and as the author of several felicitous golf books, among them "It Was Good While It Lasted". Longhurst eventually became known on both sides of the Atlantic principally for his skill as a golf commentator on television.*

Longhurst, who was born in 1909, was an interesting fellow. His public school— the equivalent of a prep school in this country—was Charterhouse, celebrated before and after Longhurst's day for its dominance in the annual Halford-Hewitt tournament which decides the British public school golf team championship. Longhurst, who had started golf at an early age, played for Charterhouse. In 1927, he entered Cambridge University, and he captained the Cambridge golf team in 1930. Longhurst was not a sufficiently talented player to be a force in the British Amateur Championship or to make the Walker Cup team, but he was a good enough player to win the 1937 German Amateur championship at Bad Ems. During the war, he served in the British army until December, 1943, when, as the Conservative candidate, he was elected a Member of Parliament for the Acton Division of Middlesex. He became a formidable public speaker. After the war, when a career in politics did not pan out for him, he resumed writing golf for the Sunday Times. *He was very skillful. Limited to eight hundred and fifty words, he managed each week to come up with a crisp, entertaining commentary on the game that was written with a dry wit and a cosmopolitan tone. One pictured countless upper-class Englishmen far from home—in Hong Kong, Yokohama, Madras, Penang, Adelaide, Christchurch, Durban, Alexandria, Palma de Majorca, Funchal, Bermuda, Buenos Aires, Palm Beach, Sun Valley, La Jolla, Victoria, and other such watering places—picking up their* Sunday Times, *along with a gin and tonic, and turning eagerly to Henry to see what the old boy had to report. Many of his fans made certain that they got hold of his entertaining autobiography, "My Life and Soft Times", which came out in 1971.*

Longhurst's success as a television commentator rested basically on his knowledge of the game and his wry, ultra-English personality. He developed an effectively understated delivery in which he let the camera tell the story and added droll comments along the way. For example, after the viewers had seen a player hook an approach shot into a water hazard, Longhurst would add something on the order of, "Oh, dear. That wasn't one of his best." Or, when a wobbly putt just managed to catch the back rim of the cup and drop in, he would solemnly note, "That ball entered the hole by the tradesman's entrance." He also knew the value of brilliant flashes of silence.

In the chapter entitled "1918–1939. Between Two Wars", his contribution to "A History of Golf in Britain", Longhurst is in very good form. The chapter that follows it, "1945–1950. A Fresh Start", is the work of Leonard Crawley. A few year's Longhurst's senior, Crawley, another in the long line of Cambridge University golfers who went on to make golf writing their life work, was on the staff of the London Daily Telegraph and The Field. A vigorous, athletic man with a classic golf swing—he was a pupil of Cotton's—Crawley appeared in four Walker Cup matches between 1932 and 1947. One of his best performances came in the 1937 French Open in which he was the runner-up. A keen student of technique, in the practice rounds before a British Open he would usually choose to watch one of the up-and-coming American stars who was making his first appearance in a foreign land. Crawley was a good man to talk with, for he was a sound judge of talent. The weakest part of his own game was his putting. When, like Sam Snead, he ultimately adopted the croquet stroke, he benefited greatly from the change. In the last twenty-odd years of his life, Leonard and his wife Elspeth lived in the village of Worlington only a few minutes walk from the Royal Worlington Golf Club, the home course of the Cambride University golf team and perhaps the finest nine-hole course in the world. During the week, if he happened to be free, Leonard would often wander over to the practice ground at the club and work with some of the undergraduate players on their ball striking. He was like a kindly uncle.

"Women's Golf", the last of the historical chapters in this volume, is the work of Enid Wilson, the English golfer who won the British Girls' championship in 1925 and the British Ladies' championship in 1931, 1932, and 1933. When her years as a player drew to a close, she became a golf writer, a superior one. Typical of Enid Wilson, her compact history of women's golf in Britain is meticulously researched, nicely organized, and written in a clear and pictorial style. It covers the scene from the organization of the Ladies' Golf Union in 1893 down through the 1920s and the classic rivalry between Cecil Leitch and Joyce Wethered—along with the two matches between Miss Wethered and Glenna Collett in the British Ladies' championship—and it takes the story to the start of a wholly new day with Babe Didrikson Zaharias' successful challenge for the British title at Gullane in 1947. There are passages in which Miss Wilson's chronicle reaches exceptional heights, as in this excerpt from her portrait of Joyce Wethered:

"Miss Wethered, tall and thin, shy and unobtrusive, became a student of the game largely because of the enthusiasm of her brother, Mr. Roger Wethered. When he was Captain of Golf at Oxford, she met and played with his friends, was drawn into their arguments, and must have theorized on the perfection of style and the composition of the swing in a manner which no other woman had ever done before. Playing with the leading amateurs developed her game quickly and made her impervious to superior power. From a quiet house or a secluded part of an hotel, she would come to the first tee, smile charmingly at her opponent when they met at the commencement of their game, and then, almost as though in a trance, become a golfing machine. She never obtruded her personality, and those who played her had the impression that they, the crowd and the state of the game had ceased to exist in her mind and that her entire faculties were being focussed on swinging to perfection and holing the ball in the fewest number of *strokes. The match concluded, Miss Wethered would vanish and be seen no more until the starter called her name for the next round."*

The Closing Word to this volume, "The Future of the Game", by Lord Brabazon of Tara, is a really lifting performance: it affords the reader the opportunity to observe an extraordinary mind in action. During the Blitz in the early years of the Second World War, Lord Brabazon—then J. T. C. Moore-Brabazon—was the Minister of Transport in Churchill's Cabinet. Because of the skill with which he handled that assignment, he was given an even more important one, Minister of Aircraft Production. He was one of the men who really won the war. "Brab", as everyone called him, was not unlike Churchill in many respects. A cheerful man with a sense of humor, he had a wide-ranging intellect. He was equally at home with aeronautical engineers, hard-headed businessmen, and ambitious members of Parliament. He loved to communicate his thoughts and did this most successfully, for he was a fabulous conversationalist and a rousing orator. Golf, which held no appeal for Churchill, was a significant part of Lord Brabazon's personal equation. He played it very well, delighted in the challenge a championship presented, and enjoyed the company of knowledgeable golfers. He was a long-time member of the Rules of Golf Committee of the Royal & Ancient Golf Club of St. Andrews, and he was the captain of the R. & A. in 1952. In his autobiography, "The Brabazon Story", which was published in 1956, he wrote, "When I look back on my life and try to decide out of what I have got most actual pleasure, I have no doubt at all that I have got more out of golf than anything else." This declaration is somewhat surprising when one considers Lord Brabazon's active role in developing different forms of modern transportation. One of the pioneers in aviation— he was well acquainted with the Wright brothers and the Short brothers—he was awarded Aviator's Certificate No. 1 by the Federation Aeronautique Internationale. He was one of the men behind the great British automotive achievement, the Rolls-Royce. As a racing driver, he won the Circuit des Ardennes in 1907. He knew how to drive railroad locomotives, and he had the finest model railway in Britain. Not surprisingly, he was one of the men who pioneered the Cresta run in St. Moritz. He could still handle the run at seventy-four.

In 1952, when "A History of Golf in Britain" was published, there were two official golf balls: the British ball weighed 1.62 ounces and measured 1.62 inches in diameter, and the American ball weighed 1.62 ounces and measured 1.68 inches in diameter. It was generally agreed that the British ball bored better through a wind and that the American ball sat up better on the fairway and putted better than the British ball. How much better did it putt than the British ball? Lord Brabazon, characteristically, decided to test the two balls himself.

". . . I made an automatic hitter of a putt, a rather heavy tripod with a swinging pendulum, which one could adjust, not only from the point of view of swing-back, so as to get the striking of the ball absolutely the same every time, but also for direction by means of an aimer with micrometer setting. Having installed the tripod machine firmly on the green you could direct the ball to a definite position, absolutely, and you could rely on a repetition not only of the stroke in strength but in direction, with unfailing

regularity. Now we know that in our game if you could always hole a six-foot putt that would be very good putting, so I started with a six-foot putt and tried to see what was the percentage of failures at six feet both with the English and American ball. It may startle you, especially you good putters, to be told that at six feet, both with the American ball and the English ball, you can stay there all day and every single one will go in, without exception, for the whole afternoon. Never mind what the slope of the green is, once you have set your machine right, the ball will go in; every time. The second experiment was at twelve feet. That is quite a respectable putt, and the experiments with the English ball showed that twenty out of twenty-one would go in, but with the American ball twenty-four out of twenty-five went in. My experiments were extensive and I can assue you that those results are correct. It is interesting to note, although I am quite prepared to be contradicted in this, that what goes wrong in a putt occurs in the first eighteen inches of its movement."

Just a bit farther along, he has occasion to remark:

"I mention these tests to impress, on all aspirants to great skill, what end of the game should be given most attention.

At present you find most people concentrating on the long game, whereas if we could all hole six-foot putts and put twenty-four out of twenty-five in the hole from twelve feet, what remarkable players we should be."

Not long after this, Lord Brabazon goes on to say: "The trouble about the modern golf ball is that the very hard hitter gets an enormous increase in length over the ordinary hitter." He proceeds to note, "If you take the record of Sam Snead, when he won the championship at St. Andrews he never played wood with his second at any time. Well, that is really reducing golf courses to an absurdity, nothing else." He is all too aware that the day of the 7,000-yard course has arrived, and this leads him to make a rather interesting suggestion:

"This continual lengthening of courses is a thing that clubs object to very much. Consequently you have got to consider in the future what is going to be done about it. First of all, I believe it was a mistake to do away with the cross bunker. It is a very funny psychological thing that if anybody drives into a cross bunker they always think that it is rather bad luck, whereas if they hit over a green all they say is that they have misjudged the distance. It would seem to me that it is a highly desirable thing to introduce the cross bunker again and make people play definitely controlled shots, and it would compel them to play a long second shot, instead of playing the second shot with a seven or eight iron, which the very long driver generally does today. It would introduce that wooden club second shot which was one of the charms of the early game. If we could get that back, I think that would be an advantage."

Moments later, he is off and winging in another direction:

"Now we come to the length of holes. I quite agree that the length of holes is dependent on the efficiency of the ball and how hard people hit it, but, as you look through your career of golf, the only real pleasure is the two-shot hole. If you try to recall the three-shot holes which are really good ones all through the golf courses you have played in your career, you will not remember many more than three good ones. I recall one very well, which has disappeared; this was the seventeenth at Prince's, Sandwich. And I consider

the long hole 'in' at St. Andrews one of the most remarkable of all three-shot holes. But they are very rare, and usually three-shot holes on most courses are of the most insipid and ludicrous type. They consist of a drive, a full brassey and a chip, which is not a very interesting form of golf—in fact, it is the sort of dull golf that women play when playing from the back tees on men's courses."

For myself, this may be the high point of Lord Brabazon's reflections on the present state of golf, but his mind is filled with other possible changes that might be introduced to make golf in Britain an even more enjoyable game. For example, he likes the growing American preference for routing new courses so that the ninth hole, as well as the eighteenth, returns to the clubhouse. He thinks that new golf clubs would be wise to situate their clubhouse so that it affords, as the Royal & Ancient's does, an excellent view of the play on the first and eighteenth holes; he makes amply clear how instrumental the steel shaft has been in raising the overall standard of golf; he is a bit uneasy about the presence in the United States of skillful amateurs who are supported by a patron; he astutely attributes the lower scoring in professional golf in the United States to the increasingly high standards of wedge play and putting; he advises British golf clubs to make certain that women members know that they are genuinely welcome, for otherwise they "are not going to allow their men to go there"; he would like to see an increasing number of public courses in England, and it would not displease him if better instruction were available for young players; and he has a very good word to say for the trolley the average British player trundles behind him—after all, he was the first golfer to go out on the Old Course with a trolley.

Some forty-odd years ago when Lord Brabazon wrote this thoughtful piece, golf was a different game than it is today. Now the top professionals, using clubs with graphite shafts and metal heads and playing the latest version of the Overall Distance Standard ball that was introduced in the United States in 1976, swat their tee shots some three hundred and forty yards down the fairway. Is it a better game now or a poorer one than it was in mid-century when Lord Brabazon, gazing into the future, put his thoughts and conjectures down on paper in his character-istically stimulating way? In any event, it would be helpful if Brab were around today. We could use the counsel of a foursquare fellow who seemed to comprehend the game of golf in its entirety and to visualize its best expression.

One of the ablest young men in British golf today is Robert Green, the editor of Golf World, *a monthly magazine whose headquarters are in London. (It has no connection with the American weekly,* Golf World.) *A companionable fellow with a wide-ranging mind and endless energy, Green has kindly written the Afterword for "A History of Golf in Britain."*

Herbert Warren Wind

A HISTORY OF
GOLF IN BRITAIN

BERNARD DARWIN | HENRY LONGHURST

H. GARDINER-HILL | LEONARD CRAWLEY

SIR GUY CAMPBELL | ENID WILSON

HENRY COTTON | LORD BRABAZON OF TARA

With a foreword by

SIR GEORGE CUNNINGHAM, GCIE, KCSI

CAPTAIN (1950-51) OF

THE ROYAL AND ANCIENT GOLF CLUB

OF ST ANDREWS

CASSELL & COMPANY LTD

LONDON

CASSELL & CO LTD
37-38 St Andrews Hill
Queen Victoria Street
London EC4

and at

210 Queen Street, Melbourne
34 Clarence Street, Sydney
PO Box 9, Wellington, NZ
263-7 Adelaide Street West, Toronto
PO Box 275, Cape Town
PO Box 1386, Salisbury, S. Rhodesia
122 East 55th Street, New York
15 Graham Road, Ballard Estate, Bombay, 1
Islands Brygge 5, Copenhagen
Gartenstrasse 53, Düsseldorf
Avenida 9 de Julho 1138, São Paulo
PO Box 959, Accra, Gold Coast

First published 1952

Printed in Great Britain by the
SHENVAL PRESS, LONDON AND HERTFORD
F.951

FOREWORD

BY SIR GEORGE CUNNINGHAM, GCIE, KCSI

THE honour of writing this foreword has fallen to me as present Captain of the Royal and Ancient Golf Club. The honour is no ordinary one. For this book will, if I am any judge, be a classic in the literature of golf. The names of the contributors, famous for playing the game and for writing on it, are sufficient earnest of that.

There is a wealth of fascinating reading here for everyone, whatever his taste. Whether his fancy turns to the early history and implements of the game, to heroes and heroines of today and yesterday, to incidents and stories of famous matches, or to the ways of hitting a golf ball, he will find in these pages what he seeks.

A word as to the Royal and Ancient Club itself, which has been given an honoured place in this book. The reader will learn how it has happened that the Royal and Ancient is now looked upon as the ruling authority on golf. Both of their privilege and their responsibility all members of the Club are keenly conscious. They also know how much, in discharging their trust, they have owed and will always owe to the goodwill and co-operation of all other Clubs and Golfing Associations. It is fitting here that I should make acknowledgment of this debt.

CONTENTS

OPENING WORD

THEN AND NOW   BERNARD DARWIN

CLOSING WORD

THE FUTURE OF THE GAME   LORD BRABAZON OF TARA

THEN AND NOW

OPENING WORD
BERNARD DARWIN

Then and Now

'THEN' from the point of view of my title is about the middle of the '80s, 1884 or 1885, when I was eight years old or so and had to the best of my belief just begun to play golf. I state the fact thus guardedly because, though I can remember a time when I did not play, the actual beginning has wholly vanished and I first recall myself as, in my infantile way, experienced, if not expert, already familiar with the delicious odour of a professional's shop, compounded of pitch and glue and cobbler's wax, and with the thrilling sight of the vice and the file and the glowing fire and a half-finished club or two standing to dry on the table. Needless to say, I am not relying on those earliest memories alone. They have been looked at retrospectively through grown-up eyes and reinforced by much diving into old books and talking with old golfers. Nevertheless a few of them are so vivid that, young as I was, I think they are by this time of some little value on their own account, as memories of a period in the story of golf which comparatively few can now recall. They are memories, I should add, of golf in England, for it was not till some thirteen years later that I first made a pilgrimage to Scotland. From the point of view of this chapter England is the more important of the two because,though Scotland was very far from unaffected by the rise in golf's popularity, it was naturally in England, where the game had been before so little known, that golf took on the character of a passion.

I think it is fair to place the coming of the boom in the middle or later '80s. By way of example, the *Golfing Annual* was first published in 1887 and I have been laboriously counting the golf courses enumerated in the second number, that of 1888. There are altogether 73 in Scotland, 57 in England, 6 in Ireland and 2 in Wales. On some of the Scottish courses, such as Musselburgh and Bruntsfield in particular, there played a number of clubs, but 73 was the total number of courses recorded in the home of golf and some of these were comparatively new and primitive. This club directory occupied in all 138 pages. Now move on eight years and look at the volume for 1896-7. It is grossly swollen in girth and the club directory takes up 477 pages.

Moreover, of the English clubs there were really very few that had been founded before the '80s. Inland there was Blackheath, of course, going back at any rate by tradition to James I and his courtiers: there was Wimbledon in 1865 and Crookham in 1872. I must not forget the Old Manchester Club which had begun to play on Kersal Moor in 1818, but was at any rate for a while in an almost dormant state. At the seaside there were the two great courses, Westward Ho! (1864) and Hoylake (1869), but when my infant career began there was no Sandwich and no Deal: Seaton Carew was relatively venerable—it was founded in 1874; and then in the early '80s came Felixstowe, Bembridge and Yarmouth.

If there was one year in this period more fruitful than another, I judge it to have been 1887, but however that may be, it is obvious that golf came with a mighty rush towards the end of the '80s. It is difficult to say now how much the fact that Mr Arthur Balfour, as he was then, was an enthusiastic player, increased golf's popularity. Perhaps it only hastened a movement that was inevitably on its way, but that this gallant and romantic figure, the Secretary for Ireland in perilous times, was to be seen playing with guardian detectives hovering on the links, unquestionably had its effect. Mr Balfour's feats at golf had their place in the London papers, which as yet would scarcely afford a line to the most eminent of champions. There was a sentence that used to be treasured by some of the less reverent at North Berwick: 'The Premier made an unfortunate start, put his ball on the rocks and took eight to the first hole.' That referred to a subsequent date in Mr. Balfour's history; the detailed fervour with which the Press pursued him on the links had begun a good deal earlier.

Whatever the exact cause, I think there is no doubt that the great golf boom had begun before the end of the '80s and that the game's popularity surged steadily forward from that time. People often talk and write as if it was the coming of the rubber-cored ball in 1902 that caused it, but I am convinced that this is not so. No doubt this ball, however disastrous the more severe may deem its advent, made the game easier and pleasanter for the rank and file, and so increased the number of golfers; but golf had long since been invincibly on the march and there would in any case have been no stopping it. It might not have achieved quite so world-wide a conquest but its empire would have been a mighty one. This is an opinion to which, rightly or wrongly, I am wholly wedded, and I am glad to see from his book that my old friend, J. H. Taylor, who can give me five years and has a knowledge and experience of golf second to none, agrees with it.

It has often been told how in those comparatively early days of golf in England there was a fraternal feeling amongst golfers which caused them on slight provocation to fall into one another's arms. They felt themselves members of a small community of the chosen, cleaving fast to their own revealed faith, mocked at by a coarse, ignorant outside world. To see another man with clubs in the railway carriage rack was inevitably to fall into conversation, whereas today his clubs mean no more than his umbrella, unless indeed we are afraid he may talk golf to us. We feel towards him rather as did Mr. Michael Finsbury: 'Rather cheery on a desert island but on a railway journey insupportable.' If the grown-up English golfer had this feeling of arrogant dissent, as it were worshipping at a strange altar up an obscure backyard, the small English boy golfer was still more conscious of being one of the persecuted elect, since he had so few companions. Had our family golfing holiday been spent on a Scottish course there would have been plenty of other boys to play with, but at Felixstowe, where we went for several years, I ploughed a very lonely furrow. I only remember two other boys and they were monsters of fourteen or so, I should guess. One said, for I heard him, that I 'didn't play badly for a kid', while the other thought there was about me 'too much swagger swing'. At any rate neither of them ever offered to play with me. By the time I was myself thirteen or so, at Cromer or Eastbourne, I found some kindly grown-ups with whom I could more or less hold my own, but there were, unless my memory is altogether at fault, very few golfing small boys.

And for that matter there were not many golfing young men. A boy's notions on the subject of age are absurdly untrustworthy, but I should say that most of the players at Felixstowe were more or less middle-aged. Mr. Mure Fergusson, the one great player who occasionally shed the light of his countenance on the course, must by my present calculations have been about 32 or 33, and I should think most of the players were decidedly older than that. Again apart from Mr. Mure Fergusson and a lesser but considerable light, a certain Mr. Duncan, with a rather flashy style (here my older knowledge comes to my aid), none of the players had, I imagine, begun golf till well after they were grown-up. There was about their swings nothing of the 'young insolent fearlessness' (to use Mr Hutchinson's fine phrase) of which Willie Fernie, then the professional there, gave so perfect an example. They were for the most part rather conscientious and painstaking in their methods. Very few had even relatively low handicaps, and between them and such a golfer as the great Mure there was a vast gulf. Such at least is my impression. Of course there were in England some very good young men players indeed. Horace Hutchinson and John Ball make two obvious examples, and at such a place as Hoylake, which was an academy of golf with fine examples to imitate, there was a still younger generation growing up (Harold Hilton was then fifteen or so) that had imbibed golf from early youth with the Cheshire breezes. Again, the University Match had been instituted some six or seven years and the very first Oxford side had contained two of the best golfers who have ever played in the match, Horace Hutchinson and Alexander Stuart, but they were wholly exceptional. Most of those who played for the universities in the '80s were the mildest of golfers. In the year 1887, on the night before the match, the Oxford captain walked into a friend's room and asked him if he had ever played golf. The friend, afterwards Lord Russell of Killowen, said he never had. 'That's a pity,' replied the Captain, 'because if you ever had I'd have asked you to play against Cambridge tomorrow.' Further, 'to witness if I lie', the records show that the match was played only seven a side that year, since Oxford were one short.

If not young in years, the Felixstowe players were young in enthusiasm. There was something agreeably schoolboyish in the pervading belief that a red coat denoted a certain standard of achievement. It was not a very high standard, demanding no more, I fancy, than that a man should once have gone round under 100. I do not mean to say that this rule was as rigidly observed as that which forbids a boy, below a certain school eminence, to roll up his umbrella or turn down the collar of his greatcoat, but prematurely to launch into a red coat was like going into tails when your height hardly justified the abandoning of jackets. It was a free country but that sort of thing should not be done. I do not know whether it was the fact of Tom, Dick and Harry taking to the red coat that gradually gained for it an unpopularity in higher circles. In a snobbish world—and aren't we all, or nearly all, a little snobbish about colours?—I incline to think it was. When I went up to Cambridge many people there bought red coats with light blue collars and those of us who were in the team added the university arms in gold and ermine on the pocket. Oxford similarly had red coats adorned with dark blue, but some of the team were not ashamed to do without them. Presently, after my time, the Cambridge red was changed into grey. Oxford, again the first to put away childish things, played sober-suited like ordinary Christians, and soon Cambridge followed their example. And now for a long time past there have been no coats of any colour. Generally speaking the taste for distinctive golfing attire has been steadily dying out. I well remember at the Amateur Championship in 1903, Angus Macdonald, who reached the semi-final, being resplendent in a red coat and a black velvet cap. He was more than dutifully wearing the uniform of the Edinburgh Burgess Society, now Royal Burgess, which was enjoined by a rule of the Society on members playing on the Club Course. Today I gather that the wearing of the gold button suffices. So passes the glory of uniform.

While on the subject of clothes, I do not believe that to play in shirt-sleeves was quite so appalling a social solecism as we are now sometimes told it was. It probably was in Scotland, and to play coatless on any public occasion may have been almost inconceivable anywhere; but the dreadful thing was done in humbler life. Indeed, if it had not, Mr Garden Smith, an Aberdonian, a stern man and a pillar of orthodoxy, would not have castigated the criminals in print as he did some years later. I have a distinct vision of my father playing at Felixstowe in a flannel shirt and the striped trousers of the First Trinity Boat Club, and he, though by no means a slave to convention, would not have deliberately led a crusade against all that was orthodox and respectable. Given a broiling summer's day I believe the Englishman did now and then take off his coat and brave the anger of the gods. On the other hand, I doubt if in winter he ever played in anything but a coat. If he had, I don't think an old friend of mine, Mr Brame Hillyard, later a well-known lawn tennis player, who played for Cambridge in my second year, 1896, would have remained so clearly graven in my memory as wearing a white sweater. He was not, moreover, allowed to do that against Oxford; then he must wear the red coat of decency and decorum. I am almost prepared to swear that *a fortiori* sweaters and woollies were illicit in the '80s. The golfer was not so well off in hot weather as he is today unless he utterly disregarded convention. Neither was he so well off in the cold, for he could not, as he can nowadays, put on an almost infinite number of soft, flexible woollies. He could put one woolly beneath his jacket, but to attempt more would have been sadly to constrict his swing. Assuredly, he was not nearly so well off in the wet, for there were no mackintosh coats or trousers. I shall always believe that the first man to wear those invulnerable trousers was James Braid and that he begged, borrowed or bought them from a policeman. Umbrellas were neither so magnificent in size or hue as they have since become, and club bags had no hoods. In short, the golfer who went out to play in heavy rain got wet through, the grips of his clubs became slimy and elusive as eels, and his wooden clubs generally wanted a leather face next day. Mr G. F. Smith, who improved on Mr Fairlie's irons, by twisting back the neck, once won a scratch medal at Formby with an excellent score while playing in an ordinary full-length mackintosh, but he was a very good as well as a very ingenious golfer.

What other habits, apart from actual methods of playing the game, belong to my infant memories? I think a good many people had lessons, because a good many were in the most elementary possible state. Later on I fancy there were for a while fewer lessons given by the average professional. Then the pendulum swung back again, swung farther than ever before in the direction of lessons, perhaps with this change that the pupils were not so much elderly beginners as good or rather good young golfers, serious students seriously anxious to improve. However, this is but a speculation of my own, possibly ill-founded, which I am wholly incapable of proving.

One thing I do definitely remember from my early days, namely, the custom of taking out the club professional to play in a foursome. This may have been done to some extent as a traveller used once to order a bottle of wine for the good of the house. It was the right thing to do now and then, but it was also a pleasant and beneficial one. There were, I should say, far more foursomes played as a regular thing than there are nowadays. To be sure, there are today a good many foursome competitions and there are besides certain private societies that habitually dine together to make foursome matches and bet on them to a temperate extent. Year in and year out some of the pleasantest and most exciting amateur golf is played in these matches of which the public never hears. But I am thinking not of these deliberately made matches but rather of the casual ones arranged at lunch for the afternoon. They were in my belief far commoner than today.

And it must be remembered that there were no four ball matches, at any rate as far as England and my memory are concerned. Doubtless that form of the game existed. Only the other day I found what is supposed to be the first printed reference to it, in the records of the Royal Burgess Society. It comes from one of the old match or bet books: '11 Decr. 1813. Braidwood and Simpson *v.* Reid and Mackenzie; this match to be played single-handed; Braidwood and Simpson counting holes on their own side and Reid and Mackenzie on the other. No result stated.' Therefore, the game had long been known in Scotland. To the best of my belief I first heard of it when I went up to Cambridge in 1894 from our professional Willie Duncan who had come there straight from St Andrews and told me how the club-makers and other young members of the famous St Andrews Club used to go out in the evenings and play four balls. Whether the more staid and leisurely members of the Royal and Ancient had then taken to the game I do not know, but I have looked at the *Badminton* volume and find that in the first edition, published in 1890, Horace Hutchinson made no mention of the game in the chapter on 'Match and Medal Play'. In the edition of 1911 he had altered the article only by inserting a single sentence after his account of a three ball match in which one player plays the best ball of the other two; 'four ball matches are but an extension of this idea'. That being so, I think I am justified in saying that at Felixstowe at any rate we had not in the '80s been corrupted.

Then what of ladies? I must not trench on Miss Enid Wilson's preserves, and I am in effect incapable of doing so, because I do not remember any ladies on the links in those dim ages. I certainly do recollect at Cromer in 1889 a tiny course of nine holes along the top of the cliff and have a vague vision of an occasional lady playing mild little shots there. I also recall the fact that when I returned some years later the whole of that miniature course had tumbled into the German Ocean. Here again, had I been a Scottish boy I should doubtless have seen young lady golfers, and some very good ones, too, playing on the men's links, but such a thing was a rare sight in the south. It was not, I am sure, till I was fully grown up that I saw a lady who had a real boyish swing that bespoke a youth spent on the golf course. For that matter it was in the '80s and early '90s a rare thing in England to see a man who had such a swing. The swing to be seen everywhere was a laboured, awkward, carefully acquired movement, and the then comparatively

8

rare creature, the boy golfer with something of natural dash and that 'swagger' swing of which I had been accused, prided himself on it accordingly. And I am sure it was very rare among the English ladies (the Scottish ones held aloof to begin with) who took part in the first Ladies' Championship in 1893. There was of course one obvious exception, Lady Margaret Scott, who won regularly by the length of the street, but she was in a class by herself, infinitely superior to all her competitors, having had a boy's golfing upbringing and been brought up with her afterwards distinguished brothers, Osmund, Denys and Michael. Alas that I never saw her play. I only once set eyes on her many years after she had given up the game, when she was shooting with a bow and arrow, clad in a uniform of Lincoln green. By the time the Scottish ladies had begun to enter and, a little later, the two great Irish players, Miss Hezlet and Miss Adair, had appeared, Lady Margaret had vanished, sated with victory. Her photographs show her with a perfectly natural, easy and graceful swing, something too long perhaps, according to modern notions, but then so was that of her brother Osmund, a really glorious hitter of the ball. By all accounts she was not very long, nothing to what we see nowadays, but I have always inclined to believe that blessed with that swing she could have been much longer had she needed it. I imagine that if some of the great lawn tennis players of a past age could suddenly be rejuvenated and plunged into the midst of a modern Wimbledon they would acquire a greater speed and venom of hitting than had once been necessary in their day. So I believe it would have been with this now legendary Lady Margaret. As it was she was as long as she needed, and possibly one may add as long as a sailor hat, a stiff collar, balloon sleeves, a tight waist and a long skirt allowed her to be, but here I am exposing my own ignorance and stealing someone else's thunder.

Now as to the actual playing and the implements of the game. Here I clearly must not rely on memories of my own equipment consisting of three clubs at most. I was playing before the mashie age, not long but definitely before it. I at least dimly recall its arrival, just as I do that of the bulger. I am pretty sure there was no such hybrid as the mashie in 1885, and by 1890 it had become essential. 'But a few years ago,' wrote Horace in the *Badminton*, 'it was almost unknown. Now its use is universal.' The pitching club in my earlier days was a lofting iron and the wooden clubs were still relatively long in the head and shallow in the face. I have studied yet again the lists of clubs given in two books belonging to the period, namely *Golfing*, published by Messrs W. and R. Chambers in 1887, and the far more famous *Badminton* volume of 1890. Sir Walter Simpson's *Art of Golf*, though a most entertaining book, does not to any great extent elucidate the question of clubs. In *Golfing* the whole chapter on 'The Game of Golf' occupies only some 28 pages in all. Of clubs it enumerates five wooden ones, the play-club, long and short spoons, brassey and putter and three iron ones, the sandiron, cleek and niblick.

Three more clubs said to be 'in occasional use' are all of wood, namely, the mid spoon, the baffing spoon and the driving putter. This seems to me, according to the bags that I remember, an intolerable deal of wood to one half-pennyworth of iron. I feel that Mr. Robert Chambers, Junior, who wrote the chapter, a fine golfer in his day, is going back too far. Therefore I turn to the *Badminton*, and on the first instant the picture called 'Modern Golf Clubs' gives me an unpleasant shock, for here are seven wooden clubs, including the putter, a perfect regiment of spoons, and only four iron ones, of which one is an iron putter. However, I am greatly encouraged when I turn to the text in which Horace informs me that 'a few years back the golfer did not deem himself armed at all points unless his equipment included a graduated series of spoons', but that 'in place of the numerous spoons of a nearly bygone age there has come into very general use a club that is named the "brassey".' That confirms my youthful memories. The short spoon there was as there is still, though it has lost its epithet, but all the other spoons had in England at any rate, and as regards the common man, become part of the historic past. Moreover, I think I know why Mr. Chambers was rather too archaic. He had, we are told, first published his article on 'The Game of Golf' in 1862, but it had been 'completely remodelled and brought up to date'. I can only respectfully hint that he had stopped short somewhere in the '70s and not remodelled it enough. I suggest that in England in the '80s the average golfer's bag contained a driver or a brassey, a cleek, two irons (driving and lofted), a niblick and a putter; also that the putter was far more often of iron than wood, and sometimes, alas, it was of gun-metal; generally of the kind that may today be hired for a penny on a public putting green, very upright in the lie, very straight in the face. Willie Park had not then invented his goose-necked putter, though that came soon afterwards. Neither, by the way, had Mr. Frank Fairlie designed his irons with the heel set in front so as to abolish the dread disease of socketing.

I am very sure of one thing, that the clubs with which the ordinary golfer was provided were vastly inferior to those we can buy nowadays. The good player was but poorly equipped compared with his successor, and, as for the bad player, he had to take what he could get, and it was often a thoroughly bad club, with spring everywhere or spring nowhere, and a head that 'lay off'. I fancy that a good many of the clubs in the shop were too long in the shaft and altogether too cumbrous. I possess an ancient driver which dear old Jack Morris of Hoylake gave me. It has but a single mark on it, the mark of a ball on the extreme heel almost off the face. I suppose some beginner had retired disgusted after that single attempt and Jack, who was kindness itself, had taken it back into stock. The beginner was right, if more by luck than judgment, for it is a really shocking club, and its peers could have been found in any shop in England. Mr. Chambers' manual says that 'the usual length of a play club is 45 inches', a fact that confirms my belief that many people set out to play with clubs too long for them; the tail waggled the dog. Nearly all clubs had thick grips, of horrid slippery leather, with a solid roll of some cloth, or kindred substance, underneath. This was largely due, no doubt, to the palm grip, or some variant of it, being so common. As soon as the overlapping grip with the club held more in the fingers became popular, the padding under the leather naturally became much thinner. Mr. Laidlay had used this grip, and no doubt some of his admirers in the Lothians imitated him. But it was first Taylor, and a year or two later Vardon, whose name was given to it, that made it widely known, and then the thick leather grips came down with a run. Whether thick or thin, something in the nature of pitch was needed to make it possible to hold them, especially when they were new and yellow, and the golfer carried a bit of pitch in his pocket as the billiard player carries chalk. He went into the shop to beg for a bit and the kind professional cut off a triangular piece of leather in which to wrap it; but it often escaped and made a sad, and sticky, black mess at the bottom of his pocket, a mess in which pencils might be found stuck, like flies in amber.

In the matter of golf balls I remember dimly that people spoke of 27s and 28s, which were the two common sizes, their titles being supposed to refer to their weight in drachms; but the real point of controversy was between the Gutty and the Putty, the Silvertown and the Eclipse. The Eclipse is long since forgotten; its brief and brilliant prime was in the '80s, but it survived into the next decade, for in the *Golfing Annual* for 1896-7 there is a full-page advertisement of it showing a gentleman with a cricket cap and a long curly moustache addressing the ball with an immense cleek, having only the extreme heel of the club on the ground. It was supposed to be a composition of gutta-percha, vulcanized india-rubber and cork. It was not superficially attractive, having a dull yellowish skin embossed with a pattern of St Andrew's crosses, nor did it make, when struck, the clean attractive click that the Silvertown did. As a small boy I naturally played with anything I could get or was given, and in any case my opinion of the ball's merits would be valueless. I have been re-reading Horace Hutchinson on the subject, and he was very kind to the Eclipse, as indeed he ought to have been, for he won the first two Amateur Championships of 1886 and 1887 when playing with it. It was not, I gather, a great carrying ball, but it had the compensating advantage of keeping very low against a wind; it was less liable to slicing and pulling, and it had a very long run on a hard ground. It was difficult to stop on the green, but once there it was, says Horace, 'a wonderful ball for keeping the line—far the best putting ball that has ever come into being during the half century or so of golf that I have known'.

The difference of opinion over the ball question arose most vehemently in foursomes, each partner declaring himself wholly incapable of playing with the ball his ally wanted. Still the Eclipse was very popular, except with the professionals, who had, I fancy, professional reasons for disliking it, and it ought to have had a long career since it was very economical. Though comparatively soft, it was hard to destroy, and it was not destructive to the faces of wooden clubs. Mr. James Balfour, Leslie Balfour Melville's father, who wrote an engaging little book of golfing memories in 1887, said in it, 'It is not improbable that the Eclipse will be the ball of the future.' And then, when its prospects were apparently so bright, misfortune rather mysteriously overtook it. According to Horace, the manufacturers wanted to make it harder and 'began to make it less good'. Clearly, from that advertisement, the ball struggled on into the '90s, but its day was done. My only definite recollection of it is of having run out of balls when in an impoverished state at Eton (the greedy river devoured many balls) and buying a single one in a photographer's shop. It was old and yellow, with a dirty complexion, and I could scarcely get it off the ground. I had not recognized it at first, but it was an Eclipse. If, like its predecessors, it was 'sunk beneath the watery floor', I am sure I wept few tears and to the best of my belief I never saw an Eclipse again.

As compared with the modern player, he of the '80s was starved for golfing literature, especially didactic literature. The pleasant little weekly *Golf*, in its scarlet cover, the forerunner of our present *Golf Illustrated*, had not yet appeared, and the daily papers might be searched in vain. There was Mr. Clark's *Golf: a Royal and Ancient Game*, but that was rather a book of history and did not profess to teach golf. To a grown-up student it is fascinating, but not to eager youth. The only books I had any knowledge of were first of all Horace Hutchinson's *Hints on Golf*, an entertaining little book, published in 1886, which became famous for a single phrase, 'Golf is not agriculture'. Then there was in 1887 Mr. Chambers' book before mentioned, followed by Sir Walter Simpson's *The Art of Golf*, and then the *Badminton* volume edited by Horace, with contributions by others, including Sir Walter, Arthur Balfour and Andrew Lang, and, as I think, deplorable comic pictures by Harry Furniss; I cut them all out of my copy at an early age. The *Golfing Annual* first appeared in 1887, but the articles in that were seldom didactic and too often facetious. In fact, the aspiring student had but few theories with which to bemuse his brain and was perhaps none the worse for that.

The Chambers' book, *Golfing*, regarded as a manual of instructions, is beautifully innocent. It gives not one but half a dozen examples to illustrate the method of scoring, it being apparently thought that such terms as 'the odd' and 'the like' and 'one off two' were terribly hard for the poor Englishman to understand, so that they must be rammed into him by main force. It describes the various clubs at some length and has something to say about the stance, but as to the swing we are

12

told no more than this, that a little practice will soon teach 'that indispensable free motion of the arms which allow of the club having full and easy play'. There are also two pictures of a gentleman with a bowler hat and a right elbow lifted on high in exquisite agony, and that is really all as far as learning is concerned; but there is some general reading, such as the well-known and amusing verses describing the different holes at St. Andrews and a story called 'How I won my pulpit', which I am incapable of criticizing, having loved it now too long.

Sir Walter Simpson's book is a golfing classic in its not too technical aspects. It is the wittiest of books, and no one has ever penetrated so deeply into the follies of the golfing heart, the wild hopes of having discovered the secret and the despair of losing it again. His golfer who 'makes a fetish of his big toe which he believes to be the God of driving' stands for ever mocking us down the ages. No man ever laughed at us so delightfully for all the foolish things we do in trying to learn golf, but I doubt if he taught us many wise ones in their place. Horace Hutchinson says of him that 'there were many strokes in the game of which he had no idea', and I suspect that rather cruel verdict of being in the main justified. He had himself, by all accounts, an elaborate and laborious swing, an imitation of the real thing rather than the thing itself. I have always liked a story of him playing at Hoylake on a windy day and making very heavy weather of it, while his adversary, Mr Bob Hutchison, was cunningly cheating the gale with a half swing and low cleek shots. 'Look at Mr. Hutchison,' said his Scottish caddie, 'he's no playin' a proud game.' But if Sir Walter was not, I think, a great teacher, he wrote a book for which we should ever be grateful.

And then soon after him, in 1890, came the *Badminton*, and that for me at least, and I think for many people, marked an era. I do not remember that on its first appearance I read the instructional parts so assiduously as I no doubt ought to have, for it was called 'Elementary Instruction', and in my youthful vanity, being then fourteen and a seasoned golfer, I did not regard myself as elementary. But there were the chapters on famous links and famous players and Sir Walter Simpson on 'Out of Form' (my vanity did permit me now and then to be out of form). Those three were perhaps my favourites, but if I pored most lovingly over them, I read every word in the book, as I have often done since. I doubt if any subsequent book on golf has contained so much good writing. As far as actual teaching is concerned it preaches in many respects an outworn creed. Horace himself, though a very fine player, indeed in my view a player of unquestionable genius, had in his methods some eccentricities of genius, and never perhaps wholly appreciated the fact. So he was now and again inclined to teach heterodoxy under the belief that it was orthodoxy. Again he was to some extent misled by the photographs from which the illustrations were made. They were not instantaneous but posed and so are inevitably deceptive. Therefore, though there is still much wisdom to be found in

13

the instructional chapters, they are no longer representative of modern golfing theory, and the learner of today will hardly found his game upon them. Golf has made vast strides since 1890, and much hard thinking and many hours of practice have been devoted to discovering the best ways of playing it. What was once good sound Sixth Form learning is, even if not wholly out of date, now better suited to Shell or Remove. Yet, when all is said, I still cherish, and, what is more, still read my *Badminton*, and of most of those who write about golf today I 'only wish they had half its complaint'.

The *Badminton*, incidentally, may be said to have marked a new epoch in that it was published by an English firm and edited and largely written by an English golfer. True there had been Horace's *Hints on Golf* before mentioned: true also that the *Badminton* had highly distinguished·Scottish contributors, but compared with all its predecessors it may be said to have been an English book. Horace himself had struck another stout blow for England when he had won the first Amateur Championship in 1886, and no doubt England was beginning to stand up for herself; but she was still conscious that she was merely a pupil, learning a Scottish game in the main from Scottish masters, and was very properly anxious to conform to the standards of Scottish custom and behaviour.

There was at least one admittedly not very important respect in which England was more docile than she has since become. She was more apt to give names to the holes on her courses than she is today. Presumably, when there were so far fewer courses in the world and a golfer was likely to play nearly all his golf on only one of them, names attached themselves to well-known holes. As courses grew more numerous and golfers made pilgrimages to distant shrines, so they grew less familiar with any particular one, and the old intimate names were superseded by numbers. Whatever the reason, I fancy the early English golfers deemed it their duty to name their holes in pious imitation of the Sea Hedrig or the Corner of the Dyke or Mrs Forman's, and it is noteworthy that the earliest of the great English courses, Hoylake, has a full complement of names for its holes, to which it has always been faithful. The holes may change their place and their character but not their names. The present Hilbre is wonderfully unlike the old one but it is the Hilbre still, just as the Rushes is the Rushes purely on hereditary grounds.

I doubt whether even at Hoylake people use those sacred names as strictly as they did once, and for that matter I fear that there is a certain laxness at St Andrews —but let us forget so painful a circumstance. Once upon a time the newest of English courses tried to follow in the ancient ways, and at Felixstowe every one of the nine holes had a name, some of which have now, alas, escaped me. The second was the Gate and the last four I can still lovingly recite: Eastward Ho!, the Ridge, Bunker's Hill and the Point. Eastward Ho! has now something of an artificial sound in my ears, as if it had been too deliberately invented. I question

14

whether anyone habitually used it, but as to the last two at least let there be no impious doubts. They still sound formidably in my ears.

Generally speaking, I believe it is in vain solemnly to christen the holes of a course. Such names will soon be forgotten. Only those remain, as a rule, that have some geographical appropriateness. A committee may invent brilliant and felicitous names and be mightily pleased with themselves, only to be disappointed. Good, honest, commonplace names are what are needed. The Field, the Lake and the Royal, however sacred they have become, are superficially dull enough names, but they stick because they were rationally descriptive.

I remember that when the Aberdovey course had taken on the dignity of a club, my uncle, its chief creator, took infinite pains to name all the holes. The names were on the plan of the course; they were printed on the cards; they were on paper perfectly good names, but in fact, except for two of them, nobody ever used them and they were all forgotten in a year. The two that stuck have been used ever since—Cader for the sandhill to be surmounted at the third hole, and the Crater for the green in a hollow at the 15th. Much the same thing has happened on all the courses of England. The Maiden, Hades and the Suez Canal have stuck at Sandwich: the Sandy Parlour at Deal is in jeopardy because the green has been changed, though the name is not yet forgotten. The same may, I imagine, be said of Majuba at Burnham. Every here and there an old name sticks, but people do not now use them for conscience' sake, because they believe it is their duty and the tradition of the game to do so. It is perhaps a little sad but there is nothing whatever to be done about it.

Another reason for feeling a very proper respect for Scotland was that practically all the professionals in the middle '80s were Scotsmen. The time of the English professionals was soon coming. It was on New Year's Day 1891 that a boy of nineteen called Taylor went from Westward Ho! to keep the new green at Burnham, and within a year or so he had done a most impious deed, he had beaten one of the most famous of Scotsmen, Andrew Kirkaldy, in a home and home match over Winchester and Burnham. It was a little later, I suppose, that Harry Vardon went from Jersey to Bury, and with those two began the great school of English professionals. But in the '80s they were still too young, scarcely emerged from the caddie, and the Scots reigned in England. Those must have been exciting years for the young Scotsman longing to make golf his livelihood and having the chance of doing so if he dared the great southern adventure. I have again been studying my *Golfer's Annual* of 1888 to see what I can discover in this regard. It is a little baffling that the directory of golf clubs deals not in professionals but 'green-keepers'. Here and there there is one too distinguished to be called anything but a professional, such as Charles Gibson at Westward Ho! and Jack Morris at Hoylake. Willie Fernie, now translated from Felixstowe to Troon, has the sonorous and all-embracing title of 'Greenkeeper, Clubmaster and Professional'. In some cases that I can myself remember the man so designated was a greenkeeper and nothing else, but there are plenty of others where he was emphatically a professional golfer as well. At St Anne's, for instance, the greenkeeper is George Lowe of Carnoustie, the club proudly flaunting his Scottish origin, and three or four years later, at Huddersfield, I light on another more famous, entitled as might be a laird, Alexander Herd of St Andrews.

It is therefore a task statistically beyond me to discover how many genuine professionals there were, in our modern sense of the word, and how many green-keepers pure and simple; but one thing is clear, that in many, probably in most cases, the professional was to a great extent a man of all work who doubled the parts. Often, no doubt, he had some help on the course, but I fancy not always even that. I believe that when Harry Vardon first went to Bury he had to do the rolling of all the nine greens. Again, in Taylor's delightful autobiography we find him going off to his first professional job at Burnham, taking the sole responsibility for the keeping of the course, building tees with his own hands and generally engaging in a desperate day-to-day fight against the encroaching sand. I remember coming across an ancient account of Saunton, telling how the wind 'doth play the tyrant in this tract'. So did the wind at Burnham and nearly overwhelmed J. H. with sand, so that he finally departed to Winchester to escape that unending battle.

This was, he says, a dangerous enterprise, since Winchester only offered a six months' engagement, feeling that it could not afford a full-time professional. That was the position of many clubs and made a professional's life the more hazardous; the club might only want him for the summer season. It was by taking such a risk that Sandy Herd began his professional career, in accepting a summer engagement at Portrush. He came back to pour forty golden sovereigns into his mother's lap (like Denry Machin on his return from Llandudno in *The Card*) and declared that if such wealth could be gained he would do no more plastering. He had been both a baker and a plasterer; Jack Burns who won the Open Championship was a plasterer: David Brown, another champion, was a slater, and Douglas Rolland a stonemason. These fine players and others had worked at a trade because there were not in Scotland nearly enough professional jobs to go around. Now, with golf beginning to boom in England, came their time to cry 'Forth Fortune' and take a cast across the Border. These were all great men, but to me the greatest must always be Willie Fernie. I can see him now in his shirt sleeves and a yachting cap with a shiny peak coming out of his little shop opposite the Martello Tower at Felixstowe, waggling a half-finished club in his vigorous wrists. Once he came within inches of killing me with a villainous, low, half-topped hook, as I lay cowering in a bunker called Morley's Grave. It nearly proved my grave, too, and in my hero-worship I nearly thought it would have been a lovely death.

16

PART II

THE PLAYERS

HENRY COTTON

Styles and Methods

SINCE Sir Walter Simpson wrote *The Art of Golf* in 1887, golf has gone a long way. His book may not have been the first book on the game, but it is one of the earliest which attempted to give golf readers some theory of the game.

To show that there is really little new in golf except the equipment itself, I will quote a few words from the chapter 'Of Driving in General': 'Do I maintain, then, the reader may ask, that everyone ought to have the same style? By no means; on the contrary for you or me to model ourselves on a champion is about as profitless as to copy out *Hamlet* in the hope of becoming Shakespeare. There is no more fruitful source of bad golf than to suppose there is some best style for each individual which must be searched out by him if he is to get the best results out of himself. In a broad and general way, each player ought to have, and has, a style which is the reflection of himself, his build, his mind, the age at which he began, and his previous habits.'

Here we have written in 1887 truths which are still true today, yet many famous golfers still contribute golf books in which they pursue one theory and ignore such words of wisdom. I can only assume that they *believe* there is one system, or alternatively are catering to public demand or satisfying their publishers' request.

In the days of the hickory shaft and the stony gutty—it seems pointless to go back to the feather ball days, for there I am sure it was essential to 'nurse' the ball to stop it bursting—players began to play more as balls were plentiful and cheap and to hit the ball as hard as they could. With hard hitting came the necessity to insulate the shock, and that is one reason for the thick grips then used generally. The thick grips, leather faced clubs (so faced to absorb shock and to protect the soft beechwood heads), I feel, made gripping of the club a job for the palms and not for the fingers and hands as today.

Whilst gripping the club was not ignored in teaching golf, one has only to look at the photos of old golfers taken playing some fifty years ago to realize that the shaft slid about in the hands freely.

I am astounded that with such loose grips Harold Hilton, John Ball Junior, H.G. Hutchinson, J. L. Low and Edward Blackwell—to name but a few top players of the end of the nineteenth century—could win fame. For they held the club in the palms of both hands, left thumbs outside, and then allowed the hands to slide on the shaft during the swing—an action which we condemn strongly today. J. H. Taylor, Harry Vardon, James Braid, L. Balfour Melville, R. Maxwell, John Graham Junior, were amongst players of the same era who had grips that would be accepted as sound today. This is really an understatement, for the modern overlapping grip is accredited to Harry Vardon—although there is evidence that Leslie Balfour Melville used it first, and J. H. Taylor, using the overlapping grip, was also winning before Harry Vardon scored major successes.

'Keep your eye on the ball' is by no means a new slogan. It has been an essential part of the game of golf ever since the game started, and the fact that you could stare at the ball too much has also not escaped notice. In the 1880s, before the overlapping grip was recognized as a help to getting the hands working together, players were advised to keep their hands as near to one another as possible. To show the importance of this Sir Walter Simpson warns players that every inch the hands are apart knocks 10 yards off the length of the shot. I have never thought of such positions in terms of inches and yards, but I imagine he must have got the information from somewhere.

Style as such seems to be given a smaller and smaller place in the game, for today no one really cares if certain players look elegant when they play—only results talk. It does so happen fortunately that most of the great players today look grand when they play, but we have had winners also who appear quite unorthodox with methods which confound many accepted theories.

Years ago, style was admired, I suppose, more in life in general; now utility and efficacy have out-done sheer beauty. Style was looked upon as an essential part of the make-up of a golfer. Today, unless it justifies the end, it can be ignored.

With the exception of J. H. Taylor, who was a short sturdy player of exceptional strength for his size, all the great golfers of years ago had long free swings, and seemed to throw themselves about more as they hit. I am sure that the ball itself had much to do with this, for unless you have played a gutty ball you cannot imagine what an unresponsive object it is and what an effort it takes to drive it 200 yards. As I write this I am looking at an impact photograph (Beldam's *Great Golfers*, p. 148) of J. H. Taylor taken in 1903 at a speed of one-thousandth of a second, in which he is seen hitting the ball with a driving mashie, which fitted in his set between the cleek and the mashie iron. By today's standards the cleek would be a strong No. 2 iron and the mashie iron a strong No. 4 iron, so the driving mashie would be a No. 3 or thereabouts with a medium deep face. Taylor hit that particular shot 150 yards—a very good shot for those days. Beneath the photo

116

of a drive taken at the same period it mentioned the shot as being of 200 yards in length.

The surprising thing when getting down to make a study of styles and methods of today and yesterday is that they are fundamentally so nearly similar that the hints of yesterday can apply today and tomorrow. Here is a series of 'Do's and Don'ts of the day' written nearly fifty years ago (with my comments after them) which remain as enlightening to today's reader as they did no doubt to the reader in knickerbockers, cap and Norfolk jacket—the golfer's dress of those days.

Don't take the club back too quickly. This advice can surely never change.

Don't hurry downward swing but allow the club naturally to increase speed. This can be the old way of saying 'swing the club-head', a slogan of today which brings in countless dollars to a few instructors in the USA.

Don't think of the circle described in the swing as being vertically up and down the line of flight of the ball, as in cricket. Golfers claimed most of their successful adherents from the cricket field, but already in these days the path of the club-head was seen as not being a circle but a looping movement. This shows that all the astonishment expressed by the golfing world on discovering Bobby Jones' perfect flowing swing was looping as it was flowing was a display of ignorance, for it was already known years earlier that a golf club-head did not follow a perfect circular route.

Don't swing any club so far back as to lose control of it. Today we might say, do not overswing: or, as I wrote in my first golf book when talking of the three-quarter swing, that it was preferable to hold on to the club all the time, and be restricted by the flexibility of the left wrist to a less than full back swing, if to swing to the horizontal meant letting go.

Don't forget the club-head should be travelling at its greatest velocity when it reaches the ball, having gradually increased in speed, with no perceptible pause on the top of the swing. This would today be written as 'hit late', get the maximum speed at impact, but the 'no perceptible pause on the top of the swing' seems hard to explain.

Don't hit at the ball; the rhythm of the swing must not be destroyed. 'Slow back' means that time must be given to allow the club-head to gradually gain speed until the highest momentum is reached at the point of impact. This is to some extent a repetition of previous advice but 'wait for the hit' might apply. The softer, more whippy, hickory shafts needed a different timing from our modern steel shafts.

Don't in swinging back take the club-head so far out that the right elbow has to leave the side. Do not swing too upright.

Don't bend the left knee too soon with wood clubs in the upward swing. Keep the left heel down as long as possible in the back swing might be more in line with today's parlance.

Don't swing so much with iron clubs, but take them back rather more upright than in driving. Here the word upright comes in, which is self-explanatory, but a simpler expression would be use a shorter swing with the iron clubs. Iron clubs can be swung on the same arc, more or less, as the woods—they need only be more upright because the ball is nearer to the player.

Don't, in wrist mashie shot, allow the wrists to go too far through after striking the ball. A wrist stroke generally contains a little forearm. There is no such thing as a pure wrist stroke in golf, except for very short shots. Here is a distinction between the flick and the push. The wrist mashie shot is the flick, the push would be the forerunner of what today is the wedge shot. How true it is that most shots, except the little delicate chips, are forearm and wrist, not wrist alone.

Do let the wrists take the club-head back first; let the arms follow, then let the body turn from the hips; in the downward swing the body turns immediately, the wrists take the club through, pulling the arms after them, then the body turns again and faces the hole. Today we say let the arms and hands take the club back together, let the body follow, begin to unwind the body, the club follows, the body unwind checks momentarily for the club head to pass the body, then continues after impact.

Do keep the head steady throughout the swing; there should be no jumping up, either at the top of the swing or at the moment of impact. Play under the head would be a simple way of telling the golfer not to permit his head to move all over the place.

Don't look up too soon after the ball has been struck. Cricketers are apt to do this. Why only cricketers every modern reader must ask, for it is a general international complaint for which there is no certain trick cure. The only way to overcome this fault is simply not to do it.

Do look at the part of the ball to be struck, not at the ball in an absent-minded abstract kind of way. Focus on the back of the ball not just on the ball in general. Concentrate on where you are to make impact.

It might seem that I am trying to make out that there is 'nothing new under the sun' by making these comparisons which amount to very little, for the advice offered fifty years ago stands today.

I think that, as the game has grown and more people have studied it, one can put the study which has been made—and the players of the day have inspired that study—into periods. The balls and the implements as much as the players have been responsible for the trends, and the improvement in the courses has also had an effect on the technique during these periods.

It is correct to say that with the hickory shaft a bigger variety of strokes could be played willingly and unwillingly. Now the almost torsionless steel shaft of recent times has simplified stroke production. The average "dub' or 'duffer' will refute the suggestions that his counterpart of pre-steel shaft days could 'spray' the ball in a greater variety of ways than he can, but this was true because he had the torsion of the shaft to contend with.

With hickory shafts and golf balls of varying weights and sizes—a state of affairs which existed up to May 1, 1921, when a standard ball was made to Royal and Ancient specifications—players moulded their styles to suit their strength, as now, but also included in their calculations the type of ball being used. A small heavy ball suited certain methods and was difficult to get in the air, so, apart from requiring great strength to send it on its way, it was usually cut up through the green. The time from the first rubber-cored ball, the Haskell in 1902, to the adoption of the standard ball, 1.62 in. in diameter and 1.62 oz. in weight, and still unchanged today, *could be one period*. From 1921-29 when the steel shaft came in, *another period*. From 1929 onwards to today *a further period*, during which time the American influence on style and method could be more felt, for in 1932 with the breaking away from our ball (on the grounds that it made golf too easy) and the adoption of the 1.68 in. and 1.62 oz. ball (a bigger size which they still use today), a slightly different system was necessary to keep this naturally higher flying ball under the same control.

Jones, Hagen and Sarazen, brought up on hickory and the small ball, reigned supreme in world golf in the '20s and their reign overlapped into the '30s.

The methods of Braid, Vardon and Taylor which were the patterns of the day have stood the test of time for they—and I might humbly add myself to this list as a further example of a wrist golfer—have been able to keep a reasonable standard of play for long years and devote time to other things in life, whereas it seems to me that since the end of World War II, the top golfers have required to hit golf balls all day long and nearly every day in order to make their play sound enough. Walter Hagen said to me during a recent meeting we had that if he had needed to slog at the game like the present-day golfers in order to reach his form he would have chosen another profession.

Joyce Wethered was another example of the wrist-under-the-shaft golfer, getting into form with the minimum of effort. These cases might be attributed to inborn ability, but I cannot help but feel that method has something to do with it.

The very strong hitters, and there are many in post-war golf, will always need to flight the ball more than the weaker players in order to stop the ball climbing so high that it is too long at the mercy of the wind, and that is one reason for a veering towards a more closed club face, for there is a limit to the 'straight-facedness' of a driver and to the depth of face.

GUTTY BALL PERIOD

There is not much left in golf today, outside old clubs in show cases in club-house lounges, which can remind us of the golf game as it was in the gutty ball era when the game really began to develop. The game grew but slowly with the gutty, although this ball came into golf as long ago as in 1848, and in 1896 there were only sixty-one courses in Scotland and forty-six in England. Wooden-headed clubs for approaching were gradually superseded by the long-headed iron ones; and then J. H. Taylor, the first English-born player to show the Scots that golfing well was not a Scotsman's prerogative, launched the mashie—a short-faced lofted iron used for pitching.

Golfers began to score better as the gutty improved in its composition and markings, and I suppose also because players could get balls to stand up to the practising required to acquire a good swing. The unresilient gutty was a difficult ball to propel and it really wanted a terrific sweeping stroke to get it on its way; the more sweep the better for the shock of impact then seemed less. Admittedly its stony 'deadness' made play around the green a more simple matter. Scores in the old days were ridiculously high by our standards today and any attempt at making comparisons with a period almost a hundred years later must be even sillier, but a golfer whose span of life took him from the days of Young Tom Morris's Championship Belt win at Prestwick in 1870, when the course used was only twelve holes long, said that his score of 149 for thirty-six holes, three times round, was but two over par, as par by our standards was forty-nine for the twelve holes. There were stylists no doubt before Harry Vardon, but he—because his swing seemed to give as good or better results than any contemporary with less apparent effort—was known as 'the stylist'. Controlled shots have no doubt always been played and recognized as such, for shots of this type only came to be considered obsolete when batteries of iron clubs appeared, numbered even in half numbers—$2\frac{1}{2}$, $3\frac{1}{2}$, etc.—whereby it was assumed that one swing was good enough for the whole game.

The wooden putter died with the gutty ball. This club, one of the original and most used clubs amongst the few carried loose under the arm, was employed for any sort of approach shot, at times from as far as 100 yards from the hole, particularly on such hard-baked bare fairways as were to be found in certain periods of the year on links like St Andrews.

A few older golfers prize these hand-made treasures of bygone days, but as no top-grade golfer has used one for years, it can be concluded that for modern golf they are completely obsolete.

RUBBER-CORED BALL DAYS

It is obviously just a coincidence that, with the advent of the Haskell, the first satisfactory rubber-cored ball, when golf took a big leap forward in popularity, the camera became a sufficiently improved apparatus to 'freeze' the swings of the leading players and so open up the study of what took place during a golf swing.

Later the slow-motion cinematograph 'burst open' positively a number of theories, particularly the one that a perfect swing was a true circular movement, whereas in fact the swing was found to be a looping action (Sir Walter Simpson's book of 1887 had already stated this, as I have quoted). Since the rubber-cored ball turned an ordinary clumsy golfer overnight into a moderate performer (for mishits often gave as much as a 75 per cent result), the long hitters were obliged to learn control, and so came the controlled back swings for play to the pin and the use of more lofted clubs which give greater backspin and ball control.

From 1902 to 1921, players had all the scope they wanted to get the most out of themselves, for there was no limit to the size and weight of the ball which could be used and, of course, extremes were tested. Small heavy balls and big floaters all appeared, and appealed to various people; but naturally they complicated the game, for during a single round the golfer was inclined to use the small heavy ball against the wind and the larger ball down wind, seeking to get the maximum out of himself—or, if he did not do, so regretted that he had not tried.

These conditions, and the fact that artificial watering to keep the greens holding was not encouraged (the Open Championship was held as usual in mid-summer and the putting greens were often shiny brown 'skating rinks'), caused the player to learn to play all the shots, and in his never-ending search there is no doubt that the hickory shaft was a help. With the torsion of the hickory shaft and the fine adjustment of the feel of any club by filing it down the shaft, golfers could make experiments which are impossible today.

In these 1902-21 days it does appear that a successful golfer had to be a smart person, for he had to think up the exact shot he was wanting, and he had a big variety from which to pick. The hands, always very important for the part they play in the swing, took on an even more important role—a peep at George Beldam's excellent book *Great Golfers, Their Methods at a Glance*, published in 1904, will show how golfers of that day had time, with the flexible 'torsionful' hickory shaft, to *make* the shots with their hands. A pitch and run shot was played with a most pronounced turn over of the wrists, forearms and shoulders, and a cut-up pitch was played with a definite slicing-across-the-ball action, left elbow riding high. These exaggerated actions almost seem to be caricatures today and seem as dated as the acting in the first silent films. Yet little has changed fundamentally in the methods, for a golf ball, of necessity following the laws of ballistics, responds to the same spins.

Players in this era began to practise more because competition was fiercer and it became more necessary than ever to specialize; yet prior to World War I players in both professional and amateur ranks would often begin to polish up their game not more than one week before the championships. Braid, Vardon and Taylor dominated golf in this period. They had varying styles because they were of distinctly different builds. Braid, tall and wiry and, when at his best, very flexible, was 6 ft. 1½ in. tall and weighed 12 st. 6 lb.; Vardon, 5 ft. 9¼ in. and weight 11 st., was very wiry; Taylor, 5 ft. 8½ in. and 11 st. 7 lb., short and sturdy. They all played with their left wrists under the shaft at the top of the swing and this became *the* position to copy. It was not that other players did not keep the left wrist in line with the left forearm (now spoken of as the latest American method), for the photos I have included here prove this was not so; but I think that the different equipment in use at the time, and also the type and weight of ball used, had a great varying influence on the methods of the different players. Balls would fly at all sorts of trajectories, for little was known in those days of the effects of the various markings on flight and steadiness. John Ball, Junior, who had an exceptional record as an amateur in gutty and immediate post-gutty days, although he had a curious double-handed palm grip (right hand so far under that the fingers of the hand faced the sky) used 'the latest American method' then. I refer to the method by this name ironically, because I find many of our young players today breaking their backs (almost in fact) practising it, believing that it is the secret of golf and something quite new. I am certain that players of the calibre of Braid, Vardon and Taylor—the order in which I put these great names matters little—had all the shots, and used them to exercise their superiority over their contemporaries. That they tried out this shut-faced method, I am sure. Braid, in fact, due to his left hand being more on the top of the shaft than the other two, was at times a big hooker because of this tendency.

The shut-faced player can play very straight shots, of course—the records of those using this method prove it—but the records also show that very few of them escape periods, and for some long periods, when a disastrous hook has put them off their game. Many never recover their youthful form, for shut-faced golf is young man's golf, and they pursue the same method in the hope of recapturing that something which once gave them their greatest golfing days. The shut-faced player fights a hook as his 'bogey', the open-faced player generally has the 'slice' as his nightmare—to be a good golfer anyway it is necessary to have one side of the course to play towards. Although the rubber-cored ball of the era about which I am writing was a good product, it needed flighting all the time to get the most out of it, just as would a floater if used today. In those days, with a wind from the left it would be necessary to fade the ball in order to steal a few yards, and likewise to hook with the wind when it came from the right. The modern powerful tournament player can ignore almost any wind except a gale. Today players repeat one swing monotonously, finding that it is 'plenty good enough' for the vast majority of occasions.

Although the three heroes of the triumvirate I have mentioned were by no means weak men, sheer power in golf as such was not worshipped then as it later was to become. Skill reaped its reward—skill at conceiving the shots and skill in

122

executing them. When the century opened and the gutty was the ball, a whippy shaft was prized; but it was found that, for control under pressure, a somewhat firmer type of shaft was preferable and hence the straight-grained steely hickory shaft became in demand. This demand grew as the game developed in popularity. Hickory wood used in the construction of wheel spokes and tool handles, grew scarce and good hickory shafts became more and more difficult to find. When the war ended in 1918 players were using very mixed bags of clubs, and it was one of the joys of golf to search the racks of the professional's shop at each golf course visited to find a new 'super' club. Then the next task was to learn to know that club, to adjust one's game to the club, and to remember when playing it how it had to be timed and if the shot could be forced or not. Some shafts would not take an all-out hit—they had to be timed, and this timing learned. With a big bag of clubs it was more than likely that every club in action would behave differently, due to the different weight and balance. Even a good club would soon be rubbed away with emery cloth by conscientious caddies, and the non-rustless soft iron heads got lighter every day they were cleaned. So golfers had many more problems than the 1951 players.

1921-1929

I take these years following World War I as another definite period in golf because in 1921 a standard golf ball of 'not less than 1.62 in. in diameter and not more than 1.62 oz. in weight' came into being. This ruled out all the added complications of having to choose your ball for the day and the course according to local conditions, and meant that golfers had one problem solved for them. There were some faint objections, of course, but this was a sound move, for players could now set about learning to master one ball.

From this moment mechanical golf, as we were later to see and read about, was created, for all over the world golfers began to practise hard in order to learn all about this new standard ball. There were no outstanding methods of play differing widely from earlier ones, although Mr R. T. Jones, Junior, of Atlanta, Georgia, the top golfer in the game through this period and, apart from Walter Hagen, well out on his own, set the whole world trying to play golf with such a narrow stance that at times the heels were touching even for full shots. Only Walter Hagen's wide sprawly stance reminded golfers that there could be champions with other stances. Bobby Jones—as he will ever be to British golfers, although he curiously enough dislikes being called Bobby and his letters are always signed Bob—turned professional after his great 'Grand Slam' of wins of 1930. This period of narrow stance experiments by the golfing world—I used a narrow stance and persevered with it with mixed success like many others at the time—came to an end in due course, and I think that, like the 'Naughty 'Nineties'

123

or the fabulous '20s, it will never return. Jones' long lazy swing was copied, photographed in slow motion, watched on cardboard flickers and analysed by writers and students throughout the world, and had its effect on the world's golf game.

Overlapping (yet not overlapping but interlocking) the latter part of this period and the following few years, taking one into the '30s, came a best selling golf book by Alex Morrison from California, in which the interlocking grip, index finger of the left hand and little finger of the right hand intertwined and with the left thumb outside the grip, was put forward as the latest in golf. This so-called *new* grip—Vardon referring to his own grip in 1904 said: 'My grip is overlapping not interlocking'—clutched the golf world and it took quite a long time for each and every golfer to spend his quota of practice time, in the vast majority of cases without profit, in testing out the new false freedom of the wrists felt when swinging clubs with the interlocking grip. Many golfers have used this grip successfully: the Whitcombes, Sarazen and Ouimet come to mind right away, but it was not the grip for everyone, and, like a Wall Street boom, its wave of popularity did not last.

Since scores and records began to be noted, it has been obvious, in Willie Park's oft-quoted remark, 'that a man who could putt was a match for anyone'. Although, for example, Arnaud Massy and Jack White, two Open Champions, were celebrated for their putting, it was not till this period 1921-29 that the good putters began to be very much noticed. Players who, on the gradually improving putting surfaces, could regularly rely upon getting by with brilliant putting when the rest of their game was below first-class average, became more numerous, and golfers with inferior 'long games' began to win big events through skilful performances on the putting greens. How could this happen all of a sudden? Well, I should say that competition and analysis gradually showed more clearly the supreme value of good putting and the model round with thirty-six putts, two per green, was soon out of date. Thirty-three putts at the most it soon had to be, and today thirty, twenty-nine, twenty-eight and even twenty-six putts is the standard aimed at, and required in order to win.

In addition the post-war conditions found courses easier than before. Less rough had been kept because of the golf ball scarcity, and history repeated itself some twenty-seven years later—with the great difference that courses were already easier to start with. When courses are easy (whether they are short or long matters little) and with insufficient rough to punish erring shots, everything hangs on the putting. You cannot win through on a superlative long game as is possible on a punishing course. Players today are inclined to grumble about bad rough on a course, complaining that it ruins their scores—what will people think if their average is ruined? This may sound pathetic, but some professional players will actually cut out a tournament on a tough course for fear that their average will be spoiled.

As the chances of a lost ball in the wilderness became less with the building of courses on open land—for with the fast growth of the game in this period courses sprang up everywhere and ground with natural features could not always be found—the day of the recovery player (down in two from anywhere) arrived. Walter Hagen was the first of a line of great golfers who did not rely on mechanical skill like Vardon and Taylor to win and halve holes—he became a master of rolling three shots into two. He had no sand wedge to help him. He had to use, as did other players (such as Ted Ray and James Braid), who had earlier reputations for making fabulous recoveries, ordinary niblicks with 'thin' soles. Hagen, while including the explosion shot in his repertoire, had much faith in his ability to flick the ball clearly off the sand, a shot very little used today. Even from a very teed-up lie in sand, the modern professional will blast the ball on to the green, a much safer shot which has been made so for him by the broad sole of the sand iron.

I feel that the golf game owes one particular debt of gratitude, amongst many, to James Braid, and that is for the way he has kept the courses at Walton Heath as such fine tests of golf. Their popularity has in no way diminished because of the fact that a bad shot is *always* punished to the maximum—a state of affairs fast disappearing from a game which is developing into a test of strength.

During this period the matched set of clubs appeared as yet another step towards mechanical golf. The theory advanced was that you buy your set and use one swing only—get a good caddie to give you the right club and hey presto! The matched set, numbered 1-9, at first blew in from America and so did the ballyhoo with it, and our golfers wanted to learn the American swing that went with the set. This swing, under Bobby Jones' great influence at the time, was a long one, a real swing at the ball once again. I went to America towards the end of this period, in 1928 it was, in order to see why they were beating our home players so regularly, and found that steel shafts were already legal and one type of bigger ball was in use. This was the time when twenty-year-old Horton Smith was cleaning up on the winter circuit—he hardly knew golf with anything else but steel shafts and had knocked all the fancy shot-making frills off low scoring. He used a slow deliberate three-quarter swing, which he repeated mechanically for every shot, letting the ball hook slightly—even for his short mashie niblick shots. He never took three putts, and he holed a lot of 'good' ones. It was rather like the way Bobby Locke plays today, though his swing is longer and faster. Seeing Horton Smith play was quite a revelation, for I saw straight away that the day of learning to play all the shots was over—the steel shaft had made golf an easier game. Only one swing was necessary, and I had to find out as soon as possible the swing which would suit me.

125

The soft watered greens—a necessity in a country where the fixed fine weather periods of spring, summer and autumn meant many sunny days and no rain—showed that one shot, if you could repeat it, was good enough to win any event. This fact did not really register at home till the steel shaft was legalized in Great Britain, and then we too all hunted for one swing to go with our new matched sets which had steel shafts in them. At last everyone could have the exact set used by his favourite champion.

THE STEEL SHAFT DAYS—1930 ONWARDS

Gradually the top golfers began to realize that golf was a more simple game with this new standard link between the hands and the club head. It was not necessary to know or practise all the shots as in the hickory shaft days, though some of the older players never quite adapted themselves to steel. Abe Mitchell, whose play I have always admired and who was a wonderful striker of the ball, never got to like steel. He could not make himself just play one stroke. He liked to fade the ball up to the flag and found that the steel shaft let him down when he attempted to play a controlled fade or any special stroke. He missed the torsion of the hickory shaft. George Duncan was also too much of an artist to enjoy steel. As the leading players of the day were, of course, all brought up on the hickory shaft, it was only natural that there should be, for a time, a search to produce a steel shaft with the same qualities of the hickory one. This led to a series of shafts being produced which had torsion. These experiments turned out to be failures. Then it was realized that a shaft with no torsion was nearer to the ideal one. Whip it could have, but the less torsion the better. There have been various sorts of shafts from the 'limber' type built to feel like a piece of cord, through the various 'master' ranges from 'pokers to average whip', right up to the 'dynamic' range, the range of today which has given us a nearly torsionless type of varying degrees of whip which has contributed to lower and lower scoring.

As golf became an industry, and a big one at that, exploiters of golf courses realized that in order to make the turnstiles click healthily, the number of players using a course per day had to be increased. The rough began to disappear faster than ever to enable quicker rounds to be played and to give the customer a greater feeling of enjoyment. Then came World War II—with again a shortage of golf balls, making a lost ball nearly a tragedy—to finish off the trend, and when the war ended in 1945 so many golfers had got used to playing 'around the park' that the days of rough as we used to know it were ended. This open field trend has had such an effect on golf that long driving has come to be worshipped. All the top players, particularly in the USA, hit the ball 'full out' all the time and do not pay much penalty for errors of direction or expect to do so. I find open park courses tedious and boring to play. I do not mean that only I find them easier to play than good courses or that I score lower on them, but that they do not inspire me and I feel all the time that my good shots are not sufficiently rewarded. I seem to score the same on the good as on the bad. Betting, now a big part of golf in the USA, has developed to provide interest whilst playing in monotonous conditions.

In one recent US Open Championship, I read that players—and the Press were backing them—were objecting to a fringe of rough around and behind the putting surfaces, because lies were poor and accurate chipping was impossible. This rough might have been extra heavy, but rough should always exist on a golf course—it is part of the game.

Courses are easier today. The extra yardage added does not seem to compensate for this, and now there is a definite leaning towards the use of forward tees for some rounds in order to encourage low scoring for publicity purposes.

Since 1941 there had been a general trend to use and recommend a more shut-faced action in play, and this fashion was *à la mode* up to 1945. Since then, players have moved their left hands back on the shaft, opened the hand to show two knuckles, which is what I have always recommended and used. The value of this change is to make more use of the hands and to cut out some of the body unwind which had a tendency to be exaggerated and which was more than the human frame could stand up to. Practising with the steel shaft was easier because full pressure could be applied all the time without spoiling the shaft, and, given enough energy and practice, an unusual swing could be made to give results—at least while the confidence held. The larger ball, which naturally tends to fly higher, needed to be knocked down to get a boring flight and the maximum control, and so this led to the strong players closing the club face much more than British golfers had been doing for some time. The only long driver of modern times who kept his wrist under the shaft like Harry Vardon has been Jimmy Thomson, the North Berwick boy, who went to the USA and he, in consequence, hit a very high ball.

Up to 1929, I always had a practice set and a tournament set, saving the latter so as not to wear them out; since those days one set was enough. Then, of course, the restriction in the number of clubs permitted a player in competition golf was an obvious legislation, for as breakages were almost unheard of, it was silly to carry over twenty clubs round a course. Fourteen became the limit, but this had no effect on the scoring or club sales. The tendency with steel shafts had been for divots to get bigger and deeper, for no strain was too much for the steel shaft. If wrists could stand it, the shafts could. Players like powerful Sam Snead, one of the game's great players, were taking platefuls of earth with their iron clubs in order to get the maximum grip on the ball, for the USGA ruling that face markings were to be almost decorative caused the leading players to hit the ball steeper in order to grip it well on the club face. This ruling came about because for a short

127

time there was a sort of competition as to how rough a club face could be made, and a cold chisel and hammer were employed to deepen the face grooves on standard markings. The very slotted club faces, apart from ruining a golf ball at almost every stroke, caused the ball to fly lower and so there came into being a low flying pitch to the pin, which had much backspin on it caused by these face markings, and which was christened a 'wedge shot' because the club generally used was a 'wedge'. (A broad-soled niblick with a flat sole, the back edge of this club not riding high as in the 'sand wedge' or 'dynamiter'.)

The sand wedge which came out in the '30s was a sensation at the time. The first models were egg-shaped, hollow-faced clubs, with a high back edge so that the club skidded and did not dig into the earth or sand. The hollow face, which it was soon ruled 'hit the ball twice', was deemed illegal, but the form of the club has remained with us today and is to be found in the bag of every serious competitor. The technique for playing this club is to hit well into the sand (for it is primarily a bunker recovery club) behind the ball, using a full shot all the time but judging the distance the ball is to travel by the number of inches below the ball the club is made to enter the sand. All the world's leading players are experts with this type of club. This is understandable, for to be a good player in the first place, it is necessary to be an accurate hitter and a little regular practice in sand soon shows how far exactly it is necessary to enter the sand behind the ball for a given distance. Bad players are so because they are inaccurate strikers, and so they are never good bunker players and cannot expect to be until they improve their precision. The leaders of today are gifted players and can compare with any past champions, in every department of the game. Modern day writers naturally enough only extol their own generation and point out that as scoring has improved by so many strokes a round it must, therefore, be better. The experimental Royal and Ancient rules of 1950-51 caused improved scores also. But, much as I allow for the need to play better today owing to greater competition, I must claim for older generations that courses were tougher and equipment in general was poorer. I will 'bump up' the scoring by at least two shots a round if you let me provide graded rough through and around the greens, and putting surfaces which are not 'puddings to pitch into'.

I do not propose to argue here about players of today and yesterday, for comparisons are odious. But it is specialization alone which has helped to raise the general standard, as today tournament players, both professional and amateur, if they expect top honours, do nothing else but take part in competitions. The club pro rarely steps out from home and cleans up the tournament players.

Style as such is not much appreciated these days. In fact, the public in general does not seem to be educated up to recognizing if a player is an artist at his job. Only figures on the scoreboard count. A successful shot, struck as the balance is

This is not a demonstration of a 'piccolo' grip, but Harold Hilton's top of the backswing grip of the club, taken in action by George Beldam in 1903. Hilton must have had a wonderful touch to have regripped the club in the same way each time as impact approached. His record alone testifies to this: 2 Opens, 4 Amateurs, 1 American Amateur

Miss Rhona Adair, Lady Champion in 1900 and 1903, using the left wrist in line with the forearm and shut face technique, in the era when ladies' legs were not to be seen. I cannot help but comment on this fine action. If this champion were dressed *à la mode* 1952, such an action would surely be 'news'

John Ball, an Open and Amateur Champion, using a palm grip, is at the top of the swing for a push iron shot. Note lovely balance and the way hands lie on the shaft. Club loosely in palm of right hand, left wrist in line with forearm

Photographs from George W. Beldam's 'Great Golfers'
(Macmillan, 1904)

Bernard Darwin
Beldam: 'Great Golfers'

G. H. Castle
Beldam: 'Great Golfers'

L. Balfour Melville. An action photo from George Beldam's book showing the Amateur Champion of 1895 using the left wrist in line with the left forearm action

Beldam: 'Great Golfers'

Byron Nelson, 'Mr Golf' to the American nation, whose brilliant consistent golf of the early 1940s was attributed to his wrist action, which is still spoken of as 'the new American method'. Here Nelson's left wrist action can be seen. Left wrist in line with the forearm

★ *My Method* ★

By HENRY COTTON

Quite a sound method of loosening up the muscles. To swing a handful of golf clubs a few times before starting out on a round or before beginning a practice session is of great value. A few swings with the extra weight of the several clubs pulling the muscles does more to stretch the muscles than dozens of fast 'swishes' with one club

The address. Here the backswing is just beginning—head well cocked to the side, the hands dragging the club head away.

Here can be seen my own particular grip—two knuckles of my gloved left hand showing, the V of the right hand made by the thumb and index finger well on the top of the shaft. My left arm much more relaxed than that of players using the 3 or 4 knuckle grip as can be seen—it soon straightens as the swing is formed. I usually have the ball more towards the left heel than is seen in this photo, for there was a moderate breeze against and from the left and I was hitting the ball a little more from 'inside to out' to hold it into the wind when the photo was taken

The address looking down the fairway. This is an average position that I use—feet square, knees relaxed, ball well towards the left foot, right wrist slightly arched, head cocked with chin near right shoulder. Club face carefully placed behind the ball with eye looking at the back centre of the ball. Note how index finger of the right hand is crooked, so as to have maximum control

The address for a pitch with a No. 7, arms relaxed, narrow stance, ball right of centre, hands close to body. My usual overlapping grip, little finger of the right hand on top of index finger of the left hand; some players allow it also to lie between the index and second finger of the left hand

Backswing already on the way. Left heel still on the ground, but left knee eases forward as the hips begin to turn. The club shaft is still in line with the left arm and the right elbow has begun to slide around the body

The wrists are now cocking slowly and although the backswing is nearing completion the left heel is barely raised. At this point the left shoulder is pointing at the ball. The hands have taken the club well on the inside and the club face has slowly opened

A 60-yard pitch shot taken at the top of the backswing—note relaxed knees, ball nearly opposite right foot, feet almost together. The wrists have cocked earlier in this shot and the pivot is less, for I play this length of shot with my hands and arms more than many players

This is my full swing, the top of the swing for me. The left heel is just clear of the ground. I am riding on the inside edge of my left shoe at this moment. The left arm is extended, right elbow under the shaft, club face more open than shut and club head almost pointing to the hole. Some players get their hands higher than I do and that means that the right elbow leaves the side more, but providing the hands are high, this swing is long enough. Both hands fairly on the club—note my left wrist, not forced under the shaft but not in the straight line with the forearm as recently recommended from USA

Nearly at the top of the swing, the front view. Hands head-high, club head forward, my back is almost right round to face the hole as the trunk is 'wound up'. This photo gives the impression, I feel, that the feet are alive and that the weight is not locked on the heels. Left eye above is still firmly focused on the ball, the turn of the head to the right has put my nose in the line of my right eye's view of the ball

Coming down—as the right elbow slides again close to the body the club head falls back. This is the guarantee that the club head will remain on the 'inside out' path. Beginners prone to slicing get a shoulder unwind at this point which brings the club head forward, on the way to an 'outside in' attack

Coming down, another angle, the left heel snaps down, the hips unwind, the left shoulder remains high, the left arm begins to pull and the right elbow hugs the side, forcing the club head back and not forward as I pointed out in the previous photograph. At this moment the body is preparing to brace itself to permit the arms and hands to overtake it. In a shut-face method the body would be much farther through at this moment

In the hitting area, right elbow close to the side still but right hand is now applying the power. The left side is braced, chin still well back, head is still. The nails on the inside edge of the right foot are coming into play as the right leg thrusts against the left side. The acceleration can be noticed here for the inside of the wheel of the left hand is being overtaken by the rim of the club head. The light has caught the steps in the shaft

The 60-yard pitch, the down swing beginning—elbows close together, hands pulling club down. The hips are turning slightly as the relaxed knees move towards the ball. It is not incorrect to say that the knees act as supplementary wrists in these shots, they help to judge the whereabouts of the ball

At impact. This photo shows well the various important points that interest a beginner—the right hand position with the right elbow on the side and the 'inside out' hit. Note daylight between arms, right heel, head position, and the way the left hip has cleared

The ball is now well on the way. Right arm follows on to the hole, head is still down, right heel is barely raised from the ground. With a two-knuckle, left-hand grip the wrists can roll, for my method is a hand and arm one primarily. This shot can be played with the left arm 'giving' at impact, the elbow taking the shock instead of the wrist. I use this method from doubtful lies and if I am cutting up the ball

The 60-yard pitch. The ball has spun up the face of the club successfully and can be seen starting on its elevated flight. Note the position of the arms and hands, elbows close to body and not spread

Same pitch a fraction later, showing how the left wrist has resisted the hit of the right hand.
The club head continues on its 'down and through' path but the ball is now well up in the air. Head very still and shoulders and hips turning with hands close to the body

A 100-yard shot. At this stage of the follow-through the right arm is still straight and the right hand has turned over the left. The left arm is beginning to bend as the right heel is coming up —but head so far is down

The driver. The speed of the hit and the violent bracing of the body can be seen. The left shoulder has gone up and round, the head is still and the right hand has driven the club head through. The right shoulder is more back at this stage than is usually found in the case of the high handicap golfer, which is proof of the power in the hands and arms

Another driver, but from behind and a little later in the swing. Right heel off the ground but 'down', left side through but right shoulder back. This camera shot shows how the shaft is taken round the body, a proof of the way the wrists have worked. The head can now come up, there is no need to stay down further

The 100-yard shot taken from the side and behind, to show the action of the left hand principally. The right knee action and the left shoulder position are very easily remarked from this particular angle

The 100-yard shot from the front, the right shoulder is now so far through that the head could not stay down. The grip is still firm, the finish is wide, right heel coming clear of the ground as the body turns more towards the hole. Soon after this comes the position of rest so often snapped by the photographer

My usual finish, the power of the punch with the right side has taken the body right through. The arms are now coming to rest after the great effort they have made during their strenuous stretching whilst striking the ball

Nelson, Sarazen, and Hogan watch me drive at Augusta in 1948. Note my position. Then, below, note Hogan (Sarazen looking on) also just after impact

Although Hogan's position is snapped later than mine, the difference in the body position due to our difference in method can be seen. The more closed club face action of Hogan demanding more body unwind

Royal and Ancient G.C., St Andrews

*Golf at St Andrews
in the eighteen-fifties*

Left to right: James Wilson, Willie Dunn, Bob Andrews, Willie Park, Tom Morris, Allan Robertson, D. Anderson, Bob Kirk

Playing the Home Hole by the Swilcan Bridge (today in the middle of the 18th fairway). On the left of the picture is Tom Morris; Allan Robertson (dark trousers) stands on top of the bridge. Major Boothby is addressing the ball

Royal and Ancient G.C., St Andrews

Old Tom Morris, Open Champion 1861, 1862, 1864, and 1867

G. M. Cowie, St Andrews

Young Tom Morris wearing the Champion's Belt. He made the Belt his own by winning the Open Championship for the third successive time in 1870. He also won the present Open Championship Cup when it was first played for in 1872

G. M. Cowie, St Andrews

Charlie Hunter and Tom Morris in 1863

Prestwick St Nicholas G.C.

Freddie Tait, Amateur Champion in 1898, putting in front of the club-house at St Andrews. Old Tom Morris holds the flag

G. M. Cowie, St Andrews

John Ball Junior and Son. The latter was Open Champion in 1890, and Amateur Champion in 1888, 1890, and 1894

Guy B. Farrar, Esq

Harold Hilton. Open Champion in 1892 and 1897; Amateur Champion in 1900, 1901, 1911, and 1913. Watching him (*left*) is Old Tom Morris

Guy B. Farrar, Esq

Andrew Kirkaldy

G. M. Cowie, St Andrews

Willie Auchterlonie, for many years professional at St Andrews and Open Champion in 1893

The Field

Allan Robertson, 'The Unbeaten'

G. M. Cowie, St Andrews

Harry Vardon putting in his match against Willie Park at Ganton in 1899 for a stake of £200. Willie Park is standing watching his opponent

Golf Illustrated

Horace Hutchinson, a member of the first Oxford University team and winner of the Amateur Championship in 1896 and 1897

Topical Press

Topical Press J. Graham

Ben Sayers

Sport and General

Arnaud Massy, the first non-British golfer to win the Open Championship (Hoylake 1907)

Topical Press

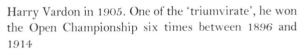

Harry Vardon in 1905. One of the 'triumvirate', he won the Open Championship six times between 1896 and 1914

Sport and General

James Braid. A photograph taken on his eightieth birthday at Walton Heath. In the game for more than seventy years, Braid won the Open Championship five times

Central Press Photos

Ted Ray, the winner of the Open Championship in 1912

Sport and General

J. H. Taylor, five times Open Champion and a member of the 'triumvirate'

Central Press Photos

George Duncan, Open Champion, 1920

Sport and General

Abe Mitchell, the greatest golfer who never won the Championship, in 1925 at Roehampton

Central Press Photos

Sandy Herd, Open Champion, 1902

Central Press Photos

Bobby Jones

Sport and General

Bobby Jones being escorted through the crowd after winning the Amateur Championship at St Andrews in 1930. This was the year of his 'Grand Slam' when he won the Amateur and Open Championships of both Great Britain and America

Golf Illustrated

Gene Sarazen
with the trophy for the Open Championship which he won at Prince's,
Sandwich, in 1932

Central Press Photos

lost, is just as valuable, we know, as the same shot played with perfect poise and balance; but for myself I enjoy seeing a real artist at work on a great course.

ON PUTTING

It does not matter whether you are Open Champion or a player with no handicap —you start level once your ball gets on the putting surface. It is not that all players do not start off level from the first tee, but in play through the green physical advantages count much—whether just much or too much is a question of opinion—but once you have in your hand a club called a putter, you can cross your legs, lean on it with confidence and say 'I can do what any champion can do— hole it or miss it'. The big difference here is that the champion holes out more putts than the others.

This fact, bordering on the very obvious as it is, has not escaped notice by anybody, but despite its being so well known, few of the millions playing golf do anything about it.

Whether it is to beat Mrs. Toppem Smith for the last place in the Bronze Division qualifying rounds veterans' section, or 'This actually for the open title', the same problems arise and maybe the same strain, but with different consequences. I like very much Sir Walter Simpson's suggestion that 'when a putter is waiting his turn to hole out a putt of one or two feet in length, on which the match hangs at the last hole, it is of vital importance to think of nothing. At this supreme moment he ought studiously to fill his mind with vacancy. He must not even allow himself the consolation of religion. He must not prepare himself to accept the gloomy face of his partner and the derisive delight of his adversaries with Christian resignation should he miss. He must not think that it is a putt he would not dream of missing at the beginning of the match or worse still that he missed one like it in the middle. He ought to wait calm and stupid till it is his turn to play, wave back the inevitable boy who is sure to be standing behind his arm and putt as I have told him how, neither with undue haste nor with exaggerated care. When the ball is down and the putter handed to the caddie, it is not well to say "I couldn't have missed it". Silence is best. The pallid cheek and trembling lip belie such braggadocio.' Here we have the final words of an interesting chapter on putting, words in a humorous vein written in 1887. Note the date: quite a time ago; in fact very few golfers are still holing earthly putts who first read his words when they were published.

How true this has always been and always will be, even if Gene Sarazen's dream of a six-inch hole came true—for it would be the same problem but from a few inches farther away.

All the various putting styles and methods used by the world's many golfers have the same objective—to get the ball into the hole as easily as possible in the

K   *129*

smallest number of strokes under all conditions. But as a general observation, I should say that putters today stand more up to the ball; fewer really crouch down to putt as was the custom fifty or so years ago.

Two photos taken from a series by G. W. Beldam in 1904 from his famous 'years-before-its-time-book'—*Great Golfers: Their Methods at a Glance*—shows none other than Bernard Darwin and H. G. Castle getting down to their putts. Bernard Darwin, now alas crippled in the hip joints with that dreaded arthritis, must recall with pride when he sees his photos with a stance so spread out as to cover nearly four feet from toe to toe, that his hip joints were one day really supple. From such a base there is certainly no question of leaning on to the ball, in fact, lots of golfers I know would lock themselves so much if they got into such a position that it would be only with difficulty they could regain the vertical again.

This stance is possibly not the one for every golfer, but I do know that there are many who have never tried getting their arms rested in such a definite manner.

Take the stance of H. G. Castle whose eyes are actually outside the ball by over six inches, too, so that he is viewing the ball from a most original angle. He has his right toe a mere foot from the ball and directly behind it. Not for him the low flowing back swing, but rather the rebound off his toe.

Few putters today get down the shaft in this way anyhow, with their hands as near the club head, but it has much to recommend it. H. G. Castle rests his right elbow on his knee as I can imagine—for I never saw him play—that his back swing was on a 'cut' path and that his right knee pushed forwards as 'he hit the ball as if he were putting with his leg muscles.

We have many arm and shoulder putters, but few players have stuck to this one type of action, with the leg muscles coming in, for a slight kick in with the right knee would add quite a bit of power to the putt and the leg could only work on one way. This knee-dip is a sort of caddie action, we would so call it today.

I have never advocated any one style of putting as being the best, for each player uses what he had the most confidence in at the time—trying to find a method that will cut out the 'Yips' at the crucial moments.

Whether pushing the ball or wristing it is better is always open to discussion and usually it only needs for us to see a player putt successfully for us to try out his method and grip.

What does influence greatly the methods employed is how to look at the line to the hole and how to line up the club face. Some do this from directly above the ball—Bernard Darwin's photo is an example of this—or look at it obliquely from the side rather, or there is a method standing well behind the ball and lining up the putt like looking down a rifle barrel and *à la* Mr Castle seen here. There can be no argument as to whether putting is better now than years ago, for today players, paid players, have to get the ball into the hole or starve, and so of necessity

130

many more back-breaking hours are spent on the putting greens than ever before. More players hole more vital putts today, not only because there are many more vital putts alone, but because so many never play without putting down the score each time they play. The only way to find out if you can putt is to putt into the hole each time.

What Sir Walter Simpson has not told in his book is 'how to fill the mind with vacancy' (a bit Irish maybe and an ideal objective, no doubt), but it is a suggestion which he equally will regard as 'doubly unnecessary' for in the vast majority of cases it already exists.

It does help to make each putt an independent affair and not a stroke followed by another with accumulating consequences: to say 'here is just a four-foot putt', not 'I have this for a four' or 'if I miss it a five will go on the card'.

No one can ever get into the skin of another player and really be able to analyse all the thoughts and emotions of others connected with putting, and to me it will ever be a game apart.

1848-1914

From Gutty to Rubber-Core

THERE are two great revolutionary dates in the history of golf in this country; the first is 1848, when the gutty ousted the feather ball; the second is 1902, when the rubber-core arrived from America and there was an end of the once usurping gutty. It seems clear that the gutty came, a little mysteriously, from London. We may accept Mr. James Balfour's account of its coming as he was one of the earliest to use it. 'My brother-in-law,' he says, 'Admiral Maitland Dougall, played a double match at Blackheath with the late Sir Ralph Anstruther and William Adam of Blair-Adam and another friend, with gutta-percha balls, on a very wet day. They afterwards dined together at Sir Charles Adam's at Greenwich Hospital and Sir Ralph said after dinner, "A most curious thing—here is a golf ball of gutta-percha; Maitland and I have played with it all day in the rain, and it flies better at the end of the day than it did at the beginning." ' Maitland Dougall soon afterwards came to Edinburgh and told Mr Balfour all about it, whereupon they sent to London for some of the balls and set out eagerly to try them at Musselburgh. Gourlay, the chief ball-maker there, came out to watch them: he saw at once that the game was up as far as the poor feathery was concerned, and having a standing order to send Sir David Baird some balls when he had any to spare, sent him six dozen.

The further story of the gutty's successful invasion has often been told and need not be elaborated. The ball-makers hated it, for they believed, short-sightedly enough, that it would ruin their business and did not realize that it would make golf far more widely popular and so inure to their benefit. Allan Robertson bribed caddies to give him all the gutties they could find in the whins in order that he might burn 'the filth'. He played a shot with one, topped it on purpose and then declared it would not fly; he quarrelled with Tom Morris, who worked in his shop, for playing with one that was given him, so that they parted company. For a little while there was hope for the forces of reaction, since the gutty had one fault; it was inclined to duck, and it only flew properly after it had been hacked with a cleek. If its economical owner gave it a hot bath to smooth away the wounds it ducked again as badly as ever. Then an ingenious saddler took to indenting the ball with the thin end of a hammer, thus producing with greater precision the effect that the gashes from the cleek had suggested. Next the moulds in which the balls were made had indentations in them, and the gutty had completely come into its kingdom. It was round, whereas the feathery had been egg-shaped, it rolled more truly, it flew farther, it lasted longer, it scorned wet weather, it cost less. No wonder that from that moment golf took a bound forward in popularity.

As we have begun with the ball it will be well to say a word on the clubs of the time. Before our period begins there had been great strides in club-making. Thorn had given way first to apple and then to beech wood; slimness and elegance had begun to refine the clumsy bludgeons of a past age. Hugh Philp, who has been called the Stradivarius of club-making, had been appointed 'Club maker to the Society' in 1829, according to the Minutes of the Royal and Ancient, and he was still flourishing and at the height of his fame in 1848. If his clubs—and there have been many forged Philps as well as genuine ones—seem to us rather lacking in power, their grace and beauty of line are unsurpassable; they are clearly the work of a true artist. Incidentally, Mr Peter, who wrote an interesting book of golfing reminiscences, tells us how he and his brother used to insert lead into the gutties when they first appeared, and were very successful with them. This, Hugh Philp not unnaturally resented, asking how the devil a man could make clubs to withstand lead.

Most of the clubs were of wood; a driver, a grassed club, somewhat set back in the face, a whole battalion of spoons, a putter and sometimes a driving putter. The niblick was then of wood, with a little head to fit into ruts, and the irons— the driving and sand iron and the cleek—were primarily meant for rough work. It seems, however, that Allan Robertson first introduced the use of the cleek and the iron for the finesse of approaching. There has been, oddly enough, some argument among those who saw him play, but the balance of evidence seems to show that it was Allan who by his example gave the death-blow to the baffing spoon. Yet the time of the real dominion of the irons was still some way off. It was Young Tommy Morris in the late '60s who, greatly daring, used the tiny-headed iron niblick with which to pitch and stop over bunkers, and twenty years after that three or four iron clubs were the most that anyone carried in his bag.

And now what sort of a golfing world was it on which there burst this new ball? It was clearly a very small one indeed according to our present notions. The author of *The Golfer's Manual*, published nine years later, in 1857, gave a list of Scottish golf clubs. He confessed himself a little disappointed in it since several clubs had not replied to his questions. There are gaps in it visible even to a modern eye; there is, for instance, no mention of the Royal Musselburgh Golf Club, which was founded in 1774. Even allowing for a few such omissions, the total of eighteen clubs is surprisingly small. It does no justice to the total amount of golf then being played in Scotland, for golf was a game of the people and was played by many who belonged to no club. It had so been played for a very long time, though we may hesitate wholly to believe an enthusiastic nineteenth-century authoress who wrote that in the seventeenth century 'every hill round Edinburgh was then, as now, famous for its golfing ground'. In 1844 Allan Robertson, from his shop, had turned out nearly 2,500 featheries, which gives some very rough clue to the play at St Andrews.

There was no doubt a good deal of golf played regularly there. So there must have been at Musselburgh, where played the Royal Musselburgh Club and the Honourable Company of Edinburgh Golfers, who had abandoned Leith in 1836. Leith certainly still existed, and for some time later, for there was a professional tournament held there in 1867, in which all the great players of the day took part. The course must then, however, have fallen from its old estate when 'Lords of Session, cobblers, knights, baronets and tailors might be seen earnestly contesting for the palms of superior dexterity', and Smollett watched the cheerful old gentlemen of eighty who 'never went to bed after their exertions without having under their belts the best part of a gallon of claret'. There was Bruntsfield, too, which was still the home course of the Edinburgh Burgess and the Bruntsfield Links Club and some other local societies. It was getting more and more crowded and congested, buildings had encroached on it, and there had periodically been quarrels with other interests, such as that in 1798 with Walter Scott, then Quartermaster of the Royal Edinburgh Light Dragoons, who wanted to drill his cavalry there. There had been a great dispute with the City Magistrates in 1843, and indeed the golfers, in particular the Edinburgh Burgess, had to be constantly standing up for their rights. Still the links were handy, so were the places of social pleasure which were so important to our golfing ancestors, and it was not till 1877 that the Burgess held their last medal day on Bruntsfield Links. So at the beginning of our period we may assume it still busy, crowded and very much alive as a golf course. There was North Berwick, too, and Crail and Leven, Montrose and Aberdeen, and Perth, which a little later distinguished itself by promoting tournaments, but the west seems hardly yet to have been awake. It was only in 1851 that the Prestwick Club was founded and Tom Morris left St Andrews to lay out and keep the green there. It cannot be doubted that golf had been played there before, but in a comparatively casual manner.

In England there were but two clubs. There was the Manchester Club, a band of exiled Scotsmen who had begun to play on Kersal Moor in 1818, and there was

134

of course the Royal Blackheath, presumed, on rather slender evidence, to be the Senior Golf Club. It seems to have been at this time in a particularly flourishing state, with new members coming in. In 1844 it had absorbed the Blackheath Winter Golf Club, which had earlier in its turn absorbed the Knuckle Club, with its mystic rites long since forgotten. Its season now lasted the whole year round, instead of merely from spring to autumn, and instead of five holes its course became one of seven, as it ever afterwards remained till golf was played no more on the sacred heath. The club was, moreover, about to embark on the rare luxury of a professional, indeed of two professionals. These were the great twin brethren of Musselburgh, Willie and Jamie Dunn. Jamie was taken into the club's service in 1854 on a salary of 7/- a week, and in 1860 Willie, who had been there then ten years, was advanced to 17/6 a week.

Still, despite the great antiquity of Blackheath, it may be said that golf was then to all intents and purposes unknown in England. It is at Scotland we must look to see how the game was played a hundred and two years ago. It is not injustice to the players to say that the dinner still formed an important part of the ritual, as it always had done, and that the evening of a golfing day was passed, to quote an old Bruntsfield minute, with 'stereotyped happiness, harmony and hilarity'. But the golf was eminently serious, at any rate at St Andrews, and was often played for large sums of money. There was doubtless jealousy between St Andrews and Musselburgh, but it seems fair to say that St Andrews was unquestionably the metropolis of the game, where on the whole the best golf was played by the best players. It became so more than ever when the arrival of the railway in 1852 made it easily accessible. It had been a different matter some thirty years before, when a boat from Leith carried passengers to Kirkcaldy, and after that they must make the best of their way on foot or any vehicle they could get.

All courses were of the roughest judged by standards of modern green-keeping, and of St Andrews in 1848 we have a detailed account, hole by hole, by Mr. James Balfour whom I have already quoted. There was a keeper of the course, indeed in 1855 there were two, Walter Alexander and Alexander Herd, 'cadies', at £6 a year between them. One of them at least bore a name to become famous in another generation, but how much did they do? Clearly there have been great changes since those days when there were but nine holes, played by both outgoing and incoming matches. The course was very narrow, beset by whins that have in many places wholly disappeared and in others have been steadily driven back or thinned. Whole tracts of the links, such as the ground to the right of the Elysian Fields, now the normal route to the Long Hole out, were then totally unplayable. I am sure that none of us today can form any real notion of what were the difficulties to be encountered. The greens again were very various in quality, and in many places extremely rough. Dr. McPherson in his *Golf and Golfers Past and Present* enumerates with pride the 'heavy surface' of one green, the 'soo-back' on another and so on. He thought that putting was much more 'scientific' in the days when the player must 'calculate every little mound and rough bit of grass' in a long putt than on the 'bowling greens' of later times. This, with all respect to the old gentleman, seems to me a little like saying that billiards is a more scientific game on the table in a village club room than on a championship table in Leicester Square.

The players of a century ago had many difficulties to contend with on the greens, but they had one advantage; the hole had no tin and players dipped their hands in it for sand to tee the ball for the next drive; under such treatment it grew definitely larger with edges here and there comfortably worn away. Tom Morris, speaking of Allan Robertson's cunning as a golfer, said that he 'aye ken'd the muckle side of the hole'. It is arguable that it is easier to hole out in a 'muckle' hole on a rough green rather than a clean-cut hole on a smooth one. If I may interpolate an egotistical experience, I played during the first world war on the Vardar Marshes in Macedonia. The greens were untouched by any green-keeping hand and the holes, dug with an entrenching tool, grew gradually more and more welcoming. However, if the putting was not perhaps quite so difficult as some people think, the accuracy demanded in the long game must have been demoniacal, such as we moderns hardly begin to appreciate.

There is something wonderfully pleasant in the picture of golfing at St Andrews in 1848. For all that some of the golfers played fiercely for high stakes, there is a suggestion of a cosy, old-fashioned family party. Some of the regular players are neighbouring lairds who have driven in dog-carts from their homes in Fife: others from farther afield, like Colonel Fairlie from Prestwick, having an eye on the seduction of Tom Morris: some are teachers from the university: some are men of business from Edinburgh like Mr. Blackwood, who has now and again to go back and look after his famous magazine, thus, to the horror of old Mr. Sutherland, 'Wasting a Monday': others like Clanranald and Carnegie, the poet, who described them all in his cheerful verse, have homes in St Andrews from which to play golf. All seem to be more or less alike in this, that they have a good deal of leisure in which to disport themselves. They have all, or nearly all, their regular caddies, more than mere caddies, rather henchmen and squires, some of whom can play a good game and are taken into a foursome if they are needed, for the line between a professional and a caddie is not at all sharply drawn.

The great figure is Allan Robertson, the ball-maker, generally recognized as the champion player who holds in some semi-official way the position of professional to the club. In his shop, still working as a journeyman, is Tom Morris, now 26 or 27 years old, a good player and ready to challenge the champion, if the champion will take up the gauntlet, which he seems indisposed to do, preferring perhaps to have Tom as a partner in a foursome. The great Willie Park, first of a

136

famous family of golfers, has very likely come from Musselburgh, and all these three are much sought after by the gentlemen as foursome partners, for a foursome is the game chiefly played. A leisurely party in every way are these gentlemen, for they do not begin to assemble and make their matches till about eleven o'clock. On the other hand, once they have started they are full of energy for they often do not stop between their two rounds but have a short rest and a snack at the Ginger-Beer hole, and then forth again. That is the regular routine of everyday golf. The two great festivals are those of the Spring and Autumn Medals, when all, or nearly all, the best amateurs assemble, for the Autumn Medal of the Royal and Ancient constitutes in popular estimation something of an unofficial championship. Apart from the important medal round, moreover, this is the season of big four-somes, carefully made and heavily betted on, with professional partners.

How good were these great ones of their day? Perhaps the question in that form suggests the right and only answer; they were the great ones of their day. It is utterly foolish to compare scores, for courses and clubs and balls have changed out of all knowledge. Perhaps it is foolish even to express the most hesitating opinion, but I will venture nevertheless. I feel that we must wait nearly twenty years, till Young Tom Morris arises, before we reach one so palpably filled with golfing genius that we must assign him a place in the small company of the very great golfers. To say this may seem to go contrary to a rule I have often proclaimed, that to compare players of different generations is essentially futile, but in this instance I cannot help it.

Allan Robertson was obviously a player of great skill and of an easy and beautiful style, but also obviously he lacked power as compared with his rivals. It is contrary to all golfing experience that a man should be quite at the top of the tree if he is at a really serious disadvantage in point of length and power. It may have been possible in Allan's day when rivals were few. Willie Dunn had clearly the advantage of him in length: so had Willie Park, a great player but apparently lacking stamina. As to Tom Morris, we know that his backers were ready to put down the money if Allan would have played the match, and he would not. The situation is rather similar to that which arose in the world of billiards when the first John Roberts, the daring young man from Manchester, challenged Kentfield, who had long been regarded as the unchallengeable champion. Kentfield, wisely no doubt, refused to play him, and equally there can be little doubt what would have happened if he had. It is clear that Allan was an unsurpassed artist at the game, but that he was never beaten, as is alleged, was partly due to the fact that he refused to run the risk. That his famous round of 79 at St Andrews, the first ever played there under 80, must have been in the conditions a truly remarkable one is beyond a doubt.

The great professional match of the time (1849) was that often described between Allan and Tom and the two Dunns over Musselburgh, St Andrews and North Berwick. The result is well known, namely, that Allan and Tom pulled the match out of the fire at North Berwick, winning by two holes after being four down with eight to play. All possible glory be theirs, and especially Tom's, for Allan had at times been very weak. It is just worth remarking, however, that these matches were reckoned by courses and not by holes. The Dunns began by winning at Musselburgh by 13 up and 12 to play. If the reckoning had been as it would be today, there would, humanly speaking, have been the end of the match.

Now a word as to the amateurs, some of whom were beyond question very fine golfers in their day. John Wood of Musselburgh, of whom it was said that it was 'a study in the fine arts' to see him strike the ball, was a little too early for our period, but not so Sir Robert Hay and George Condie. My own impression is, however, that the really outstanding amateurs were Mr. (later Captain) John Campbell Stewart of Fasnacloich and Mr. George Glennie, who was for many years the honorary secretary of Blackheath and a beloved and monumental figure in that club, surviving till 1886. Up till 1853 the Autumn Medal had only twice been won with a score of under 100, to wit 99. The Silver Cross in the spring had been won with 96. Suddenly in the autumn of 1853 Stewart put all their scores in the shade with a 90. Nevertheless, Dr. McPherson declares medal play was not his strong point and that he was essentially a dashing match player. His score of 90 only survived for two years, for in 1855 Glennie won with 88. How good a score this was may be judged by the fact that it was not beaten in the autumn till Horace Hutchinson did 87 in 1884, when the course must have been definitely easier and a new era had begun. A few years later, in 1857, these two, Stewart and Glennie, united forces to play for Blackheath in what may be called the first open amateur tournament. It was a foursome tournament for which there entered pairs from eleven clubs, and was played at St Andrews. The two swept through with supreme dominion, beating Perth by 8 holes, Innerleven by 12, Bruntsfield by 6, and finally the Royal and Ancient by 7, thereby, as a Blackheath Minute proudly declares, 'Constituting this Club the Champion Golf Club of the World'. A year later came the first open single tournament, also at St Andrews, which was won by Robert Chambers *secundus*. He beat in the final a certain Mr. Wallace of Balgrummo who had driven all his victims mad by his slow play. Chambers was not so tamed. 'Give me,' he said, 'a novel and a camp stool, and I'll let the old chap do as he likes.' The Bruntsfield Links Club duly held a dinner to rejoice over him as 'The Champion Golfer of Great Britain', being thus one degree more modest than the Royal Blackheath.

ENTER YOUNG TOMMY

I would willingly linger for ever over these agreeable old gentlemen, but I must

138

not emulate Mr. Wallace of Balgrummo. We must pass on to the coming of Young Tommy Morris and his debut in 1864. The Open Championship had been four years in existence, the Prestwick Club having presented the Belt to be played for over Prestwick. It had been won so far three times by Tommy's father and twice by Willie Park. In 1864 Tommy was thirteen, too young it was thought to play in the grand tournament at Perth. However, the match, which has since become historic, was made for him to play 'Master William Greig of Perth, juvenile golfing celebrity'. He astonished everybody, including Master Greig, by his fine golf and it was clearly only a matter of time before he would leave everyone else behind. 'I could cope wi' Allan mysel',' Old Tom said in after years, 'but never wi' Tommy,' and there would soon be no coping with him. In 1867 he tied with Willie Park and Bob Andrews (the Rook) for first place at Carnoustie in a tournament in which all the best professionals played, and won the play off. In 1868, when he was either 17 or just 18, he became champion, and there was no other champion for four years.

Not only did this young hero, barely emerged from boyhood, win: he won with scores that had never been approached or thought of before, and he left his opponents many strokes behind. Thus, in 1868, he won with 154, in 1869 with 157, and in 1870, when he made the Belt his own by this third successive victory, with 149. A man generally wins a championship by the narrowest possible margin: Tommy for the three years he won the Belt was on an average nine strokes better than the runner-up. No doubt he had comparatively few competitors, though also no doubt some of them were fine players, but his scores are convincingly eloquent as judged by the par score for Prestwick as it then was. In the biography of Old Tom Morris will be found an interesting disquisition on this point by Mr. William Doleman, in his day one of the best of the amateurs and an interesting figure in several ways. As a youth he had been a seaman and had sailed out of Sebastopol under Russian gun-fire. Yet he took part in an Amateur Championship at Sandwich in which I, *moi qui vous parle*, myself played. I remember well the look of the old gentleman surveying the not very distant flag with an enormous pair of field-glasses, before deciding on his club. It was said that in another championship about that time he had said to his youthful adversary, 'I mind well the day your grandmither was married.' At any rate he was a fine old golfer of long experience. I make no apology for being momentarily seduced down a bypath by him, and return to the point. Prestwick was in Tommy's day a twelve-hole course, so that the championship consisted of three rounds. Mr Doleman calculated the par of the course as it had then been hole by hole as 49. Tommy's rounds were 47, 51 and 51. Thus, for the 36 holes he was two strokes more than perfect play. Now admittedly there are pars and pars, and a par four hole may demand two very fine, long accurate shots, or maybe no more than what is vulgarly known as 'a kick and a spit'. Still, Prestwick was in the forefront of courses and we have no right to doubt Mr Doleman's calculation. So much being admitted, in an era when the implements of the game and the standard of green-keeping were so vastly inferior to those of today, a score of only two worse than par play was a wonder that can still speak for itself. It was to my mind beyond all argument a tremendous performance, to be fairly compared, as far as comparison is possible, with any of those that have come after it. It convinces me that Leslie Balfour Melville gave me the right answer when I once asked him, tiresomely enough, how Tommy compared with Harry Vardon. After a moment's thought he said, 'I can't imagine anyone playing better than Tommy did.'

As far as one can now judge, Tommy was never quite so good, certainly never so all-conquering again, after his third win in the Belt. It may have been simply that, as is often seen, he raised the general standard of what was thought possible and so compelled his competitors to improve. Certainly he was still recognized as the leading player, but he seems to have become, in comparison with his greatest years, only *primus inter pares*. I have an impression that his health and fitness were not, towards the end of his tragically short life, quite what they had been. After he had won the Belt there was a year's interregnum and then the present Cup was given to be played for at Prestwick, St Andrews and Musselburgh. Tommy won it in 1872 in a score seventeen strokes higher than in 1870, in weather that was clearly difficult. In the next three years the championship was won by Tom Kidd, Mungo Park and Willie Park, with no very remarkable scores, and Tommy can hardly have been in his old form to allow it. About those three years none of his eulogists have much, or indeed anything, to say, and then on the morning of Christmas Day 1875 he was found dead in his bed. He was twenty-four years old.

And now what kind of a player, from a technical point of view, was this immensely great golfer? We have few photographs to help us save the one of Tommy addressing the ball for a half shot with an iron, which was clearly the model for the figure on his monument in the cathedral churchyard at St Andrews, a figure which seems instinct with golfing dash and power. There was alas! no instantaneous photography in his day and we have to gather what we can. By far the best account that I know is by Mr. Everard in the *Badminton*, but we may pick up a little elsewhere. Obviously he was a player of tremendous dash, with a rather forcing, or at any rate forceful, swing, not quite so long as was normal in his day, and a capacity for putting a little more into a shot when it was needed. I take it there was something fiery and almost flamboyant about his style, first from the fact that he is said to have broken shafts merely by waggling them, secondly from Old Tom, his father, telling Horace Hutchinson, when he first saw him, that he reminded him of Tommy, and Horace's style was certainly flamboyant rather than peaceful. He was, we are told, great in any form of recovery from bad stances or bad lies, and in playing all sorts of forcing shots with the iron niblick, with its then minute head, which he also daringly used for playing short pitches. I think it was Mr. James Cunningham who told me of seeing with awe and terror Tommy using this club to pitch from the Elysian Fields over the big bunker on to the green of the Hole o' Cross. His iron play is said to have been uniformly magnificent, but by all accounts it was his putting that, as it were, put the coping stone on the rest of his game, and gave him that inside turn against all his rivals and particularly his nearest competitor, Davie Strath. He used a wooden putter, having the ball so near his right toe that he looked as if he must hit it with the club; his left toe pointed at the hole and he stood well up with knees nearly straight.

He is said to have deliberately hit the ball high, coming near to half topping it; he was an essentially bold putter, never being afraid of running past and rather unfilially laughing at his father who, he said, would be a good putter if the hole was always a yard nearer to him. He took very great pains over short putts—another respect in which his father was reminded of him by Horace Hutchinson. Finally, and that is of course the test of a great putter, since everyone can putt well sometimes, he was consistently good.

THE SECOND COMING OF GOLF IN ENGLAND

There was a subscription raised among golf clubs for a monument to Tommy, and among them were just four English Clubs: Blackheath, Westward Ho!, Wimbledon and Liverpool. That fact reminds me that I have gone a little too far ahead and must now retrace my steps some ten years or so to see the second coming of golf in England. The pride of place belongs by just one year to the Royal North Devon Golf Club and Westward Ho!, the first seaside golf course in England. The story is well known how in 1864 General Moncrieffe came from St Andrews to stay with his cousin, Mr. Gossett, the Vicar of Northam, and being taken by his host for a walk across the Burrows to the Pebble Ridge he exclaimed, 'Providence obviously designed this for a golf links.' It was not for Mr. Gossett to oppose the providential plan; he was fond of games and had athletic sons who needed amusing, and he set to work at once to organize a club. General Moncrieffe was a useful liaison officer with St. Andrews, and clubs and balls were forthcoming from Tom Morris's shop. Presently that sage himself came down to advise on the course, and in later life all he could remember of it was that there was a terribly steep hill to climb after the day was done. Johnnie Allan came as professional, the first Scotsman after the twin Dunns to make the great venture. Captain Molesworth, generally known as the Old Mole, a famous character and a match-maker of great shrewdness, had three sons, all good players and Arthur very good. Horace Hutchinson was living near by and was beginning as a schoolboy to show great promise; players came from Blackheath and from Wimbledon; there were

141

one or two tournaments in which the most famous Scottish professionals took part.

A year after the foundation of Westward Ho! came that of Wimbledon. The original members who played on Wimbledon Common were all members of the London Scottish Rifle Volunteer Corps, and the club, the London Scottish Golf Club, was first of all merely subsidiary to the Corps, as were the football and curling clubs, and its every rule had to be submitted to the Commanding Officer, Lord Elcho, an admirable but, as it subsequently appeared, a somewhat arbitrary nobleman. In course of time the club was thrown open to those who did not belong to the Corps and far outnumbered those who did, but Lord Elcho would not budge a foot; the minority must still have the supreme power. The end was inevitable, a partially amicable split, the formation of a new London Scottish Club distinguished from the old one only by inverted commas, and a new Wimbledon Club, soon afterwards to become Royal Wimbledon. Of the Royal Wimbledon two of the moving spirits were the well-known Scottish golfers, Mr. Henry Lamb and Dr. W. Laidlaw Purves, later to be one of the founders of Sandwich. It is a belief of the club, and it is a point on which nobody is likely to contradict them, that these two were the first to establish the custom of giving three-quarters of the difference in handicap in match play. Incidentally, it is interesting to go back a little and note that in May 1870 the Committee decided not to employ a professional till September, but announced that they 'took a favourable view of Young Tom Morris's application for the post'. Tommy in fact never took up the job. He was at the time twenty years old and at the zenith of his youthful fame, since in 1870 he made the champion's belt his own by his third successive victory. Perhaps Old Tom thought him 'ower young' for this voyage of southern exploration. We shall never know. It need only be added that Wimbledon (which since 1908 has played on its private course in Caesar's Camp) has remained one of those London clubs which most faithfully preserve the oldest, best and friendliest traditions of golf.

In 1869 came perhaps, if it be not invidious to say so, the most momentous of these three foundations. It was in that year that there came into being what is now the Royal Liverpool Golf Club, with its links at Hoylake, breeding place of mighty golfers, a club that has been second to none in enterprise and to whose pioneering spirit are owed some of golf's most cherished and now almost venerable institutions. It was in May 1869 that Mr. J. Muir Dowie, who is for ever commemorated in the name of the seventh hole at Hoylake with its little triangular green on the very verge of perdition, sent out a circular letter. It called on the recipients to join a golf club with a subscription of 10/- a year and to attend a meeting at the Royal Hotel at Hoylake.

Hoylake in those days consisted largely of the hotel aforesaid, in the eighteenth century the resort of fashionable bathers, but since then somewhat fallen in the world, a farm and one or two houses, a rabbit warren and a race-course. Of the race-course all that now remains are the names of two holes, not so often used as of old, The Stand and The Course, and, I think, one or two fragments of posts on the way to the eighteenth. Save at the time of the race-meetings Hoylake lay wonderfully solitary. George Morris, Old Tom's brother, came from St Andrews to lay out the original nine holes and brought with him his young son Jack to be professional to the new club. The place seemed so dead alive that his heart bled for the boy to be left in loneliness, and he suggested taking him home again. Jack, however, was made of stern stuff; he stayed there, occupying himself in making balls in a loose box at the Royal until the golfers began to appear. He stayed there till he died, full of years and honours, a life member of the club and a beloved Hoylake monument. By October the first competition had been held and once more the older clubs sent forth missionaries to cheer and encourage the youngest born; there were players from Blackheath, Manchester and Westward Ho! An interesting winner was one then designated Mr. John Ball, Junior, who was the father of *the* John Ball. He won the Hulton Cup with 135-36-99. Evidently golf and the Ball family were naturally intended for one another, for within a year Mr. Ball's handicap had fallen from 36 to scratch and still he could win. The time was to come several years later when the Royal Hotel at meeting time would ring with his challenge, 'Me and my son'll play any two,' a gauntlet not so often taken up, and he himself was to reach the semi-final at the first official Amateur Championship to be played at Hoylake in 1887. Incidentally, golf did the Ball family a good turn in that they then and for many years afterwards owned the Royal Hotel, and it was there that the club had its rooms and held its dinners until the present club-house was built about 1894.

Young Tom came to Hoylake in its early years and duly won a tournament, and there was another held in 1892 in which most of the distinguished Scottish professionals took part. It is of one of these occasions that a pleasant little story is told of Jamie Anderson, who, having suffered from the extreme narrowness of the first hole, then the second, where it skirts the out-of-bounds field, exclaimed, 'Ma God, it's like playing up a spout.' Some of the best amateurs from Scotland came, too, as they did from London and Westward Ho!, and there were famous convivial evenings in the bar parlour of the Royal. Golfers in England during the '70s and early '80s constituted to some extent at least one family, and with club subscriptions so minute as they were, it was no uncommon thing for a golfer to belong to Westward Ho!, Hoylake, Blackheath and Wimbledon, as well as the Royal and Ancient and the Honourable Company and go happily medal-hunting at all of them on dates carefully arranged so as not to clash.

Doubtless, this blossoming of golf in England, though as yet local and spasmodic, was the cause of its beginning at Oxford and Cambridge. At Cambridge some earlier efforts had been made, I believe, on Midsummer Common, and pioneers had even explored the heath at Royston, but the club was founded in 1875, as was that of Oxford, the two courses, both chiefly notable for mud, being respectively at Coldham Common and Cowley. I am not sure whether Oxford had one pre-eminently pious founder, but Cambridge certainly had in the shape of W. T. Linskill, later a very well-known character at St Andrews, and the subject of many pleasant legends. He went up to Cambridge in the '70s, to Jesus, and since he showed no signs of passing his little-go his father and mother, so at least the story goes, took a house there till he should do so. They died there many years later, their hopes still unfulfilled. Meanwhile he played a great part in promoting the first university match, four a side, on Wimbledon Common, and untrammelled by any nonsensical rules as to date of matriculation, he continued to play for Cambridge till 1883. Oxford won the first match by 24 holes to none, and it is noteworthy that in those days when golf was barely known, the side could yet boast two golfers as distinguished as have ever played for Oxford since, Horace Hutchinson and Alexander Stuart. Let it be added that in 1879 Cambridge produced one F. G. H. Pattison who beat the great Horace by five holes, and to show that this was not too gross a fluke halved with him in the following year. He must have been, and I have been told that he was, a very good golfer, but he lives only through this feat, and no other trace of him has ever been found.

AFTER TOMMY

Now we must get back to the more serious golf of Scotland and the championship after Young Tommy's death. His closest rival and friend at St Andrews had been David Strath, a grand golfer who never won the championship, and, like Tommy, died young. He had a great chance of winning at St Andrews in 1876 and the story is worth telling as showing how comparatively casual were championships in those days. Bob Martin was leading with 176 and Davie Strath needed two fives to beat him. After two strokes at the 17th he was within a full wooden club shot of the green. The players in front of him were still putting but he lashed out gaily, hit someone on the putting green, and through this rub of the green was saved from the road and got his five. Having victory now in his pocket he took a sad six at the last hole and so tied for the championship. Not so, said Bob Martin's supporters, for Davie had broken the law by playing on the couple in front of him, and, moreover, his marker had not kept his card properly. After much solemn deliberation it was declared that the 'tie would be played off under protest'. Apparently, rough justice was done; Bob Martin must have won the tie, for he is recorded as champion.

He won again nine years later, but meanwhile the two great players were Jamie Anderson of St Andrews and Bob Ferguson of Musselburgh, who each won the

144

championship for three years in succession. Anderson I take to have been not unlike J. H. Taylor, in an almost incredible accuracy and in mastery of the pitching shot, but he clearly never had J. H.'s power. Bob Ferguson was the stronger and more solid golfer, and a great player with the cleek, with which he once won a match against Tommy Morris similarly armed. He all but achieved a fourth victory since he tied with Willie Fernie and led him by one stroke coming to the home hole—a one-shot hole—at Musselburgh in playing off the tie. However, Fernie holed an immense putt for two and his opponent had a four. Bob Ferguson afterwards had a bad illness and never again made a serious show upon the links, ending, as he had begun, a caddie on his native Musselburgh. Willie Fernie won in 1883 and I had better briefly complete the champions of the '80s before going back to the amateurs who are now clamouring for notice. Three of them were scarcely professionals at all in the ordinary sense, for Jack Simpson of Elie, a mighty driver and a most dashing player, was a stonemason, David Brown a slater, and Jack Burns a plasterer. These men were, it is not unfair to say, of the old happy-go-lucky kind of professional, not far removed from the caddie. Of a very different type, a man of education and ambition, was Willie Park, Junior, who won in 1887 and in 1889 (after a tie with Andrew Kirkaldy), and was among golf's leading figures first as a player and then as a pioneer of golfing architecture. Park was sprung from a race of professional golfers and brought up at Mussel-burgh. It is rash to dogmatize, but he was probably as good a putter as ever lived, at any rate in this country. He had practised scientifically and assiduously, and his wonderful holing out more than made amends for the rather erratic nature of his long game. Judged by modern, and indeed by any standards, he was a most un-trustworthy driver, lacking the power of carry and capable of a smothering and most destructive hook. But his putting and his determination kept him going, for he won two championships and came very near to a third, when he just failed to tie with Harry Vardon, then in his most invincible mood. He was ever ready to throw down the gauntlet for a money match, but here he was less successful, for H. Vardon annihilated him by his long game, and Andrew Kirkaldy also beat him with some severity in a notable match over four greens. As he gew older Park became known not so much as a player as a golfing architect. He was indeed one of the first to deserve that name. The earlier race of professionals, when called upon to lay out a course, had proceeded rather on the principle of Mr. Wemmick, 'Hullo! Here's a church. Let's go in. Hullo! Here's Miss Skeffins! Let's have a wedding.' If they found a hill they drove over it, if there was a hollow they put a green at the bottom of it. Willie Park on the other hand had the genuine artist's eye for golfing country. Sunningdale and Worplesdon, amongst other fine courses, owe to him their original design, and so does Huntercombe, a delightful place, which was the love of his later life, though for him an unfortunate speculation.

L

Andrew Kirkaldy, as has been said, beat Park in a great match and, though he too continued to be for years a notable golfing figure, he falls more naturally into his place here. As early as 1878 he had been second to Jamie Anderson in the championship. Soon after that he enlisted, for some reason which, like the birth of Mr. Yellowplush, is now 'wrapped up in a mistry'. Having served his time and fought at Tel-el-Kebir he returned to St Andrews and, save for one or two brief and temporary engagements in the south, never left it again. He was rough, dour and aggressive, the very reverse of a courtier, but with some honest and downright qualities that were decidedly endearing. His conversation, moreover, though most of his sayings cannot be recorded, was racy and amusing; amusing, I think, not at all necessarily because he meant it to be. He acquired the reputation of a wit, but many of his supposed witticisms were, as I imagine, uttered in solemn and deadly earnest. He was, if not a wit, at any rate undeniably a character, and as he grew older this reputation a little unfairly overshadowed his fame as a golfer. He was a very fine golfer, especially in a match—he was no great lover of scores— and over St Andrews. His swing was in his prime considered notably short, as indeed it was compared with those of his contemporaries, but it would not today be out of the common. It was very rapid and of no one could it more truly be said in the familiar metaphor that he hit the ball like the shutting of a knife. The stories of Andrew are numberless, but to me almost the most characteristic—and it is entirely printable—is of his match with Andrew Scott at St Andrews. As he holed his putt on the 16th green to become dormy two, he raced to the next tee calling aloud in a formidable voice, 'The door's locked noo.'

Three other very fine golfers, no one of whom ever won the championship, may be dealt with in the same period, Archie Simpson, Willie Campbell and Ben Sayers. Archie Simpson had by all accounts a most beautiful swing and was twice second in the championship, but I fancy Campbell was the more alarming golfer— he beat Archie heavily in a four-green match—and indeed for a year or two I doubt if there was anyone so good. He had an extremely rapid swing, even in a day when Scottish swings were certainly not leisurely, and he was a very fine putter with occasional bursts of positively demoniac inspiration in the matter of long putts. On one occasion he had the championship at Prestwick in the hollow of his hand, and then came a fatal encounter with a bunker at the 15th hole. Someone has told me how on that day after play was over he went into Charlie Hunter's shop and found Willie Campbell and his caddie, each seated on an upturned bucket and weeping bitterly. He later went to the United States and remained there. The third of them, Ben Sayers, was a more familiar figure to later generations, a tiny little man who had begun life as an acrobat, and could manage his small body and his long club with almost acrobatic skill. He was in fact a very fine player and might well have won the championship. 'Give me a wind,' he said before one meeting at Muirfield, 'and I'll show you who'll be champion.' That fortunate breeze never blew for him, however. He was once thought to have tied but a recount showed that Jack Burns had won. He was constantly opposed to Andrew Kirkaldy in big matches, when Sayers, with the celebrated Big Crawford to carry for him, had none the worst of the exchanges. He was a shrewd, amusing little man, wonderfully keen, a great salesman and—one metaphor seems imperiously demanded—as cunning as a basketful of monkeys.

THE FIRST AMATEUR CHAMPIONSHIP

And now to the amateurs and to the beginnings of the Amateur Championship. It was the Royal Liverpool Club that began it, as they were later—in 1902—to begin the Amateur International. In 1884 it was proposed by Mr Thomas Owen Potter, a famous honorary secretary of the club, that a tournament should be held 'open to all amateur golfers in the week of the spring meeting 1885'. A special committee was formed and the first question they had to deal with was a rather delicate one, since there was then no official definition of an amateur. Douglas Rolland, a stonemason from Elie, who was not then a regular professional, sent in his entry. As he had been second in the Open Championship and taken the money prize, it was simple enough to say he was not an amateur, but then a few years before John Ball, as a boy of 14 or 15 had gone up to Scotland to play in the Open Championship and had gained sixth place, for which the prize was the vast sum of 10*s*. He had asked his chaperon, Jack Morris, what he should do with it: Jack had advised him to put it in his pocket, and that he had done, as would any rational boy. Clearly there never was a purer amateur than John Ball, and yet the two cases seemed superficially on all fours. The distinction was drawn—it was a fine one no doubt—and Rolland's entry was refused. And that for those who like legal history is why the amateur definition until quite recently laid down that an amateur must not, after attaining the age of 16, have played for a money prize in a competition.

This tournament was not then recognized as a championship, though nearly all the best amateurs of the day played in it. It was only many years after that it received this recognition, and the winner, Allan Fullarton Macfie, was retrospectively canonized as the first amateur champion. He was hardly expected to win, not being rated the equal of John Ball, Horace Hutchinson and one or two others, but he was a very good player, beautifully accurate if without any great power, knowing just what he could do and attempting no more, and a most deadly putter. The draw was rather unsatisfactory, since it left three in the semi-final, of whom Macfie rested in peace while Horace and John went out to cut each other's throats. John Ball had in those days hardly attained his full match-playing qualities and was apt to disappoint his admirers, who thought, and that rightly, unutterable things of him. He was two up at the turn but lost by two holes, and then Horace,

147

having made his great effort, could do nothing right in the final, and Macfie, wonderfully blameless and holing everything, won by 7 and 6.

Next year, 1886, the Royal Liverpool suggested to the Royal and Ancient that this tournament should be officially established as the championship. Twenty-four clubs were associated in the buying of the cup and the managing of the championship, each club being entitled to appoint a delegate. The first championship was to be held at St Andrews, and on the eve of it let us look at the select band who might provide the winner. There were some seven or eight of them, and there can be no doubt at all that they were good. I come now to those whom I knew myself, with some of whom I played and all of whom I saw, though they were all of course very considerably older than I was. I have also had the advantage of many talks with Horace Hutchinson on the subject and the opinions on which I venture will be coloured by his. The eight best players, I suggest, were Horace Hutchinson, John Ball, J. E. Laidlay, Leslie Balfour (afterwards Balfour Melville), S. Mure Fergusson, Alexander Stuart, A. F. Macfie and F. A. Fairlie. Inside this body of eight there was an inner circle of three, Hutchinson, Ball and Laidlay, and of those three Ball was by common consent the best. It took him some little time to get into his stride and do himself justice, for he did not win until 1888, but in the long run his record was incomparable, and I am sure that even in early days both the other two had the feeling that he at his best had something they had not quite got, that he had in a unique degree the power of putting in a thrust not to be parried.

Of the other five, Leslie Balfour won one championship, the only one which John Ball ever lost in the final, and Mure Fergusson was twice runner-up. On records I think they come next. Leslie, a notable all-round player of games, had a fine and orthodox swing that looked likely to last him for ever and did endure a very long while. Mure's style was less attractive: I doubt if it could be called attractive at all, though it was eminently powerful, and he could go very crooked on occasions, but he had a fine dour courage, a great power of recovery, and was a magnificent holer out at a crisis, standing up to the ball and seeming to compel it to go in by sheer force of character. I ought to add that Horace put Alexander Stuart ahead of these two and next to the leading trinity. Undoubtedly he was very good with a smooth and graceful style, but he gave up competitive golf comparatively young, and so for myself I can give no opinion. Neither, for that matter, did I see either Fairlie or Macfie play more than a shot or two.

There can be little doubt on one point, that these, the best young amateurs of the first championship, for they were all at least reasonably young then, marked a very decided advance on the leading Scottish amateurs of the '60s and '70s. It is a thing not to be proved but, I think, generally recognized. Some of them at least were to all intents and purposes as good as the best professionals, and I shall soon be coming to a tremendous day when John Ball, the first Englishman and the first amateur, won the Open Championship, and so disclosed new and hitherto undreamed-of possibilities.

Even before he had achieved this earth-shaking victory, I believe John Ball had opened the eyes of golfers to new possibilities in the matter of long shots hit straight up to the pin. I know this was Harold Hilton's view, and there could be none more worthy of attention. Some years later, when J. H. Taylor first appeared, his extraordinarily bold and accurate play up to the flag may have set up a higher standard, but I fancy that it was John Ball who had first shown the way. John Ball is one of those golfers whom it is very difficult to estimate, because not only did all Hoylake golfers worship him devoutly, admitting no comparison, but in a lesser degree all those who ever saw him play fell under the magic spell of his golf. I do not think, however, that anyone will seriously dispute that he was the greatest amateur golfer that this country has yet produced. His stance was a little stiff and his grip of the right hand apparently though not really unorthodox, but his swing was the true poetry of motion, the most perfectly smooth and rhythmical imaginable. He had a remarkable control of all his clubs, and a power of hitting the ball low through the wind that was unequalled in the gutty days, when it was so intensely valuable. He was a grand iron player, using a comparatively straight-faced iron even for lofting shots: a good approach putter but not always trustworthy over the short ones. In his youth he had great power and was capable of a tremendous carrying shot at a crisis, such as that over the Dun bunker against Mure Fergusson in the final of a championship. Later, when I knew him, he relied rather on a blameless accuracy and straightness, and he had always a great capacity for rising to the occasion. He was not, any more than any other great player, free from nervousness, but the beautiful trueness of his swing pulled him through in the most desperate moments.

Horace Hutchinson had not John Ball's perfect swing but his style was in its way a fascinating one, with its flamboyant or, to use his own word, bombastic freedom and remarkable looseness of the wrist, and indeed looseness of his entire frame. The handle of the club was given an amount of play in his right hand which would today be looked upon with horror, and his right knee gave very perceptibly under him. This excessive freedom may have made for unsteadiness, but it seemed to have this compensating quality that he could swing 'or high or low' and adapt his swing wonderfully to any kind of uncomfortable lie or stance. Nobody was ever better at improvising a stroke for some difficult or, as it looked to the too confident adversary, impossible occasion. He putted as he did everything with this noteworthy freedom of wrist, and though he had an occasional bad day, he holed on balance far more than his share of good putts. So did the third of this great trio, J. E. Laidlay. 'I suppose I must trust to a pitch and a putt,' was a remark

149

often quoted by his familiars, and no one was better justified in his trust. He was a beautiful pitcher, in his time as famous for his skill with the mashie as J. H. Taylor was later, and the ensuing putt had a horribly stealthy and insinuating way with it. The ball, struck with that little light old putting cleek, his boyhood's club at Loretto, looked as if it must be short, but it crept on and on and toppled into the hole at last. His style was a peculiar one, or rather his stance was peculiar, with the ball far away in front of his left foot: the swing itself was sound and normal enough. It was written of him that 'his wretched imitators swarm on every links of the Lothians', and no doubt his was a method to be perhaps admired but not copied. The results were admirable beyond all possible doubt, and it is an ironical circumstance that he ought to have won an Open Championship in which he was second, if his putting, of all things, had not for once forsaken him. Incidentally, he was the first golfer known to have held his club with the now common overlapping grip which has been labelled with the name of Vardon.

After Horace had won his two championships, the belief of Hoylake in its hero was at length justified, and the two Johnnies, Ball and Laidlay, divided the next five championships between them, Ball with the lion's share. Peter Anderson, a young St Andrews University student who soon afterwards went to Australia, surprisingly beat Laidlay in the final of 1893 and Leslie Balfour Melville, triumphing at the 19th hole in three matches running, beat Ball in 1895. And then in next year's final, played for the first time over 36 holes, we come to the first victory of one of two very great players of a slightly younger generation, who were destined constantly to be compared with one another. At Sandwich in 1896 F. G. Tait beat H. H. Hilton by 8 up and 7 to play. The two were as near as might be of the same age. Hilton was born in 1869, one of the great vintage years of amateur golf, and Tait is generally assigned to it, though in fact he was born early in January 1870. They had both, and Harold Hilton in particular, been very well known for some years before this encounter. Hilton had already been in two finals, in 1891 and 1892, losing to Laidlay in one and Ball in the other. More than that, in 1892 he had followed the example of the other great man of Hoylake and won the Open Championship in the teeth of all the professionals. Freddie Tait had blossomed a little later but had done outstanding things. He had already beaten Hilton in the Amateur Championship at Prestwick in 1893, losing a great match afterwards to Laidlay: he had beaten the record of St Andrews with a 72: he had been very unluckily beaten after a tie by Rolland in the amateur and professional tournament at Sandwich, when Rolland had gone on to beat the new champion, Taylor. He was emphatically the hope and pride of Scotland, where he was as much adored as John Ball was at Hoylake. And as between these two players it must be owned that the Scotsman had much the better of the perennial argument. Hilton could not do himself any kind of justice against Tait; try as he

150

would a deadly paralysis would creep over him against this one opponent, while Tait went from confidence to confidence against Hilton and cheerfully annihilated him.

Apart from this personal ascendancy Tait was, I think, the greater match player. It was the game he liked and that suited his temperament and his methods. He won plenty of medals, often with fine scores, but it was the man-to-man combat that was for him the game of golf: the other he compared rather scornfully to rifle-shooting. Match play suited him both because he had something of the same gift as John Ball of putting in on a sudden a terrific thrust, often in the nature of a recovery, and because he could now and then make a disastrously wild shot which was very expensive in strokes. I have seen Tait described by some who never knew him as a 'slashing' player. I can hardly conceive of a worse-chosen epithet. He had great length when he wanted it but as he grew older he kept this power of hard hitting under rigid control. And his swing was easy and smooth almost to the point of gentleness. In his best games there were no recoveries because none were needed, but now and again something—perhaps it was his right hand held so far under the club—could produce a vast hook or slice. Then he did have to recover and could do so in a way to break an enemy's heart. Anyone who saw his match in the semi-final of the Amateur Championship at Hoylake in 1898 against John Low will agree that here was the art of recovering carried to really outrageous lengths. Tait was a fine iron player, especially of the kind of iron shots that were needed at St Andrews in days when the course and the greens were keener and barer than today, and he was a very good and especially a very bold putter with a lofted putting cleek. No one ever gave the hole a better chance.

It was clear from his bearing at once gallant and light-hearted that he enjoyed the fight and as certainly he enjoyed the crowd, though he never for a moment played to it. By comparison I do not think Harold Hilton greatly enjoyed single combat, though except in that one instance, he was no mean fighter. 'I could fight pretty well myself,' he once said to me, 'when I could see the humour of it.' It was in score play, however, that he was to be seen at his best, and this country has produced no amateur who was his equal in it. Neither has it produced any one amateur or professional who studied and practised the game so scientifically, who observed it so closely and knew it so thoroughly. He did not make a simple game of it, since he constantly tried experiments and was never wholly satisfied with the straightforward 'bread and butter' shots, however perfectly played. He loved perhaps better than anything else to acquire complete mastery of a wooden club. At the same time this varied skill was no mere virtuosity. He had a practical reason for all he did; and he habitually gained in length by bringing in his drives from right to left. And yet he won one Amateur Championship, at Prestwick in 1911, when the ground was fast and length did not matter compared with straightness, by an exactly opposite shot, a slightly fading drive. In that same championship he showed a power of stopping his iron shots on the hard dry greens that scarcely anyone else there could compass. As to his putting he was a very good putter when all was going well but was inclined, like other much more fallible human beings, to putt a little short at a crisis.

Harold Hilton was a great master of golf and let it be remembered that he won the Open Championship not once but twice. The first victory at Muirfield in 1892 may have been rather a lucky one in that the course was then new, rough and short, and perhaps hardly fit for a championship; but there could be no question as to the second at Hoylake in 1897, when the Triumvirate and Herd were in their glory. Moreover, only a single disastrous mistake, an eight at the short Himalayas, prevented him from winning a third time at Prestwick in 1898, and years later at Sandwich in 1911, in a second blooming, he was right up in the hunt up to the very last hole. The Amateur Championship eluded him for a long while and he did not win it till 1900 when both John Ball and Freddie Tait had gone to the South African War, the latter never to come back. But he won three times afterwards, and his record of four wins is second to John Ball's of eight. Moreover, in 1911, when he was forty-two years old, he made a lone pilgrimage to the United States and won the Amateur Championship there, always a great feat in the other man's country.

Before Ball and Tait had gone to the war they had played perhaps the most famous of all Amateur Championship finals, at Prestwick in 1899. It has been often described and every golfing schoolboy has heard of Freddie's great shot out of the water in the Alps bunker at the 17th hole, followed by an equally good, though less dramatic one, played by his opponent from the hard wet sand close to the boards. In the morning the match had seemed as good as over with Tait five up at the 14th and Ball unable to hole a putt. The leader by his own account thought it was over and eased off a little, a mistake for which he afterwards condemned himself, saying that it had taught him a lesson. Ball got two of those five holes back before lunch, and then, after a putting lesson on the home green from Harold Hilton (I can see him now vividly enough, with a variety of clubs strewn around him), he set out to catch his man in real earnest. After ten holes he had squared the match. At the eleventh he missed a putt and was one down, but Tait instantly hit a grotesque hook over the crowd and clean over the Pow Burn out of bounds from the twelfth tee. With two to play, John Ball was one up. Then came the famous 17th halved in five, and Freddie with a wonderful pitch and run and a good putt saved his bacon with a three at the 18th. Finally, as all the world knows, John Ball holed a putt, not an enormous putt but a very, very good one, perhaps 8 feet, perhaps 10, for a three at the 37th. From between somebody's legs I believe I saw him strike the ball, but I only heard it go in.

152

A NEW GENERATION

Hilton and Tait had broken in on the preserves of the Ball, Hutchinson, Laidlay generation, and now they were to be attacked in their turn by a generation some seven or eight years younger than themselves. Among these younger challengers two stood out, Robert Maxwell and Jack Graham, the one a Scottish player alike by birth and breeding, a product of the East Lothian, the other a Scotsman by blood but purely English in his golfing upbringing at Hoylake. Jack Graham was beyond any doubt the finest amateur golfer who never won a championship, and a far, far better player than many who did. His failure to do so was partly a matter of temperament—he hated to disappoint year after year the high hopes of his friends; partly perhaps the result of his working hard at his business in Liverpool and so being quite unaccustomed to a week of continuous golf. The golf that he enjoyed and excelled in was the round on a summer evening, when he would come back from Liverpool, exchange his town coat for one of ancient tweed, take out four or five clubs and some old balls and run round Hoylake in about an hour and a half with a chosen friend. Then he was wholly magnificent and the scores he could do, and constantly did, in such circumstances were terrific. He would regularly play very well in the international match which preceded the championship, overwhelming some wretched Englishman by many holes, but as the championship itself wore to its close he seemed to grow tired (I believe he slept badly on these occasions) and gradually petered out. If ever he could have reached the final, a 36-hole match would have given him full scope, but that was what he never could do. And so he must go down to history, as do certain athletes who are great runners but poor racers. Technically he was a player of marked idiosyncrasies, standing with the right foot far advanced and the hands noticeably far back in addressing the ball, a method having a curious beauty of its own to which no photograph I have ever seen did any justice. His iron play was especially fine, and, like all the best Hoylake players, he was master of the wind that blows there so fiercely. He certainly did not lack courage, but he did lack hostility, being by nature a gentle, friendly creature, liking private golf and playing public golf rather from a sad-eyed loyalty to his admirers. He was killed fighting in the first war, most deeply regretted by all who knew him.

Robert Maxwell was not unlike Graham in having no relish for the publicity of championship golf and no love for the attendant crowd; he, too, preferred peaceful games with his friends. But he had great physical strength and could compel himself to fight hard and dourly once he was in the ring. A beautiful player he was not, but he was immensely strong and accurate, and I think few today realize what a very great and formidable golfer he was. His wide stance with the right shoulder notably far down and the right hand under the club, together with some hint of a lurch in his swing, suggested power rather than straightness, but he went very straight indeed and was in particular a master of the shot held up into a strong right-hand wind. He was the possessor of a tremendous iron shot onomato-poeically called a 'dunch', but he also had a wonderfully delicate touch near to the green in what his friends termed 'Bobby's pussy-cat shot'. It was perhaps typical of his stay-at-home nature that he was definitely more alarming at Muirfield than anywhere else and won both his championships there, but he was a great golfer anywhere and more than once finished very high on the list in an open championship.

Of much the same generation was one golfer whose exact status in golfing history will always be a question for argument. This was A. J. T. Allan, a young Edinburgh doctor who won the championship at Muirfield in 1897 and died before he could defend it next year. The story is well known how he came down each day by train from Edinburgh to Drem, whence he bicycled several miles to the course, and how he played in his ordinary shoes with no nails in them. I never saw him and can give no opinion, but this much is certain that for a year or two before his surprising win he had been doing a series of notable scores on Edinburgh courses. Whether or not he had sufficient power to be one of the really great I do not know, but clearly he had remarkable accuracy and a tranquil and courageous temperament. His victim in this final was James Robb, then of St Andrews but afterwards for many years of Prestwick St Nicholas. Robb had a most successful career, winning one championship, being twice runner-up and four times in all in the semi-final. He was hardly an impressive player with a rather short snappy swing and was neither a very long nor a very straight driver; but he was a sound iron player, and above all a lovely putter. His name is not often mentioned when great putters are enumerated, but I am very sure it ought to be. Having regard to his record I doubt if there has been one better.

And now, before I come to the end of the nineteenth century amateurs, to return later to those of the twentieth, there are two I must mention. One was of the 1869 vintage, John Low. John was once runner-up in the championship, beaten only at the last hole at St Andrews by Harold Hilton, and was twice beaten in a semi-final, once at the 21st and once at the 22nd hole, each time very unluckily. That was a fine record which he owed mainly to his magnificent putting with the wooden putter, but also to his fine fighting qualities, his mastery of strategy and his power of keeping the ball in play. Yet John Low's position in golfing history depends rather on his qualities as a man, his fine intellect and delightful sense of humour, his power of making friends and his deep love for the old traditions of the game, which he never ceased to uphold. He was for years Chairman of the Rules of Golf Committee and did admirable work in that office. He was, with Arthur Croome, one of the founders of the Oxford and Cambridge Golfing Society, which now more than fifty years old has played no inconsiderable part in the history of amateur golf. He led the Society side that went to America in the early years of the twentieth century and returned to warn us of the imminent peril of invasion. Of all those in my time who deserve the title of elder statesmen of golf the name that comes first to my mind is that of John Low.

The other, of much the same vintage, was Edward Blackwell, one of four famous St Andrews brothers. We are apt to think of Ted Blackwell as of a later date, partly because he lasted so long and played for Scotland when he was much nearer sixty than fifty, partly because in his young days he spent most of his time farming in California. In fact he was born in 1866. His name will always be synonymous with colossal driving and he was not only immensely powerful but had a swing which for combined grace and fury of hitting was glorious to behold. The curious thing about his driving was that he was inclined to slice rather than hook. If he had learned in his youth to hit 'from inside out' and drive with a shade of draw, he would surely have driven the ball off the face of the earth. He did not, however, trouble his head overmuch about such niceties but went on his simple way rejoicing in his strength. In his later years he became a notably good holer-out with an aluminium putter, just as in his younger days he had been a notably bad one with a cleek. If he had mastered this art a little earlier Walter Travis might not have beaten him at Sandwich; but that is another story to which we shall come later, and anyhow there are always 'ifs and ands'.

THE TRIUMVIRATE

I am afraid it is unavoidable that I should be like a man playing on a pair of kettledrums, turning from side to side, now to the amateurs and now to the professionals. So now, having taken the amateurs to the end of the nineteenth century, I must go back ten years or so and trace the epoch-making arrival of the famous triumvirate Taylor, Vardon and Braid, and their constant rival, Alexander Herd, who with them made up what a piquet player called the *quarte major*. Herd was the eldest, born in 1868, Vardon and Braid in 1870 and Taylor in 1871. 1893 seems to me the material year, for it was then that Taylor burst upon the world and to some extent started a new era. Between that year, however, and the year in which I ended my professional survey several things had happened. In 1890 the Open Championship had been won for the first time by an Englishman and an amateur, John Ball, and after him Hugh Kirkaldy, a grand slashing St Andrews player who died before he was thirty, had won in 1891. A second Hoylake amateur, Harold Hilton, had broken down the ring fence and won at Muirfield. Herd tied for second in that year; he had won a professional tournament at St Andrews and was at any rate in his own country well known, and yet it was Taylor, the young man from the West Country, who set Scotland alight in 1893 and made this Prestwick championship a landmark.

From working on the course at Westward Ho!, where he had already made

155

some local mark, Taylor had gone to Burnham as professional and greenkeeper. When there he had been matched in a home and home match against Andrew Kirkaldy, then doing a temporary job at Winchester, and had beaten him. Andrew, both to excuse his defeat and from a natural generosity to the young, had sung the praises of his conqueror. So when Taylor appeared at Prestwick, nearly all the best players made a dead set at him and one and all retired abashed before him. His extraordinarily straight driving, his long shots played boldly right up to the pin, and his deadly pitching with a mashie all marked him out as something of a new phenomenon in golf, and when he began the championship with a 75, a record round and three strokes lower than anyone else's, he seemed to hold the championship in his hand. Perhaps he thought so himself, and if so he had a rude awakening; the rain came down in torrents, drenched him to the skin and washed away his hopes. He began to miss putts, his second round was 89, and he finished far down the list, the winner being another young and then relatively unknown player, Willie Auchterlonie, now a beloved monument at St Andrews. It had been a sad set-down but perhaps a useful lesson, and all those who had seen Taylor play realized that his victory must be only a matter of time.

That was two years before the first occasion of my seeing him, when he came to play at Worlington, near Newmarket, and I imagine that my impressions were much the same as those of many other people who watched him spell-bound for the first time. He stood then very 'open' for his wooden shots, his right foot being, I think, perceptibly farther forward than in his later days. This, coupled with his comparatively short swing, and sternly controlled follow-through, together with the immobility of his feet—he always upheld 'flat-footed golf'—made his style extraordinarily different from that of the typical Scottish professionals and gave the impression, to me at least, of a man playing his driver as if it were a mashie. There was a noteworthy sameness in his method of playing all his strokes, and he seemed to make of golf a game of almost monotonous simplicity. Whether it was precisely a beautiful style or not it was a fascinating one in the crispness and cleanness of hitting and the arrow-like straightness of the ball's flight, and I have never asked for anything more aesthetically satisfying than to watch J. H.

In 1894, it was apparent that he had profited by the Prestwick disaster and was now steady as a rock. He led almost from the start and save for a shaky hole or two in the last round gave his admirers no anxiety. Sandwich was then comparatively new, a rather rough, wild stretch of great golfing country with a home-coming very, very long for the gutty ball. Taylor's winning score of 326 now looks abnormally high, but it was the best score in a field of all the best golfers, and those who only know today's course and today's game must take its merits on trust; they are, through no fault of their own, incapable of judging it.

Taylor was now the cock of the walk; Herd could and did hold his own with him in the many exhibition matches they played together, but Taylor was *the* player and he showed it in 1895 when he won the championship for the second year running and that at St Andrews, a course that rash critics thought he would never be able to play. They were good prophets in that he never really liked the course; there were features of it that went against the grain with him, but he could play it superbly and won two of his five championships there. In this year he began by putting himself apparently out of court with a first round of 86, but he hung on and on and gradually cut down Herd's lead over him to three strokes with a round to go. A storm of rain in that last round destroyed poor Herd who was out in the very worst of it. It drenched Taylor, too, though he had less of it to endure, and it did that which was for him much more important, it drenched the greens. He pitched and putted on them with splendid boldness and sailed away to win by four shots.

With Taylor's second year as reigning champion the two other members of the triumvirate may be said to make their first appearance. True, both had already played in a championship and each was known to a small circle of good judges as a golfer of great possibilities, but the general public knew little of either of them and it was a rather ironical circumstance that each of them owed his early fame to a match with Taylor; the man they were trying to dethrone gave them a helping hand. It was in December 1895 that Taylor was billed to play an exhibition match of 36 holes against one James Braid on a course of singular muddiness, long since a victim to the builder, West Drayton. Braid, a cousin of Douglas Rolland, one of the uncrowned kings of golf, came from the same nursery of fine players, Elie. His parents had not approved of golf as a career; he had been apprenticed to a joiner and had worked both at St Andrews and Edinburgh, where he made a considerable reputation as an amateur. Then, having acquired the security of a trade, he had cut loose and taken a job as a clubmaker at the Army and Navy Stores. I remember the rumours of this mysterious player—I hardly knew his name—who was to be seen at weekends on suburban courses hitting the ball incredible distances. With the match at West Drayton all these rumours were confirmed. After a close and splendid struggle the champion was dormy two, but Braid by dint of superior length could get up at each of the last two holes and saved his bacon with two great threes.

Braid was a made man; he soon left the Stores for Romford and in 1897 he was second in the Open Championship, beaten by Harold Hilton by a single stroke. Yet his real time was not yet. It was not till a new century had dawned that he came into his kingdom and won five Open Championships in ten years, nor is the reason in the least mysterious. James was a terrific driver and there was no finer iron player alive; in temperament he was resolute, patient and imperturbable; but he had one weak spot, he could not putt. He worked hard to overcome his weakness;

157

he took to an aluminium putter instead of a cleek, stood still instead of 'knuckling' his knees as all Scottish caddies had once done, adopted a long smooth stroke, and instead of putting, to use a phrase of his own, 'like an auld sweetie wife', became a very, very good putter with a diabolical capacity for holing the middle-length ones. Then he was for a while irresistible, but I am anticipating, for it is Vardon's turn next. And with him I come to a golfer to whom I may apply that most ungrammatical and most eloquent sentence which John Nyren wrote of David Harris—'who between anyone and himself comparison must fail'.

HARRY VARDON

Vardon had come from Jersey several years before and was beginning to be known, but it was Taylor who made him famous by going north to Ganton to play him in an exhibition match and coming back defeated by 8 up and 7 to play. The championship of 1896 at Muirfield which first set Vardon on his victorious path deserves relatively minute description. After one round he seemed out of the hunt for he had taken 83. It was Herd once more who was the menace, for he had raced right away from his field with a 72. In the afternoon he collapsed dismally with an 84. Taylor led the field with 155, Herd with 156 and Vardon 161. Next morning Vardon had a 78, Herd a 79 and Taylor 81. So now Herd led Taylor by one stroke and Vardon by four. Again he collapsed and took 85. Taylor, a very tired man, led the field with a final 81. And now came Vardon to the last tee with a four to win. After a moderate tee shot he looked at the big cross bunker guarding the green, pondering whether or not to put it to the touch, while James Kay of Seaton Carew signalled violently to him to play short. He had not asked for advice but he did play short, got his five and tied for the championship. The play-off was a curious one. After eight holes Vardon led by six strokes, but by the end of the round the six were reduced to two. At the first hole after lunch the lead had wholly vanished, for Vardon hooked out of bounds and took five to Taylor's three. Then, just when he might have been expected to weaken, he gained a stroke at each of the next three holes; he was never headed again, holed a long putt for a three at the 17th to make sure and won by three shots.

Vardon was not even yet the invincible and incomparable golfer that he was soon to become, but he was a long driver with plenty of power, a beautiful iron player and, contrary to the belief of those who only saw him in his later years after his illness, a sound putter. He was not yet so good as in his great years and he was most emphatically not so elegant a player. 'These Vardons are not pretty players,' said Mr Everard on first seeing Harry and his brother Tom. I remember well the first time I ever saw him, at Ganton, a month or two after his triumph; I was puzzled rather than attracted by that pronounced lift of the club in the back swing with the right elbow inclined to wander at its own sweet will. I am glad to have my memory confirmed by Taylor who has written, 'In his early days Harry Vardon had a most ungainly style. A lift in his back swing violated the principles of accepted orthodoxy.' And yet, within a comparatively short time, Vardon's swing was generally accepted as a perfect model of beauty; there was still the suspicion of a lift, but it had been modified, the right elbow occupied its orthodox position and the whole was an example of ease, grace and rhythm, above all rhythm. How much his style actually changed and how much people grew used to his heterodoxy and were swept off their feet by its prodigious results, I am not prepared to say, but that there was a change is, I think, beyond doubt. His overlapping grip, exactly the same as Taylor's and that of an earlier master, Mr Laidlay, was soon known as the 'Vardon grip' and was too hastily believed to be a panacea for all known golfing ailments.

In the next year, 1897, when Harold Hilton won at Hoylake with Braid a stroke behind, Vardon had a temporary set-back, but in 1898 and 1899 there was no holding him. At Prestwick, Willie Park made a gallant effort, failing only by a single putt, but in the following year at Sandwich the only possible question was who would be second; nobody doubted that Vardon must win, as he did very comfortably. During those two years he went up and down the country winning tournaments and matches and trampling down his adversaries like some ruthless juggernaut. Nobody could touch him, and in one 36-hole match at Newcastle in County Down he beat Taylor by 12 or 13 holes, and poor J. H. could only say, 'I played my game, sir. I played my game.' His power with both wood and iron was immense; he had a driving mashie that became a by-word; but it was perhaps more than anything else his full brassey shots up to the hole that were so overwhelming. The brassey was not atrophied in those days; Vardon could reach in two strokes holes that cost most other men two and a pitch, and his brassey shots ended as near the hole as did their pitches.

After these two all-conquering years Vardon went on a prolonged tour in America. He always thought he had left a little something of his finest game there and certainly he never mowed down his enemies in quite the same way again. He came back from America to play in the championship of 1900 at St Andrews, and played well enough to be second, but St Andrews was not his course, he never liked it, and this was one of Taylor's ferocious years when he gave his enemies to the dogs and vultures. He led from the start, finished with a tremendous 75— it *was* tremendous with a gutty—and beat Vardon by eight shots. In 1901 Braid won his first championship, at Muirfield, by three shots, and within a few years he was to be almost as invincible as Vardon had been; between 1901 and 1910 he won five championships, an unapproached achievement. But now with 1902 comes an event, far greater than any one man's prowess, since it affected the whole world of golf, the coming of the rubber-cored ball.

159

THE DEATH OF THE GUTTY

The ball had been invented by a Mr.Haskell in America in 1901. Taylor had played a few shots with it at Wheaton near Chicago before meeting Vardon in the American Championship and decided not to swap horses, a decision he has ever since regretted. Horace Hutchinson had, I believe, experimented with it here, at Forest Row, but it only burst on the general public, and that as a most surprising bombshell, with the Amateur Championship at Hoylake in May 1902. How little it was known I may illustrate by an egotistical story. At Euston station, on my way to Hoylake, I met a friend from the north who asked me if I was going to play for England in the international match instituted for the first time that year. I said I had some hopes. 'Are you going to play with the Haskell ball?' he went on, and I answered, 'What is that?' He said I should make a great mistake if I did not use it, and we parted. When I reached Hoylake I found that a certain number of the players had been better informed than I had and had secured a Haskell or two, but no more were to be had for love or money. Charles Hutchings and Sidney Fry were two who played with it; they reached the final of the championship and Charles Hutchings won it at the mature age of 53. From that moment I do not think any reasonably good prophet could doubt that the gutty was doomed. It was true that some people could not at first master the new ball's eccentricities on hard ground and disliked its feeling of lightness off the club, but its added length, the ease of getting it up into the air, and the fact that it made many a half hit shot as good as a better, were irresistible attractions. There were certain wise voices raised against it, but they were as those crying in the wilderness. John Low never ceased to hold that it had spoilt the game; Mure Fergusson is another deserving to be honourably remembered among the die-hards. The professionals began by declaring that they would not use it, but their motives were, perhaps unjustly, suspect, even as had been Allan Robertson's when the gutty had first appeared. And then it was one of their own number who had been among the fiercest up-holders of the old ways who went back on his resolution. Sandy Herd was playing a practice round at Hoylake with John Ball who gave him a Haskell with which to try some shots. He was instantly converted and had the courage of his opinions. Alone among the leaders of his profession he used the Haskell in the championship and he won by a single stroke. It was certainly an ironical circumstance that he who had so unquestionably deserved to be a champion should owe his solitary success to this mixture of luck and shrewdness. At any rate with Herd's victory the battle was over. The only question was that of buying a Haskell, whatever the price, and the man with Haskells to sell had the world at his feet. Some virtue had gone out of the game for ever, but it was a pleasanter and easier game, and what will ever deter mankind from pleasant paths and short cuts? In a very few months, except for some remote courses or some economical people who had a stock to get rid of, the gutty was as dead as the feathery. There arose various other kinds of rubber-cored balls, and those who had the selling of the Haskell in this country brought an action against another firm of ball-makers. It went to the House of Lords, where they were defeated, contrary, as it has always seemed to me, to what is rashly called natural justice. So now scores grew lower and lower and tees were gradually put back, and there began that unceasing struggle to keep the flight of the ball within reasonable limits and restore some splendour to the so-called two-shot hole.

The same year, 1902, which saw the coming of the Haskell saw the first Amateur International Match between England and Scotland. It was originally promoted, as had been the championship itself, by the Royal Liverpool Club and was put on an official footing in the following year. It was played on the Saturday before the championship, ten a side by 36-hole singles. It began by being very popular; then, perhaps because of the regular superiority of Scotland, interest in it began to fade and there arose a feeling that the championship was sufficiently hard work without another gruelling day's golf added. The match was abandoned in 1913 and 1914, but played again in 1921. Its subsequent history, however, together with that of the international tournament in which all four countries take part, must be for others to tell. The interest in the first match in 1902 was unquestionably great and of the younger players who took part there are some that ought to be named. In Scotland there was Fred Mackenzie, a really beautiful player from St Andrews, who later turned professional for a short while and could never play as an amateur again. St. Andrews, however, knew him well for years as a grand golfer. On the England side were Osmund Scott, H. C. Ellis and J. A. T. Bramston, all three golfers of really high class, and Johnny Bramston, one who would, I think, have been in the very highest but for his illness and too early death. Brought up among the fierce winds and the spiky rushes of Westward Ho! he had the power and the style and all the shots, together with a fine boyish confidence. Given health I think he must have ranked with Maxwell and Graham.

THE AMERICAN CONQUEROR

It was in 1903, the year after that first international, that Maxwell won the first of his two championships at Muirfield in a manner that left no room for doubt, but 1904 is a year that cannot be thus so briefly dismissed. This was Travis's year, when the little middle-aged man from America, with the black cigar, who began by being so lightly regarded, humiliated us all at last, and that on his merits. It it a sad but undeniable fact that Walter Travis and British golfers did not hit it off, and when he went home to America he said very unpleasant things about Sandwich and its members. As far as I know he is the only American golfer who has ever had cause to complain of a lack of friendliness, and it would be the simplest thing in the world to say it was his own fault. But I am afraid that would be neither generous nor quite true. Admittedly his was a difficult character, he did not appear to welcome advances but rather preferred to be left alone. Nevertheless, I have always had an uncomfortable feeling that we ought to have tried harder to penetrate that uninviting reserve, and gave up the effort too readily.

Whatever Walter Travis was as a man, and it is clear we did not wholly understand him, he was a truly remarkable golfer. He had not begun the game young, he was essentially a made player, he was gifted with no great power, although he had always a little something up his sleeve; but he had drilled himself into great accuracy of striking: he had a fine, hostile, match-playing temperament and he was a supremely good putter. To a great extent it was the putting with the centre-shafted Schenectady putter that did it: I have never seen better unless it was from his younger rival and near namesake, Jerome Travers. But he was also very skilful and accurate with all his clubs. It is evidence of his relative shortness that in the final he needed a spoon for his second shots to the second and twelfth holes; it is likewise evidence of his accuracy that each time his ball finished within a few yards of the flag. The diabolical accuracy of those shots through the cross wind (Travis had something of a black and Satanic air) remains with me as if I had seen them yesterday.

He began by beating H. H. Holden of Hoylake after an unfortunate incident in which he had quite justifiably claimed a hole. There was another incident when he beat James Robb. He had a fool of a caddie (he surely should have been given a good one) who, misunderstanding what he was told, suddenly picked up his master's ball on the green. He was told to put it back, Robb said nothing and the hole was played out. Travis was, we thought, really going to be beaten at last, when he was two down with four to play against a good Irish player, Harold Reade, but he finished perfectly and won after all. Then he had to play Hilton, who might put an end to him, but Hilton was in no state of health for such a battle and Travis won easily. That was in the last eight, and now the American terror began to stalk across the links. In the semi-final he met Horace Hutchinson, who, armed with a driver of some 46 inches long, had been enjoying an Indian summer of golf. In the morning he had beaten Robert Maxwell after a great struggle at the 19th. In the afternoon he was palpably exhausted. As Andrew Kirkaldy said to him later in the day, pointing at Maxwell, 'Yon's your murderer.' Travis was three up at the turn and then gave some chances that Horace was too tired to take. Travis won by 4 and 2 and now Edward Blackwell was the last hope of his countrymen. It was not a sanguine crowd that went out to watch the final. It was true that in point of length Blackwell could metaphorically drive the American's head off, but the fairways were that year very narrow and the grass at the side so long and thick as to defy the strongest man. A single yard into that deadly hayfield and all the yards that Blackwell had gained were wasted. Of course in the short game there was only one in it and Travis began more lethally than ever by holing everything. He was four up at lunch and, keeping his lead with a horrid incvitableness, won on the 15th green. Somebody ought, it seemed, to have been able to stop him, but in fact nobody could. He was, within his own limitations, a great golfer.

I think my best plan now will be to continue the story of the amateurs till 1914 and then go back to the professionals and watch the triumvirate expire in a blaze of glory. Between 1904 and 1914 three championships were won by John Ball, two by Harold Hilton and one by Maxwell. The new champions were, in 1905 at Prestwick, Gordon Barry, a student of nineteen at St Andrews University, with a huge swing, to be rigidly cut down later in life. He was full of confidence and an admirable putter. If this was something of a flash in the pan it was a very bright flash. In 1906 Robb won at Hoylake over Lingen in a final famous for the mediocre play on both sides. In 1908 E. A. Lassen from Bradford surprised everyone by winning, but showed it was no fluke by reaching the final again three years later. He was a fine putter and played the game with a cold, inhuman concentration not easy to combat. The last champion before the war, J. L. C. Jenkins, was undoubtedly the best player of that year, a fine, confident, attacking golfer and a masterly iron player, who, but for a wound in the war, would, I think, have been more prominent in later years. So much for the relatively lesser lights. Of the three great men, Hilton beat two very good golfers in Lassen and Robert Harris in his two finals, and with returning health had come back, if not to all the dash and fire, at any rate to all the skill of his best days. Maxwell's win over Cecil Hutchison at Muirfield produced a match never to be forgotten by those who saw it. The golf was so faultless, the speed at which it was played so great, that they seemed to be playing not a championship final but one of the friendly, almost casual games which they had often played together on the links of the Lothians.

If Hilton's was a great revival so was John Ball's. He was by several years the elder of the two and had not won since he had beaten Freddie Tait in 1899. In 1907 at St Andrews he beat C. A. Palmer, in his younger days a famous bicyclist, a most plucky and determined player who in his middle age had resolutely made himself into a golfer with the help of the rubber-cored ball. Three years later the championship was on his own Hoylake. He took it into his head he would like to win another medal and his golf in the final against C. C. Aylmer was the most perfectly flawless and accurate that I personally ever saw him play. Two years later again at Westward Ho! came his swan song in a match fully as dramatic as that at Prestwick thirteen years before.

In 1910 at Hoylake there had suddenly appeared in the English team an artisan player, Abe Mitchell of the Cantelupe Club at Forest Row, one of a redoubtable

163

clan of golfers bred on the forest. Horace Hutchinson had vouched for him and rumour reaching Hoylake in advance had declared him a prodigious player. As soon as he appeared there was no doubt about it. If by no means so polished a golfer as later in his professional days, he had crushing power and was brimfull of golf. He went through that championship like a devouring flame till he met John Ball in the semi-final and that was too much for him.

Now two years later they met again, this time in the final at Westward Ho! Again Mitchell had swept more or less triumphantly through the field. Not so John Ball who had become in his relatively old age a rather lazy starter. In the sixth round he had been five down with seven to play and then three down with three to play against F. S. Bond of Wimbledon, but he had pulled through at the 19th. That had been the spark and now he was fairly alight. It was clear that Abe Mitchell would have the advantage in length; Westward Ho! is a long course, and in the morning round he ended three up. John Ball was credited at lunch-time with one of those prophetic utterances of his which had a knack of coming true. If, he said, he could hold his enemy for the first three holes in the afternoon, he might just do it. A wet and stormy afternoon came to his aid and in fact he got one of those three back. Soon he was right on Abe Mitchell's heels, as he had been on Freddie's at Prestwick. With the match all square with three to play John miraculously got round a stymie to halve the 16th, but missed his second to the 17th, and that was one down. Both were within 4 feet or so of the last hole in three. That for the championship! It was destined to be the nearest that poor Abe ever came to winning one. He missed it, and after a half at the 19th he put his tee shot into a ditch in front of his nose at the 20th and all was over. John Ball had won once more, for the eighth and last time.

OPEN CHAMPIONS

I left the professionals when Herd, taking to the rubber-cored ball in the very nick of time, had won the championship. From that moment there was no question of any of them kicking against the pricks and refusing to use it. Nor, though the new ball was supposed to make the game easier for the weaker brethren, was there any sign of the leaders losing their grip. From 1902 to the beginning of the first war there were twelve championships and the triumvirate accounted for nine of them, Braid four, Vardon three and Taylor two. The new ball may have helped Taylor a little, since he had not quite the length of the other two and was naturally getting no longer with the years. Vardon may have lost a little of the advantage he had once possessed in those long wooden club shots up to the green; but generally speaking the *status quo* was not greatly disturbed. Three players managed to break into the small and select circle of champions, Jack White at Sandwich in 1904, Arnaud Massy at Hoylake in 1907 and Edward Ray at Muirfield in 1912.

1848-1914: *From Gutty to Rubber-Core: Bernard Darwin*

Jack White has the distinction in history of being the first man to win the Open Championship with a score of under 300, namely 296. He was a wonderfully fine putter. He had neither the physique nor the power nor the consistency in the long game of his great competitors, but he could keep more or less within reach of them by this beautiful putting of his, and since he was second and third on other occasions in the championship he must not be grudged his one victory. Despite his brilliant score, as it then undoubtedly was, he won only with the skin of his teeth, for both Braid and Taylor chased him to the last gasp with tremendous finishing rounds, each being left with a three to tie at the last hole and each taking four. Jack White was a nephew of Ben Sayers and had much of his uncle's mixture of shrewdness and enthusiasm. Nobody could make or sell a club better, and his seriousness was as portentous as it was delightful.

Arnaud Massy, born at Biarritz in 1877, the first foreigner to win our Open Championship, had all the bodily advantages that Jack White lacked. He was, I believe, half French and half Basque, but he had all the physical characteristics of the Basques, that race of great game players; he was a mountain of a man and carried himself like a grenadier. With his odd little flourish at the top of his swing—men called it his 'twiddledybit'—Massy was a really glorious striker of the ball, having not only great power but the greatest delicacy of touch on and round the green. Sprung of fisher folk he was bred among Atlantic winds and revelled in them, and I recall him once before a championship hoping it would blow hard enough to blow down every tree in Sandwich. In point of skill and strength he was, I think, the equal of any of the golfers of his time, but he lacked something of their quality of steadfastly pegging away. He was a little too palpably in high or low spirits, and his game fluctuated accordingly. Massy had a fine swashbuckling air and a cheerful, chuckling way with him that were most engaging. His account of his career as a bomb-thrower at Verdun, where he was wounded, was as picturesque as his description of his matches against rich Spanish visitors at Nivelle, matches which nearly always landed a pleasing number of francs in his pocket. Almost the last time I saw him he told me explosively of one such match which had been all square with one to play. Massy's ball at the home hole pitched out of bounds and the Spanish adversary thought that here at length was a measure of revenge; but the ball bounded back into play and Massy won the match and the money. 'Ma God, sir,' he ended confidentially, 'he was angry, sir.'

Massy had been to this country before his victory, for Sir Everard Hambro had discovered him at Biarritz and sent him here to improve his golfing education at North Berwick, where Ben Sayers had conceived almost unutterable thoughts of his greatness. He had, moreover, beaten some of our best men in a tournament at Cannes. Still, though our complacency as regards the amateurs had been disturbed by Walter Travis, our professionals were generally thought to be at home invincible. Massy headed the qualifying rounds and that was a shock; he led by a stroke after the first two rounds, and now the danger was imminent. With a round to go Taylor had wrested the lead from him, but Massy came again and, with a fine steady round through the wind he loved, won by two strokes.

Massy was always formidable after that and desperately hard to beat on his native soil, but here he only once again came near the championship. That was in 1911 at Sandwich when he tied with Harry Vardon. There never was such a championship as that for the poor reporter who must needs be in six places at once. Harry Vardon, his health fully restored, was making a great come-back, and with a round to go seemed assured of victory. Then he lapsed with 80 for his last round, and the whole pack were on his heels—Taylor, Braid, Herd, Duncan (just coming into the picture as infinitely dangerous but as yet something too volatile), Ayton, Robson and above all Harold Hilton. Any one of these might do it and Hilton would, humanly speaking, have done it but for a corner of a bunker— I curse it every time I pass it—which he could not see. They all failed and last came Massy wanting a four. He played the hole perfectly, with two wooden club shots against the wind, and tied. And then in the play-off next day he fell into a desponding mood, was thoroughly out-played and picked up his ball on the 35th green.

Edward Ray, of much the same age as Massy, had been well known here ever since he had first appeared, a rough, crude young golfer of obvious possibilities, from his native Jersey. In 1903 he reached the final of the *News of the World* tournament, then instituted for the first time, and gave Braid a hard run for it. He was constantly well up on the list but some one wild, disastrous shot seemed always to creep in, nor was this altogether surprising. He was a huge, lumbering figure of a man who lurched into the ball with every ounce he possessed. True there was a fine rhythm about it but a lurch it was. Ray's philosophy of striking appeared to be comprised in his advice, possibly apocryphal, given to one who wanted to hit the ball farther, 'Hit it a bloody sight harder, mate.' His approaching again, done largely with a graduated series of niblicks, though capable of astounding results from hayfields and over tree-tops, was yet not wholly convincing. To some extent no doubt these were eccentricities of genius; moreover he did, in course of time, modify his lurch so that his body came nearer to occupying the same space during the swing, and he had, rather surprisingly, a delicate touch on the green. In the year he won at Muirfield he was on those three days the best man in the field, and in the year of his reign as champion he was consistently successful until he was beaten into second place by Taylor at Hoylake with wholly unbeatable golf. In 1913 he tied with Vardon and Francis Ouimet at Brookline for the American Open Championship, to lose, as is now a part of history, on playing off, and in 1920, though that is outside my period, he won that championship at Inverness. Judged by results, and that is by far the best way to judge, there is no doubt that Ray was a very fine golfer.

THE END OF A LONG REIGN

To all the victories of the triumvirate I have not space to do full justice. Vardon's win at Prestwick in 1903 was an extraordinary achievement, for he felt so ill that he several times thought he should be unable to finish at all. He was in the grip of the disease of the lungs which was to send him to a sanatorium and from which it took him several years fully to recover. Of Braid's four wins I should choose that of 1908, also at Prestwick, because I saw it and because his score of 291 then seemed almost incredibly good. In fact his golf, admittedly in fine and easy weather, was almost perfect. He won with the utmost ease and that despite an eight at the Cardinal, where twice the ball glanced off the sleepers of the bunker and so out of bounds into the waters of the Pow Burn. Yet the greatest win by any of the three was, I think, that of Taylor at Hoylake in 1913. He had come right back into the picture when he won at Deal in 1909, and won very easily, but I put the Hoylake victory first. To begin with Taylor only qualified by holing a thoroughly nasty putt of 5 or 6 feet on the last green to save his neck. After that he played such golf in storms of wind and rain as I have never seen nor hope to see again. At the end of the first day Ray, the holder, led with 147, with Taylor lying nicely up, a stroke behind him, ready to pounce. The next day was truly appalling; all the exhibition tents had been blown down and presented a ruin of ropes and flapping canvas, the rain came in great flurries, swept across the links by a wind that even Hoylake admitted *was* a wind. For those who know the course, it took Taylor, as he has told in his book, two full shots to reach the corner of the field at the first hole; it took him three drives and then a running shot of 60 yards to reach the third hole. In that weather J. H., his cap pulled well down, his coat collar up, his chin stuck out, his feet flat on the ground, went round Hoylake in 77. In the afternoon he was two strokes worse and he holed the Briars (the sixth) bang in the teeth of the gale in three, laying a driving mashie shot stone dead. I saw that shot and the glory of it so dazzled and blinded me that I have nearly forgotten all the rest. There are some opinions I do not mean to change and that was the greatest golf I ever saw.

Finally, the long reign of the three great men may be said to have come to a great end at Prestwick in 1914. Each had won five championships, each wanted to be the first to win six, and could they have looked into the future this was their last chance. At the end of the first two rounds, it seemed that one out of two of them must fulfil his ambition: Vardon led with 150 and Taylor was second with 152. Being then on the Championship Committee I was present when the draw was made for the last day's play and can testify to our emotions when the names of Taylor and Vardon came out of the hat together. With the knowledge of what a Prestwick crowd could be, how big, how unruly, how difficult to control as they swirled around the Cardinal and the famous loop, how inevitably they would all follow this one couple, there was an immediate and universally felt temptation to put the names back and take another dip into the lucky bag. It could not be done; much agony would have been saved if it could have been, but we should have lost the historic remark of the Scottish miner, who being appealed to to make room for the players to pass exclaimed, 'Players be ——d! I've come to see.'

The course, as I remember it, was fast but rough, bumpy and difficult. In the morning Taylor played magnificently, 74 against 78, and led now by two strokes. He had got his teeth in and I never thought to see him let go. Still less did I expect it when he had gained another stroke and ought to have gained two in the first two holes after lunch. That stroke came back at the Cardinal, which Vardon played grandly in four—a telling blow at the moment—but it was the fourth hole that did it. There was a new bunker right in the middle of the course, placed, by the cruel ingenuity of James Braid, just where a straight tee shot had once securely finished. Vardon hooked far away into safety but Taylor, taking the narrower way, was bunkered near the Pow Burn. The ball lay clean enough. More often than not he would have put the ball on the green, but now he fluffed the shot, the inexorable burn was waiting, he took seven to the hole and Vardon led again by two. That was the end and Vardon had won his sixth championship.

Before I leave the *quarte major* I must go back a little, to 1905, for the great international foursome which they played over four greens. Scotland is never lacking in patriotism. I do not know that it felt at first quite so venomously patriotic over this match as it had done over Park and Vardon, but it soon whipped up its feelings to fever heat. England, too, was not without a more tranquil partisanship, and everybody, whether Scottish or English, was glad that after so much exhibition golf here was a real old-fashioned foursome for hard money, worthy of the days of Allan and the Dunns, and the undying feud between St Andrews and Musselburgh. There was a huge crowd for the first 36 holes at St Andrews and when, after a fine close struggle, Braid and Herd ended two up their supporters carried them off the field in triumph. It was a sadly short-lived triumph. With the second part of the match at Troon the Scotsmen were 'withered and strown'; from two up they finished twelve down, and all was over. The two Englishmen played magnificently but even so it was an astonishing catastrophe that overwhelmed the two Scotsmen, on whom some of their supporters turned unkindly. It might never have happened again if the two couples had played each other till the crack of doom. 'It's no possible but it's a fact,' said Ben Sayers of one of his own defeats, and that is the only possible comment. At the next stage at St Anne's the Scots rallied bravely and reduced the lead from twelve to seven. The last two rounds were to be at Deal and now once again Harry Vardon was seized with illness and it seemed very doubtful if he could play. It was a day of storm, too, and driving rain, as bad for him as any day could be, but he rose to the occasion; he and Taylor were in their Troon form again and won the match 13 up and 12 to play. It is curious to reflect that if the score had been reckoned on the system of Allan's day, that is to say by courses, there would have been not this resounding victory but a stalemate, since each pair had won on two courses.

Finally I must say a word or two about some other very fine golfers who, without winning the championship, came very close to the crown. The *News of the World* tournament, with its 18-hole matches, gave the lesser lights an occasional chance, and though the big men kept a tight hold on it for the most part, there was every now and then the chance of a surprise. There was George Duncan, destined to be the first champion after the war, a really lovely golfer, like Harry Vardon in rapid motion, a true golfing genius but having a little too much perhaps of the poetic temperament and in his earlier days given to going up like the rocket and coming down by the stick. His best days were to come, though he did win the *News of the World* in 1913, and so he must be dealt with by my successor, as must Abe Mitchell as a professional. With Duncan there played in several big foursomes Charles Mayo, who later went to America, a remarkable golfer of no great strength or dash, but on his day an uncannily good holer-out, with a great power of painstaking. He and Duncan boldly challenged at one time Braid and Vardon and at another Braid and Taylor, but the task was each time a little too great. Then there was Fred Robson, who perhaps belongs rather to the post- than the pre-war period and has now, after a second war, become so famous a coach that people begin to forget what a fine golfer he was. It was in fact in 1908 that the then almost unknown young man from Bromborough with the red head suddenly came through into the final of the *News of the World* tournament at Mid-Surrey and had to meet Taylor entrenched in his own fastness in the final. Nor did his audacity stop there, for, playing with the greatest dash and having decidedly the legs of his illustrious enemy off the tee, he went in to lunch three up. In the afternoon he was caught and passed but came back nobly and took his man to the very last green. How well, after 42 years, can I see J. H. taking out his handkerchief to mop his brow before attacking a putt for the match on the 35th green—and then missing it!

Another very fine Cheshire golfer was Tom Ball, one of the great Hoylake clan of that name, who died during the war. He had apparently no physique and looked rather white and frail, but he had plenty of length and was an outstanding putter, with a stroke at once crisp and gentle. He was second to Braid, divided from him to be sure by a long interval, at Prestwick in 1908, which was, I think, Braid's greatest year. Then in 1909 on Braid's own course of Walton Heath he reached the final of the *News of the World*, where he met Herd. It could hardly be that one of the old gang could be beaten, and yet he was. The first eleven holes in the final were halved, but then Tom Ball went away and won quite easily.

There were Tom Williamson from Nottingham, George Pulford from Hoylake and Rowland Jones from the Isle of Wight, good golfers all. And now I have kept a particularly good one for the last, James Sherlock. Sherlock learnt his golf on the short and muddy little course at Hinksey, near Oxford. He could juggle with the ball on the mud, but he could hardly learn to be a long driver there. When he became the professional at Stoke Poges his game was submitted to a natural process of stretching, and if he never became a great hitter, a part for which he was not built, he drove far enough to hold his own in the best company. In one year, 1910, when he beat Duncan in the final of the *News of the World*, it might fairly be said that he was the most successful golfer of the year. He had a style of engaging simplicity, never seemed to be using any great power of cue, as it might be called in another game, was always doing things in the easiest and most straight-forward manner, constantly escaping notice in being as good as he was. But one fact about him could not escape notice, namely that he was a really splendid putter, eminently simple and natural in his methods, wonderfully consistent in his results. And with him I bring my gallery of now ancient heroes to a worthy end.

1918–1939

Between Two Wars

THE OPEN CHAMPIONSHIP

A T the end of the first war, George Duncan was 36 and Abe Mitchell 32. For some years, discounting the American 'invasion' which was to change so radically our ideas of golf on this side of the ocean, these two as a pair became to Britain what the great triumvirate of Vardon, Taylor and Braid had been as a trio.

Mitchell and Duncan: their names were coupled, the two of them travelled, played countless exhibitions and contested together. Yet as golfers they were as poles apart. Duncan mercurial, inspired, temperamental, capable of flashing the ball out of a bunker with his spoon and missing the next short putt—or holing a long one—before the crowd round the green had so much as settled themselves for the stroke. Mitchell, stolid, more simple, lacking the fire and eccentricities of genius but hitting the ball, as his disciples will declare, as it will never be hit again.

The historian must be allowed at times to confess partiality. Abe Mitchell was the first great golfer I ever saw and, perhaps because he was the first, he remains to me, in a way, the greatest. Posterity will ridicule such a verdict and no doubt rightly. Mitchell will not go down to history with Jones or Hagen or even, in our own country, with Cotton, yet when you had seen Mitchell hit a golf ball you felt you had seen the very backbone of the golf swing and that all others were mere elaborations or variations. He stood with his feet rooted to the ground, grasped the club in a pair of massive hands, and quietly and with little outward effort gave the ball a tremendous, two-fisted clout with his arms, hands and wrists. Little more to it than that, but woe betide the poor spindle-wristed mortal who tried to do likewise!

In the first serious tournament after the war, on the Old Course at St Andrews,

171

Mitchell and Duncan tied, and no more fitting result could have been imagined. After this preliminary skirmish they came to Deal for the first post-war Open in 1920. With hickory shafts and a ball short by comparison with today, Deal was a battlefield for giants, and Mitchell's 74 and 73 saw him six strokes ahead of the field and thirteen ahead of Duncan's two 80s. The final day probably set the seal on Mitchell's career as a championship golfer. Due to start late, he was human enough to arrive early at the course to 'see what was doing' and to hang about the club-house. Meanwhile Duncan, with nothing to lose, was out almost first. Not only did he finish in 71, but he had done it a few minutes before Mitchell was due to start. Mitchell opened with three putts. More strokes slipped away and on the 5th he had a seven. Then came a long chilly delay as the waiting couples piled up on the 6th tee. He battled on but the long haul home took further toll and he finished in 84. Every stroke of his huge lead was gone, and with it not only that championship but also, as his best friends and worst enemies—if he had any, which is doubtful—would declare, all championships to come. Nevertheless there are many who, if they were permitted again to hear a hundred players driving off, would back themselves blindfold to tell which was Mitchell.

Duncan defended his title the following year on the Old Course at St Andrews, but never quite looked like holding it. The winner was a Scotsman, Jock Hutchison, and it was in his hands that the old championship jug made the first of its many journeys across the Atlantic. It was a remarkable championship for many reasons. Hutchison, for instance, in his first round of 72, which led the field, holed the 8th and 9th in a total of three. He had a one at the 8th and was within inches of another at the 9th. Then there was Roger Wethered treading on his ball in searching for it and losing a penalty stroke in the third round. This, since he and Hutchison later tied, has always been said to have lost him the championship, a proposition which is to my mind as ridiculous as to suggest that Hutchison's 'one' won it. If a solitary shot could be said more than another to have lost the championship for Wethered, one could more fairly suggest his second to the 18th in the last round when, after a fine drive, he pitched short into the Valley of Sin and took five. Even so, 71 was a great score. Hutchison, with 70 to tie, did it and was perhaps the only man in the field capable of doing so.

The play-off was what the boxing promoters, I believe, call a 'natural'. Britain *v.* America, Scotland *v.* England, amateur *v.* pro—and the Old Course on a summer Saturday. The heart said Wethered, the head said Hutchison, and as usual the head was right. Wethered hung on well enough in the morning with 77 to 74, but fell away in the afternoon to lose by a total of nine. He had covered himself with glory and the fact that he tied is itself imperishable, yet in a way it is as well that things went as they did. On the final day Wethered, six strokes behind after two rounds, wanted to catch the evening train south in order, of all things, to play in a cricket match! The authorities, suspecting as little no doubt as did Wethered himself what was to follow, made room for him and his partner in an earlier place in the draw. Whether it was in force then, I do not know, but there has for many years been a rule that starting times may not be changed on the day of play. Had he taken a serious view of his chances, one may be quite sure that it would not have entered Wethered's head to make such a request, for it is widely reckoned an advantage to get one's blow in first and set a target for the other man to shoot at. Anyway, Wethered's 72 in the morning put him, at 225, within three strokes of the leader, Sandy Herd, and a stroke ahead of Hutchison—and the rest we know.

And now comes the moment to introduce, shall we say, the second greatest golfer and assuredly the greatest 'character' in the game between the two wars— Walter Hagen. Here again I must confess partiality. As to Hagen's record it remains in the professional world unchallenged. Today success, in America at least, is judged largely by dollars earned. Hagen earned, and spent, dollars running I dare say into the half million mark, but he won the titles as well—the American Open twice, the British four times, and the match play championship of the United States four times in a row. Yet for all that, it is Hagen, the man, who will be remembered more than Hagen, the golfer.

All the same Hagen's golf was very much in keeping with Hagen, the man. It had about it a fallibility combined with impertinence that endeared him to the 'common man' of golf and caused him to be followed by huge galleries irrespective of his chance of success. People crowded to be with Hagen while he took 80, while the winner holed the course almost unaccompanied in 67. He had in a strong and enviable degree the faculty of dismissing from his mind any subject he found uncongenial—the fact equally that he had just put his second into a bunker, or that he was due on the tee at half-past ten, or that there were at the moment insufficient funds to pay the hotel bill. He reckoned to hit three or four downright bad shots in the course of a round; he then hit them and at once forgot about them. Perhaps because he had more practice at them than most, perhaps because they stimulated his sense of the theatrical, there was never a man to equal Hagen at the recovery shots that turn into a four what had seemed at best a five and possibly a six. In one of his Sandwich championships he played six rounds without a six despite being bunkered beside the green four times with his third shot.

Hagen became a legend in his lifetime and if some of the stories that will for ever be told of him are apocryphal, they pass muster because they so easily *might* have been true. One thing I think is unchallengeable, namely that he was largely responsible for the change in the status of professional golfers as a whole. As Gene Sarazen says: 'All the professionals who have a chance to go after the big money today should say a silent thanks to Walter each time they stretch a cheque between their fingers.' When he first came to England, it was not customary for pro-

173

fessionals to lunch in the club-house. I cannot recall there being any great resentment about this but it made no sense to Hagen, who drove in the thin edge of the wedge by arriving at the course in a hired Rolls-Royce and having a man-servant dispense a picnic champagne lunch in front of the club-house window. Sarazen is also fond of telling how they were staying for the 1924 championship at the Adelphi Hotel in Liverpool. Hagen had taken 83 in the first qualifying round and was in imminent danger of not playing in the championship at all. When they emerged from the hotel together, a crowd had gathered to see the Lord Mayor in his robes of office. It did not occur to Hagen that they could have assembled for any purpose other than to salute Hagen, and he thereupon mounted a small platform and waved appreciatively to the multitude. There would be little point in recounting this trivial though characteristic episode if the central figure had then failed to qualify— but he did qualify and he did go on to win the championship. And as he left the 72nd green at Hoylake, having nonchalantly holed a putt of 9 or 10 feet to win by one stroke, he let fall perhaps the most typical of those utterances so fondly cherished by the connoisseurs of 'Hagen stories'. Pushing his way through the crowd, a newspaper correspondent said to him: 'You appeared to take that putt very casually, Hagen. Did you know you had it to win?'

'Sure I knew I had it to win,' said Hagen, 'but no man ever beat *me* in a play-off!'

As one of the confessed connoisseurs, I must resist the temptation to linger with further tales of Hagen and return to Hagen the golfer, who with two United States Opens behind him, one in 1914 and the other just after the war, appeared first on the English scene in 1920, finishing in comparative obscurity, and again for Hutchison's championship in 1921, when he made a more pronounced but not yet formidable impact. Next year he was back again at Sandwich—what a pity, incidentally, that the lure of the dollar has sapped the crusading spirit in the great American professionals of today—and here he entered upon a reign of glory that was to last until the '30s. After two rounds he led with 149. Then he slipped back with a 79 and with Barnes and Charles Whitcombe was in second place with one round to play, one stroke behind Hutchison. His last round was his best, a 72, and none of the others could match it, though Barnes was within a stroke. All was over, or so it seemed, when strange tidings reached the crowds round the 18th hole. George Duncan, it was said, was up to his tricks. He needed a 68 to tie and, what was more, was in the process of doing it. The rumours for once were true. At hole after hole Duncan was slashing his second shots up to the flag, putting again and again for a three, though rarely, alas, getting it. With the crowds swarming out to meet him, Duncan needed one more four for his 68. He drove far down the middle, leaving himself the kind of spoon shot of which he was the supreme master. He hit it well, too well perhaps, and instead of fading in to the flag it held its course to the left of the green. His hurried chip showed that, while it may be good to 'miss 'em quick', it is possible to miss 'em too quick; a gallant unprofitable spurt was over, and Hagen was the champion.

He defended his title at Troon, a pleasant, not unduly fierce, links beside the sea on the west coast of Scotland, which was not to see another Open for twenty-seven years. This championship of 1923 was memorable for the fact that for years afterwards it was to remain 'the last time an Englishman won'. The hero was Arthur Havers, then professional at Coombe Hill and 26 years old. Some ten years previously, just before the war, he had achieved the remarkable feat of qualifying for the Open at the age of 16. At Troon he played three admirably steady rounds of 73 apiece, and they left him one stroke ahead of Joe Kirkwood, two ahead of Hagen and three in front of Macdonald Smith. Kirkwood, an Australian who later settled in America, became famous all over the world for his trick shots, and indeed what he could do with a golf club, fortified by his professionally excellent 'patter', was quite uncanny. The only thing he or the others of his kind could not do, it was said unkindly, though with some truth, was to hit one dead straight. At various times he was third, fourth and sixth in the championship but never did he stand in with a better chance than at Troon. He could not quite clinch it and when Havers returned a rather 'safe' 76 it was Hagen who was left in the hunt with 74 to tie. In the end, needing a three at the 18th, he sliced his second into a bunker, just in front of the club-house windows. Not for the last time in similar circumstances, he had the flag removed, but it was too much to ask even of Hagen. His ball ran close enough to the hole, however, to send shivers up the spine of British supporters and, no doubt, of Havers.

Hagen's turn came again, as I have mentioned, in the following year at Hoylake and then the Open returned, for the last time as it turned out, to Prestwick, the original home where, since 1860, the tournaments for the Championship Belt were held, until in 1871 Tom Morris, Junior, by winning three times in succession, won it outright. I did not see this championship but the unanimous verdict of those who did confirms it to have been not so much the one that Jim Barnes won as the one that poor Macdonald Smith lost. This may be hard on Barnes but that is the story, and something tells me that the history books will stick to it. Both Ray and Compston had their chances and with last rounds of 75 and 73 came within a stroke of the winner, but it is the other two whose names linger in the memory—the two exiles returning from America. Barnes had stoutly retained his English citizenship, though as a good Cornishman he would probably have declined to admit himself a naturalized Englishman either. Mac Smith, long since departed from his native Carnoustie, where he learnt the fundamentals of his lovely and now, I suppose, 'old-fashioned' swing, had become more Americanized.

Barnes, certainly the tallest player to win the Open on either side of the water—he had won the United States Open in 1921 by the length of a street, when he was

175

a dominating figure in American golf—was the lanky, rangy type whose stature is so often their biggest handicap. With a wide stance and, for a man of his height, shortish clubs he had it completely under control and, like so many big men, had a most delicate touch in the short game. At any rate he shot straight ahead of the field with a 70, leaving Mac Smith almost stranded with 76. Next morning the tables were turned, and Smith with a 69—a great score in those days—against Barnes' 77 led by two strokes. On the last day Barnes was out early, his rival late, and here was his chance. He missed it, slipping away to 79, and with a sound 76 Smith was five strokes ahead. Out went Barnes on the last lap and his 74 was good, but clearly not good enough. Mac Smith needed 78 to win, 79 to tie.

If Mary Tudor had the word Calais engraved upon her heart, so assuredly must Macdonald Smith, who died after the recent war, have had Prestwick. Colossal crowds turned out—I have mentioned these Ayrshire crowds else-where—to see the Scotsman win. In their combined determination to see the play at all costs (or, in the case of those who did not pay to come in, no cost) and to cheer their hero home, they lost him the ambition of a lifetime and, as I shall always feel, set permanently in the top of the second-class a golfer to whom no heights might have been unattainable. However, those are ifs and buts. What happened was that the hordes trampled poor Macdonald Smith into an 82 and, though he was to be eternally second, he never again looked like winning an Open Champion-ship—or at least he never, after it was over, looked likely to have won it, which is perhaps a different thing. On the other hand one cannot help feeling that in the same circumstances Hagen, even if it had taken him five hours, would have got around somehow in 78. The winner is the man who finishes first, and there never was a championship that 'ought not to have been won by someone else'.

So continued the successful retaliation by the Americans for the long years in which golf in the United States had been dominated by players from the home of the game on this side. The pupils turned masters with a vengeance, and now the sons of the former masters sit at the feet of the men who learnt from their fathers.

Greatest of them all by common consent, and greatest of all time by almost common consent, was the immortal Bobby Jones—or as he has always been known in America, strange as it may seem to us in Britain, Bob Jones. His first visit to us was in 1921 and on the whole it was inglorious. Even at that time he had for many years suffered from the reputation of the infant prodigy. In 1916, when he was only $14\frac{1}{2}$, he had survived to the third round of the American amateur and had then given an ex-champion, Bob Gardner, a severe run for his money. For years the golfing world had been waiting for him, as the Americans say, to 'break through'. Already his shots were as perfect as makes no matter, but somehow he could not quite win. It was rather as though he had to 'throw a six before he could start'. He did not throw it at Hoylake where, though he won his matches in the

176

preliminary international match that was to lead to the Walker Cup, he was beaten handsomely by Allan Graham, nor at St Andrews, where he tore up his card at the Eden in the third round of the Open.

By the time we saw Jones again in 1926, he had 'arrived'. He had won the United States Amateur twice and the Open once, and had tied for the Open again, losing on the play-off. Now he arrived for the British Amateur at Muirfield. All went well till the fifth round when he was beaten by a capital Scottish golfer, Andrew Jamieson, whose fate it has been to this day to be known as 'the man who beat Bobby Jones'. It is said that Jones, had he won, would have taken the boat straight home. He decided instead to stay for the Open at Lytham and St Anne's. So, having beaten Cyril Tolley by 12 and 11 in the Walker Cup match at St Andrews, he came to Sunningdale for the qualifying rounds. Here he played what is now accepted as the nearest thing yet seen to the perfect round of golf. He holed in his 66 one longish putt for a three at the 5th and he put an iron shot into the bunker at the 13th—chipping out dead and getting his three. Otherwise, shot by shot, it was the model, flawless, flukeless round.

After two rounds at Lytham, Jones with his two 72s and that rough-cast character, 'Wild Bill' Melhorn, led the field. Hagen with 68 and 77—it was the only time he and Jones played in a championship together in this country—was one stroke behind and Al Watrous two. It so happened that Jones and Watrous were drawn together on the last day, and the championship in the end developed into a desperate man-to-man affair between them. In the morning Jones, putting somewhat ill with the 'Calamity Jane' putter which later was to be imitated all over the world, even down to the rings of binding on its wooden shaft, took 73 while Watrous turned the tables with a 69. With five to play Jones was still two behind, but the strokes came back one at a time and with two holes left they were all square. Watrous drove safely out in the proper place on the right, but Jones' ball was lying in a flat sand bunker in a wilderness of 'rough stuff' on the left, still some 170 yards from the hole, with unbroken rough all the way to the green. Watrous reached the green with his second, some way from the flag. Whereupon Jones played what is perhaps one of the two outstanding shots in golfing history. With a mashie-iron he took the ball clean and cracked it straight to the heart of the green, well inside his opponent. Poor Watrous took three putts—for which human error who shall blame him?—and with a four against five at the last hole Jones won by two shots. His club hangs on the wall at Lytham to this day, and at the back of the bunker the club have erected a kind of 'tombstone' to commemorate his feat.

Jones went home to win the American Open and returned in the following summer to win at St Andrews, the scene of his first failure, what may in a way have been the most satisfying of all his championships. He led from the start with a 68 and the title was his from the word 'go'. In the last round, when he was leading by four shots from Fred Robson, he faltered for a moment and then from the sixth onwards proceeded to do seven holes in twenty-four shots. The rest was a triumphal procession and he was carried shoulder high from the last green by a crowd moved as much by affection for the man as by admiration for the golfer.

The next two years were Hagen's, as mentioned elsewhere, and in 1930 Bobby Jones was with us again for the last time, more determined, one may be certain, upon winning the Amateur for the first time than the Open for the third. This he did, at St Andrews, after one or two appallingly near squeaks on his way to the final, though his victory over Roger Wethered over 36 holes was never seriously in doubt once he got there. George Voigt, for instance, an American amateur of almost professional quality, had him two down with five to play and lost the match, one can say in retrospect, by driving out of bounds at the long 14th. Then there was his never-to-be-forgotten match with Tolley. Did Bobby's second to the 17th, when they were all square, hit a spectator at the back of the green, where they were allowed to stand in those days—nowadays they are herded behind the wall— and bounce back to the green? Or didn't it? People saw it do so with their own eyes. Others standing equally nearby saw with their own eyes that it did not. At any rate they halved the hole in four and, with another four, Bobby won at the 19th.

Thence to Hoylake for the Open, and the heart upon which Hoylake will one day be found to be engraved will assuredly be that of Archie Compston. After two rounds Jones led by a stroke from Fred Robson. He added a 74, which was sound enough, but Compston had flashed into the lead with a 68. What is more, he was in a position to set the pace for the final round. He opened with two fine shots and three putts. A five at the first at Hoylake is no disaster for any man, but other fives followed, and sixes, too. Bad led to worse, and poor Compston slithered down the slippery fatal slope to an 82. This tall, leonine, unaccountable man was a great golfing artist, worthy of a championship, but, like Macdonald Smith after Prestwick, he never looked like winning again. Meanwhile all was going well enough with Jones till at the long 8th there arrived from a blue sky a seven. Looking back on it, he can hardly have believed it to be true. In two shots he was nearly on the green. He fluffed his chip, the next was nothing to write home about, and the end was the inevitable 'and three putts, seven' of the handicap golfer. Moistening his lips and looking not unlike the condemned man, he mounted the slope to the ninth tee and fought his way grimly home for a 75. It turned out to be just good enough.

Jones returned to America to win the Amateur and Open Championships there, too. All four in one year. The grand slam! It was an achievement which has no equal in golf nor, so far as a layman may judge, the equivalent in any other game. At the end of it all, Bobby retired altogether, finally, completely, almost the only sporting figure to do so at his peak and with no second thoughts. He had indeed no more worlds to conquer and the rest must have been anticlimax. He was as near the perfect golfer as the game is likely to see, not merely in the perfection of his strokes but in the fact that his golfing manners, too, were perfect and every single soul who met him or watched him liked him. Physically he was, if I may use the past tense—and he is at the moment of writing, at the age of 48, battling with some malicious ailment of the spine which may prevent his ever striking a ball again—of a short and stocky build, but possessed of an amazing suppleness which enabled him to hold his left arm straight and high up behind him on the back swing and to finish with his right arm equally straight and high in the follow-through. His sense of rhythm, timing and balance was, I should say, unique. A continuous film of all his competitive play would probably fail to reveal him at any moment, even in high winds, off balance. Talking of films, he has left behind him a series which I saw again only the other day. They reveal not only the gracefulness of his play but also a complete absence of the fuss which seems indispensable to the experts today, all of whom Jones would have beaten into the proverbial cocked hat. He played to a sort of drill which never varied. Having looked towards the hole, he set the club behind the ball. His feet fell into position. One more glance; one small waggle—and away it went. Nothing more.

Gene Sarazen has said of Jones that he had the finest mind of any competitive golfer. He was a brilliant student at college and an extremely able lawyer and business man and 'he had, along with a great golf game and great fortitude, great intelligence. . . . Jones was able to master his temper and every other problem that lay between him and consistent superlative performance. . . . In a unique and wondrous way, Bob quietly unleashed the most furious concentration of any golfer, in those days when it was Jones *versus* the field'. Sarazen also pays this delightful tribute: 'Bob was a fine man to be partnered with in a tournament. Congenial and considerate, he made you feel you were playing with a friend, and you were.' To which I will add only that by his superb skill and unfailing charm Bobby Jones probably did as much to draw Britain and America together as all the diplomats combined.

For three more years after Jones had retired and Hagen had passed his prime, the ancient jug which is the championship trophy was to make its way back across the Atlantic. Next time it was in the hands of Tommy Armour—the best pair of hands in American golf, if I may quote Sarazen again. Armour, an Edinburgh Scot, had gone to the States with an amateur team in 1922. He found the pastures green and stayed there, and, after a spell as secretary at the Westchester-Biltmore Club, turned pro. 'As an amateur,' says Sarazen, 'he was just a fair amateur. When he turned professional, he made himself into a magnificent professional. This may happen in other sports, but it rarely happens in golf. . . . Some of his other distinctions are that he says more words per round than any other golfer and is the slowest player in the entire world.' At any rate Armour built himself not only into

179

a great golfer but into a 'character'. Now well on in his fifties, he remains both. When he came to Carnoustie for the 1931 Open, he had already won the United States Open four years before, holing a tremendous putt on the last green to qualify for the play-off. He was undoubtedly a fine iron player, but behind the build-up which dubbed him the greatest iron player in the world one can detect the hand of Armour. The truth is that his wooden shots, hit with a terrific crack and straight as an arrow, were every bit as good. Until the last round at Carnoustie, when Armour came from behind with a 71, all eyes, including those of the Prince of Wales, were on a small dapper, smiling South American, José Jurado. A brilliant golfer, Jurado had three years previously been right among the leaders after three rounds, only to fall away with an 80, and had yet to prove that the 'Latin temperament' could survive the full 72 holes. Now after two rounds here he was in the lead again, bracketed with the new young hope of England recently returned from a voyage of discovery in America, Henry Cotton. Close on their heels were Armour, Farrell, Sarazen and Macdonald Smith. At lunch-time on the last day Jurado, 73, led with 220. Macdonald Smith was 223, and Armour, Sarazen and Percy Alliss third at 225, Cotton having fallen away with 79. Armour got his blow in first, and a thumping good blow it was, with his 71. The others could not quite match it, so now everything lay with Jurado—75 to win. 76 to tie. As he neared home, he faltered. He did not 'blow up', but he took fives at the holes where ordinary mortals are happy enough with a five, but champions must somehow extract a four. So at last he needed a four to tie. The 18th at Carnoustie is a desperate finish. It needs a long drive, and a long second over the burn with an out-of-bounds fence on the left edge of the green. Jurado hit the drive to perfection, and a brassey would surely have seen him home. To the consternation of his friends he elected to play short with an iron. He pitched up well but not quite well enough—and then, when he had tapped in his putt for a five, there broke upon him for the first time the excruciating news that he had needed a four to tie. Had he known—as, poor fellow, he ought to have known—he would assuredly have gone for the green. Perhaps he would have hooked it out of bounds; perhaps he would have dropped it to watery disaster in the burn; perhaps he would have hit it to the heart of the green and holed out for a three. Only one thing is certain. He would not have played short. So there became engraved yet another name on another heart, and another great golfer never looked like winning again.

Having borrowed so many of his opinions of other people, I now come to Gene Sarazen himself. The son of immigrant Italian parents—his original name was Eugene Saraceni—he had been first caddie, then assistant, and had shot suddenly to the top by winning the United States Open at the age of 20 in 1922. To show it was no fluke, he won also the professionals' match-play championship and, what is more, went on to beat Hagen in a 72-hole match which one may be sure the great man was not anxious to lose. Writing his reminiscences a quarter of a century later, Sarazen headed the chapter on Hagen: 'My hero, my rival'. Sarazen was, and still is, a stocky, olive-complexioned, dark little man of engaging disposition who has always been a favourite in Britain, perhaps because we remember him from the days when the great American players thought the British Open more worthy of their attention than is the case today. His first appearance among us he has described as the most crushing blow his self-esteem had ever received. As American champion he came to play at Troon in 1923. His first qualifying round of 75 was fair enough. On the second day he started early when 'a cold driving storm was sweeping off the ocean with such fury that the fishermen in the town were not allowed to go out, and the waves were hurdling the sea-wall and washing up to the side of the championship course'. Later the wind dropped and low seventies began to come in. Sarazen with an 84 failed to qualify by one stroke. He said he would come back 'if he had to swim across', and he was as good as his word. In future years, experiments with his grip caused his game to lose some of its edge. He finished 2nd, 9th and 4th in the championship, but it was not until 1932, at Prince's, that he came back into his glory. He was the winner from the start and his 283, though twice equalled, was not beaten until 1950 when three calm, sunny days made Troon a more simple proposition than the normal championship course. I can see him now, accompanied by old Daniels, his caddie, to whom he pays an almost emotional tribute in his book, and beaming all over his face, as he came with a huge gallery to the last green.

I like particularly the remark of Daniels when, after starting with three fours in the last round, Sarazen suddenly socketed his second to the fourth. Putting the club back in the bag, the old man observed, 'I don't think we shall be requiring that one again, sir.' Sarazen went back to the States to win the United States Open with a final round of 66. As to his method, it was, I think, more essentially simple than any I have seen—both feet on the ground, both hands wrapped firmly round the club, no frills, twists or fancy bits; the elementary, straightforward, simple way to play golf. Perhaps that is why, having won his first championship with 288, he was still finishing high up in a big American tournament with 286 some twenty-eight years later.

The next year, 1933, was a Ryder Cup year and we won. Now at last the tide had surely turned and for the first time in ten years the championship would stay at home. Yet when it came to Friday evening at St Andrews, two Americans had tied and five were in the first six. Sarazen himself was a stroke away, due largely to a disaster, both physical and psychological, at the short Eden hole. He himself describes it as 'the most torturing experience I have ever gone through in golf', and, if only for that, it deserves mention. He drove into the Hill bunker, a deep, cavernous affair below the sloping green, behind which is the estuary of the river

Eden. Two ineffectual blows left him still there. He played sideways and at last holed a rattling good putt for his six. He and his partner had with them two markers, one an ex-woman champion of Scotland. At this point a steward, who turned out to have been unable to see the bottom of the bunker, suggested that Sarazen had taken seven. A first-class 'incident' developed both in the club-house and the Press. It turned out that the steward in question had probably counted as a stroke the brandishing of his club by Sarazen after one of his bunker shots. For the sake of the record let it be said that both markers clearly counted six and there remains no possible doubt whatever that this was the figure. The whole unfortunate affair was a classic example of the virtue of minding one's own business. The two who tied were Densmore Shute and Craig Wood, the former with four admirable 73s, the latter ranging from 68 to 75. One by one, Cotton, Easterbrook, and above all Diegel, had their chance but fell away. The ground was running very fast—I recall little puffs of dust as the ball pitched and bounced—and at the Long Hole Out poor Craig Wood drove into a bunker about 100 yards short of the green and took five. This fantastic stroke measured some 15 yards under a quarter of a mile! In a play-off of no more than academic interest Shute won by five shots.

And now at last, with no silver lining visible in any quarter of the firmament, our fortunes changed. In 1934, it is true, the tide of the American invasion was on the ebb and few of them were present at Sandwich. Looking back on it, this was perhaps fortunate for Henry Cotton. Lest this sound uncharitable, let it be said that, although this will for ever be remembered as Cotton's year, the true and complete consummation of his powers did not come until three years later, when, in perhaps the most rigorous conditions under which the Open has ever been played, he defeated the whole array of the American Ryder Cup team at Carnoustie. Sandwich, however, was beyond question the more 'sensational'. Cotton's opening rounds of 67 and 65, to say nothing of a qualifying 66, set a standard not yet equalled in the game's history. I remember well the finish to that second round when, incredible as it seemed in those days, he needed only a couple of fours to equal his 67. On the 17th he holed from perhaps 10 feet for a three and on the 18th was no more than a yard or so from the hole with his second. The details deserve to be recorded, and here they are:

Out 4 3 3 4 4 4 3 4 4—33.
Home 4 3 4 4 4 4 3 3 3—32. Total 65.

In the meantime Padgham had had a 71 and a 70—and was nine shots behind!
The morning of the last day was blustery with squalls of rain and occasional hail, and in these conditions Cotton's 72 was admirable. Kirkwood gained a stroke with 71 and Syd Brews, an Englishman long settled in South Africa, gained two

with a 70, but it only remained now for Cotton to amble home as he liked. They say he ate something that disagreed with him for his lunch. Certainly the circumstances were not such as to aid digestion. Be that as it may, he turned up on the tee for the final round with the appearance not so much of a conquering hero as of a man on his way to the gallows. A five at the first did no harm; four, three, four was everything to be asked for; and then the deluge. A six at the fifth, a stroke dropped at the Maiden, another six at the 7th, and out in 40—with the sterner half to come. Anyone who is to come home in reasonable figures at Sandwich must virtually begin with three fours—and Cotton took three fives. Seven over fours and three long holes in a row to come. This really was agonizing and none who saw it will forget it. If this sort of thing did not stop soon, and one saw no reason whatever for it to do so, we were about to witness the most appalling 'blow-up' in recorded history. However, stop it did, at the next hole—a hole which to the victim must remain for ever blessed in the memory. He could not reach it in two, but he pitched up perfectly and holed the putt for a four. Another followed at the Suez Canal, and another at the 15th, which can be five of anyone's money, and now he was home. Yet when he missed a short one on the 18th, thus failing to break the record, it seemed only a fitting anticlimax. His win was hailed as a great triumph for Cotton, and so, in a way, it was, but it was incomplete. There was better, far better, to come.

Cotton spent the following year adding steadily to his stature, and for 17 holes could be said to have dominated the next championship at Muirfield. He needed a four for a 66, and one had the idea that this time there was going to be no mistake, either about this round or those to follow. He hooked his drive slightly into that admirably placed bunker on the left and was tempted to go for the green. The result was a six and somehow he was never quite the same again. With one round to play, Alfred Perry was 211, Charles Whitcombe—perhaps this was to be his year at last?—212. Whitcombe took 76, and there was the ball at Perry's feet. He had not been in the running for such honours before nor did he seriously look like winning again, but let no man say that Perry's win at Muirfield was a fluke. He holed the course in 72 to win by four shots and equal the record, but it was not so much his score as the way he got it. I never saw a man less frightened of winning—even when he had nearly reached the first green in two and then taken six—and it warms the heart to remember the way he did it. His curious grip, with the fingers of the right hand hanging loosely from the club, and his rather 'agricultural' scythe-like movement that swivelled him round on his left foot, distracted attention from the fact that in the fundamentals he was sound as a bell. Above all, he was sound of heart. At the 14th he was bunkered and without a tremor hit the ball right home with a spoon. At last he needed a five and a six to win. It might have been a moment for caution. Narrowly skirting the bunkers at each hole,

183

scorning the safe line, he hit two colossal, full-blooded cracks with wooden clubs to the heart of the last two greens and strode cheerfully to the club-house.

There was no doubt about it: 1936 was Alfred Padgham's year. Almost his alone. He won everything. Nearly all the professional tournaments—excepting the match-play championship, which he had won the year before—and then the Open. No man, I think, unless it were Jones himself, made golf look more effortless and simple than Padgham at this time. His huge hands seemed to envelop the club, so that he wielded it as a wand. Though his backswing was short, he never seemed to hit hard at the ball, yet it flew off with a resounding crack and he was among the longest hitters of his day. It was his putter, though, that won him the honours in 1936. He stood with his hands held well away from the body, the club, as it were, hanging from them, and rolled the ball smoothly along to the hole, into which, with unbelievable regularity, it disappeared. Good things cannot last for ever, and at Hoylake it was my impression that Padgham's longer game, after his long and brilliant season, was beginning to tire. He was getting his figures but not according to the book, and it was his putter that was hanging on to the end. On the final stretch it was a duel between Padgham and James Adams, the Scotsman with the long, flowing 'St Andrews' swing and another magnificent putter. From 10 yards Adams' putt on the last green for a three skimmed the rim of the hole and stayed out. Eventually Padgham had four to tie, three to win. His high, graceful pitch flopped on to the green, perhaps 12 or 15 feet from the hole. At the last call the valiant putter did not fail and rolled the ball into the hole in the manner of a man finishing a summer evening fourball.

And so back to Cotton, and this time the full unqualified triumph. The Americans had beaten us in the Ryder Cup match at Southport and were there in full array, fortified by Charles Lacey, brother of the English professional, Arthur Lacey, and now settled prosperously in America. Carnoustie with its vast length—well over 7,000 yards—and extra bunkers inserted devilishly in the middle of the fairways some 240 yards from the tee, was a battlefield for heroes, and the weather on the last day was such that only a strong man could survive at all. Reginald Whitcombe, youngest of the brothers who have made such a mark in British golf, stung perhaps by his exclusion from the Ryder Cup, led the field with 72 and 70 against Cotton's 74 and 72. In the third round Cotton gained a stroke with 73 and Charles Whitcombe was one behind that. The wind blew and the rain swept across the course from the sea to the bleak, grey, little town and at one moment it seemed, as one pool began to join another on the hollowed green at the first, that the whole day's play might go by the board. Clubs were seen to fly slithering from the players' hands and no ingenuity was enough to keep a man's hands dry. In all this Whitcombe went round in 76 and was seized upon by photographers to pose as the new champion. Some distance behind was Cotton, knowing what he had to do

184

and playing, as I shall always look on it, the greatest single round of golf I ever saw. The man was not born who could play Carnoustie in the copybook way that day. You had to improvise the figures somehow—and no questions asked. Time and again Cotton turned the fives into fours with a pitch and putt, to such purpose indeed that I believe he only had twenty-six putts. With the rain hurling down with such fury as to silence completely the typewriters of the innumerable British and American correspondents in the Press tent, Cotton finished in 71 to win by two strokes.

Though he proved to have another championship in him after the war more than ten years later, this, I believe, was the climax of Cotton's powers. He has been a remarkable figure in the game, in many ways the most remarkable in what may be called modern golf. He had the good fortune early in life to make up his mind and never change it. He wanted to be a champion golfer and he wanted it to unlock for him doors that might otherwise have stayed closed. Like many a man who knows precisely where he wishes to go, he took sometimes an unduly direct route, thereby treading on toes which a slight detour might have avoided. He was what the newspapers like to term a 'stormy petrel'. He seemed inseparable from controversy and criticism, sometimes deserved, sometimes manifestly unfair, often merely from doing the right thing in the wrong way, but no man ever worked harder at golf nor more thoroughly earned his success. Devoted supporters who knew him as the *maestro*, and they numbered some of the most knowledgeable critics in the game, would swoon with ecstasy at the shots he could play when he tried. As an exponent of the No. 1 iron I dare say he has never been surpassed. Posterity will know him, in the same sense as they knew Harry Vardon, as a 'bad putter'. That, of course, is rubbish, though understandable for two reasons. One is that Cotton never found a 'natural' method of putting to match his truly exquisite performance up to the green. He never seemed at ease. From tee and fairway he was the master, alike in championship or Red Cross exhibition. Through the green, you marvelled at him. On the green, you felt for him. When at last he was ready to putt from 10 feet, you felt the whole thing by now to be so difficult as to be almost impossible. The second reason was that his first two shots left him, so much more often than lesser men, putting from anything up to 15 feet for a three. When he failed to hole it, the word went round, not that Cotton had got a four, but that Cotton had 'again missed a three'. The answer is, surely, that no man can win three open championships fourteen years apart, and a match-play tournament with a score of 22 under fours, and a challenge match against Densmore Shute on the longest inland course ever known with ten under fours, to say nothing of innumerable other titles, and be anything but a first-class putter.

One last word on Cotton. Aided by a wife of peculiar shrewdness, he can claim to have made a success of everything he has touched. He has prospered in a variety of business enterprises: his book on golf and golfers and his own life is outstanding in its class: when he went on the music-hall stage at the Coliseum, they kept him on for another week and increased his already fabulous salary: and he remains one of the very, very few people with whom I would sit up all night talking golf.

Only two more championships remain to be mentioned, one of them wholly unforgettable. This was at Sandwich in the following year. For two days perfect peace reigned. The sun shone benignly, the larks sang as only Sandwich larks can, and when three players had tied at 140, everything seemed set for a new record. My own memory of the last day is of being woken by the roaring of the sea and the flapping of the curtains in my bedroom beside the beach at Deal. On arrival at St George's a fantastic scene greeted the eye. The huge eight-masted exhibition tent, the biggest in the country so I believe, was in ribbons, parts already a shambles on the ground. From what was still standing, vast sails of canvas bellied and flapped in the gale. Steel-shafted clubs were twisted grotesquely into figures-of-eight, assorted haberdashery soared away into space to be salvaged later as far away as Prince's, while frenzied traders battled to pin down the remainder of their wares. If ever there was a day to 'separate the men from the boys', this was it. It was a day for short swings, fourteen stone, and two feet on the ground—a day, the day in fact, for Reginald Whitcombe. He was partnered with James Adams, and the championship turned into a duel between these two. One by one the others were blown to perdition. Nines were commonplace; four putts to a green was nothing; Padgham drove the 11th, 382 yards, and holed his putt for a two; only eleven scores in the day were lower than 80. Adams started with a lead of one. Whitcombe, unbelievably two under fours for eight holes, went several ahead, only to lose three in one fell swoop at the 9th where he took four putts and Adams holed a chip. Whitcombe finished in 75, a terrific round, against 78 by Adams, and led by two strokes at lunch. Away went both of these shots at the first hole with another four putts. At last Whitcombe was four ahead with four to play and that surely was enough. Adams retrieved one with another chip shot to the short 16th, normally something in the nature of a No. 5 iron, while Whitcombe took five. Only one ahead now, and two to play! The 17th was out of range of mortal man that day, but Whitcombe followed two heroic blows into the teeth of the wind with a low run-up that cheated it all the way, and holed his putt for a four. That settled it at last, and Adams for the second time in three years was doomed to be runner-up. To Whitcombe there remained only one danger, his old enemy, Cotton, and after his experience of the previous year his thoughts, as he waited, need no description. Once again Cotton wanted a 71. Once again it was clearly impossible. Once again it seemed as if he would do it. Cotton went out in 35. Then the word sped over the course, shouted into unbelieving ears in the gale— and truthfully as it turned out—that he had started home four, three, three. Giving

186

him a three at the short 16th, he could afford three fives. The hurricane raged more fiercely than ever. He did not quite get the three at the 16th, a putt for four at the 15th stayed cruelly out, and Whitcombe was home. His name is one without which no roll of champions would have seemed complete.

So now the tale is nearly ended and it remains only to pay a farewell visit to the Old Course at St Andrews, a fitting stage for what so long seemed to have been the finale and which mercifully turned out only to have been the interval. Here we were threatened again with invasion from an old friend, Lawson Little, now a professional; a burly newcomer, John Bulla, who was later, by his persistent and nearly successful endeavours to win our championship, to qualify as a welcome 'regular'; Martin Posé from the Argentine, who had won the French Open with an outstanding last round of 68 on the new course at Le Touquet; and, if he may be called an invader, Bobby Locke from South Africa.

Lawson shone in the qualifying rounds but was not quite his old self when it came to the real thing. Posé played well but an unhappy eight at the Road Hole where he was penalized two strokes for grounding his club on the grass behind the green, which is technically part of the hazard, put him out of the running. Locke had a 70 which also included an eight at the 14th—an astonishing performance—and in the end it was Bulla *versus* the rest. On the final day he sailed round in 71 and 73, and only Perry, Shankland, a rugged golfer who had once played professional rugby football in Australia, and Richard Burton could catch him. First Perry, then Shankland, failed to do the trick, and Burton, out late, was left with 73 to tie. Tall and rangy, Burton has, to me, a most attractive style, with the hands held high away from the body and a tremendous cock of the wrists at the top which is noticeable almost as a movement on its own. He even does it with the putting, and, though it sets the spectators' hearts fluttering, it is indeed a beautiful and graceful method for a man of his build. In the last round he was out in 35, which was more than satisfactory. He got safely past the long 14th, and now, with the multitudes pouring out to cheer on the last hope of Britain, needed two fives and two fours to win. He won the championship at the next two holes—with his putter. I suppose his putt at the 15th was 8 feet. Only those who have endured these things for themselves can know what a St Andrews 8-footer can mean at this sort of moment. We breathed again. A five must be reserved for the Road hole, of course, but that left him a five for the 16th and a four for the 18th which, down wind, he might almost reach. From the 16th tee he delivered a truly gigantic hook, all across the third fairway and nearly into the whins. His second was short and then, oh horror! he fluffed his chip. The fourth was none too good either. I remember well the ghastly silence as he stood to his putt and the roar that greeted the disappearance of the ball. Now, at last, Burton himself sensed that he was going to win. He played the sensible copybook five at the Road hole and,

187

scorning the safe line to the left, drove a colossal drive down beside the rails at the last. The only way he could lose now, thought lesser mortals, was to take a sharp-faced niblick and fluff the little pitch into the Valley of Sin. I can hear now the subdued mutterings and expostulations of the more knowledgeable watchers behind the green as he was seen to withdraw from his bag some hideously sharp-looking lofted club, and I can see also the nonchalant flick of the wrists as he tossed the ball perfectly up on to the green past the hole. He had, I suppose, a 5- or 6-yarder back from above the hole. He hit it with a firm crack down the slope and I think it must have slid at least a yard past, but already he was striding after it, as though to put any such nonsense out of its head, and the ball dropped obediently into the middle of the hole for a three—a fitting curtain to the twenty years of golf between the wars.

THE AMATEUR CHAMPIONSHIP

Among the amateurs the first world war made virtually a clean sweep in the golfing, though mercifully not in the physical, sense. For the five years up to 1914, the names on the championship trophy had read Ball, Hilton, Ball, Hilton, Jenkins. None of these could hope to reign as champion again. The field was clear, and into the arena to take their places marched a trio widely different both in temperament and method but for ever to be bracketed together. They were Cyril Tolley, Roger Wethered and Ernest (now Sir Ernest) Holderness.

Between them they won four of the first five championships after the war, and though his renown, for reasons which will appear, has lasted less long than that of the other two, it was Holderness who won two of these titles to the others' one apiece. In 1914 when Tolley was 18 and Wethered 15, Holderness was already becoming known as a promising Oxford player. Not only was he the most mature of the three when the war finished (unless in Tolley's case an M.C. and a long spell behind German barbed wire counted towards golfing maturity), but he also had that simple and, in the best sense, elementary sort of style that enables a man to leave his clubs for a year or two in the attic and, on retrieving them, to play from memory. It has been said of Holderness by Bernard Darwin, who knew his game more intimately than the writer, who only played with him two or three times, 'One never expected to see him hit a huge shot but neither did one ever expect to see him hit a crooked one.' He won the President's Putter for the first four years of its existence from 1920-1923.

A steady rise in the senior ranks of the Civil Service left Holderness too little time, though indeed he needed less than most, to remain in the highest flights of golf, but right through until the middle '30s he would emerge to play top for Walton Heath, when club sides were stronger than they are now, and nonchalantly defeat the captains of Oxford and Cambridge.

Whatever may be said in the present volume or in anything written hereafter, it will almost certainly be Wethered's fate to go down in the game's history as the man whose erratic driving prevented his reaching the supreme heights. Perhaps the fairest verdict is to say that Wethered's driving, by comparison with the rest of his game, was about on a par with Harry Vardon's putting. Both were good enough by normal standards, but not when compared with the rest. Vardon's putting was good enough for anyone except Vardon. Wethered's driving was nearly good enough for anyone except Wethered. Just as Vardon missed occasionally and 'unaccountably' from one yard, so did Wethered from time to time unloose a tee shot which earned the awe of the spectators for its splendid inaccuracy. On the other hand, his iron shots, hit with the minimum of fuss and calculation and with a reverberating crack, were a joy to eye and ear.

Tolley by contrast—and the two will always be contrasted—struck awe into the hearts of the watchers by his driving. On courses all over England, Scotland and indeed Europe, the visitor is still informed by his caddie 'where Mr Tolley drove to, when he was here'.

History is necessarily in the past tense, but it comes slightly amiss when writing of Cyril Tolley, who won the championship in 1920 and again in 1929, to say nothing of two French Opens over 72 holes against the best professionals, and then was only beaten in the semi-final by the ultimate winner, Frank Stranahan, in 1950, Stranahan's age when Tolley first won having been minus three.

If championships had been played by age groups, I cannot help feeling that Tolley would have been a constant champion. At 25, at 30, 40, 50 and now for a certainty at 55, he has been capable of beating all amateurs of the same age. His swing—full, smooth, supple, unhesitating and in every sense 'classical'—gives the impression that it will last for ever, long after the shut-face exponents of the 1950s have reverted to ten handicap.

Throughout his golfing life Tolley has been dubbed by the Press as 'majestic' and so, outwardly, he has appeared, but beneath this apparently carefree exterior his nerves smoulder. Early in life he decided that the only way to overcome 'temperament' was to affect to ignore it—a stratagem to which he probably owes his golfing longevity. Rarely at any rate has he since appeared more majestic than in the winning of his first championship at Muirfield in 1920.

His opponent in the final was Bob Gardner, an American athlete of much distinction who, apart from winning the United States Championship when almost a boy in 1909 and reaching the final again in 1916, had also held the pole-vaulting record for the world and won the rackets doubles championship of America. Tolley was three up with four to play. To the agony of his supporters two holes were lost in a row. The rot was stemmed at the 17th but a perfect four gave Gardner the 18th, and on they went to the extra hole, in those days a one-shotter.

189

Gardner, furthermore, put his tee shot well on the green. Tolley not only matched this but got inside it—4 or 5 yards from the hole, they say, but unless putts like this are measured with a foot-rule,opinions even of eye-witnesses, as anyone who writes about golf will confirm, vary up to 200 per cent. At any rate,Gardner laid his putt dead, whereupon Tolley walked straight to his ball and hit it straight in. And they do say that, having equipped himself with a five-pound note for his caddie in the event of victory, he handed it over before he stepped up to putt.

When the trio had finished, it was the turn of Robert Harris, born in Carnoustie and settled in London. He had twice been in the final—once before the war and once after it—and though he had for years been good enough to win and had won almost everything else, it was widely reckoned that now, at 43, he had left it too late. He won in the most convincing way, to be followed in the next year by the first of the 'modern' Americans, Jesse Sweetser, a well-liked figure on both sides of the Atlantic and a golfer in the true amateur tradition.

For many years the amateurs whose names figured most prominently in the championships and in the councils of the game had hailed either from Scotland or the South of England, but now the Midlands were to have their say in both. The English Golf Union, now making its voice heard, had its spiritual home in the Midlands, and the next two champions, Dr. William Tweddell and T. P. Perkins, also hailed from the Shakespeare country. These two,to the outside observer, had little in common. With his ancient wooden putter and a style which defied the text-books by aiming to cover-point, Tweddell, the weekend golfer and full-time practitioner, reached the final again in 1935, captained the 1936 Walker Cup team in America, and for years remained liable to beat anyone in the championship. Perkins was of different calibre. He took golf more 'seriously' than was then perhaps the fashion and his slow play led to a rather unhappy incident when he came to defend his title at Sandwich. At any rate he emigrated to America, turned professional, and as such had succeeded in tying with two others, as was thought, for the United States Open, until Sarazen, holing the last twenty-eight holes in 100 strokes, slipped through to beat them all.

Of Bobby Jones, who beat Wethered in the 1930 final, I have already written more than enough. Suffice it to say that it must have added to the sweets of victory to feel that he had not only captured a title that had eluded him so long but also had done it at St Andrews. And if he should have at that time had any doubts about the popularity of his victory, which he can hardly have done, the people of St. Andrews made it abundantly clear on a later occasion which he afterwards described as one of the most moving episodes of his life. Six years later, passing through Britain on his way to watch the Olympic Games at Berlin, he went to play a casual round at St. Andrews for old times' sake. No preliminary fuss was made and the fourball was a quiet and private affair—except for the five thousand people who by ten o'clock in the morning had assembled to follow him respectfully around.

His St. Andrews championship saw the end of Bobby Jones as a competitive golfer. Anyone who followed was doomed to figure as anticlimax, and Eric Martin Smith, just down from Cambridge, for whom he had played for three years against Oxford, and a happy-go-lucky golfer with a long flowing swing which, in the dying days of hickory, had once prompted a caddie to remark, 'Lucky you don't play with steel shafts, sir, or you'd stun yourself!' would be the last to take offence at such a description. His victory at Westward Ho! was a surprise, but Martin Smith had in his veins the blood of two families of golfers, his own and the Hambros, and, if he did not play a round in the sixties, he did not play one in the eighties either, and, when there came to him a chance which he might assume would not come again, he took it like a man. His opponent, John de Forest, was also a 'surprise', but when he went on, the following year, not only to reach the final again but to win it, the critics could affect surprise no more. De Forest's two finals, and his play in other events at this time, will be remembered for the unfortunate golfing malady under which he laboured. He 'got stuck'. Only those who have suffered this seemingly ridiculous ailment can appreciate fully its mesmeric effect, wherein the player gazes fixedly at the ball, motionless as though hypnotized and quite unable to move the club. It made de Forest's victories a little tedious to the watcher but took away none of their golfing glory.

To me, at any rate, one of the most remarkable achievements in the championship was Michael Scott's at Hoylake. He was 53 at the time and, though a man may be only as old as he feels, this was the beginning of the unhappy era in which we have successively lengthened the thirty-odd thousand holes of golf in Britain to fit unsought 'improvements' in one ball instead of fitting one ball to thirty thousand holes; and Hoylake must have measured every inch of 7,000 yards. Not only that, but the walks back to the far tees added fully a thousand yards of extra trudging—the tenth tee, for instance, being up in the sandhills level with the place from which the players had five minutes previously played their second shots to the ninth. One is tempted, on contemplating this farcical development, due not to the wish of the ruling body but to the research departments of competitive ball manufacturers, to wonder whether, if the manufacturers of footballs discovered a ball which, when kicked from one end of the field, would pitch at the other, every football club would rebuild its grandstands to accommodate the new ball!

Be that as it may, not only was Hoylake desperately long but there were playing in the championship several of the leading American amateurs. Scott survived his gruelling week by persistent avoidance of error and by continuously hitting the ball quietly in the middle of the club, thus taking advantage of the hard-baked ground and keeping up with more vigorous and youthful opponents. The runner-up, too, must be mentioned. It is the fate of runners-up to be almost instantly forgotten. Dale Bourn will never be forgotten. He was the gay cavalier of golf, a man who would drive into some impenetrable golfing jungle and not only find his ball tee-ed up but confidently expect to do so. His exuberant spirits and at one time classical style endeared him to golfers, caddies and spectators alike. Sometimes people were cross with him, but no one was ever cross with him for long. He lost his life, alas, in the second war. There was only one Dale Bourn—perhaps there was only room for one—but there will never be another.

And so at Prestwick in 1934, with the full strength of the American Walker Cup team who had already trounced us at St Andrews, we came to perhaps the most memorable of all the inter-war championships. In the end the final was between giant and giant-killer, but this time the story went wrong and it was the giant who did the killing. The giant-killer was a good West of Scotland golfer of somewhat frail physique who later turned professional, James Wallace. If ever a man came up the hard way, he did. To reach the final, Wallace beat five Walker Cup players, including Jack McLean—in a Scottish 'Derby' wherein both were nearly trodden under foot by hordes of wildly partisan watchers, many of whom had entered the course by the 'Aberdeen gate', i.e. without admission fee over the sandhills, and whose conduct helped to set the seal on Prestwick as a championship course. The giant was Lawson Little. He was a beefy, broad-shouldered young fellow, strong as an ox, with a shut-face method of driving that led one to fancy he might have done well in a slaughterhouse in the days before the humane killer. Like many big, solid men, Little had a velvet touch on the greens, and when this and his long game were working at their best, he was probably, with the exception of Jones himself, the most formidable amateur golfer the game has seen. At Prestwick everything was working at once and no such exhibition as his is likely to be seen in a championship final again. Even the vast Saturday crowd that poured out from Glasgow to see Scotland win—thousands arriving after the match was over—could not forbear to cheer the conqueror. He was twelve up at lunch, and in the second round started with 3, 3, 4, 3, 3. The starting time having been put forward to help him catch the boat to America, he was the winner by two records that are likely to stand for all time—14 and 13, and twenty past two. His figures deserve to be quoted and here they are.

Out 4 3 3 4 3 3 5 4 4—33.
Home 4 3 5 4 3 4 3 4 3—33. Total 66.
Out 3 3 4 3 3.

Little went home to win the championship of the United States, and in 1935 was back again to defend his title at Lytham, still as formidable as ever but with a noticeable psychological change in that this time, instead of thrusting his way to the top, he was already on his pedestal, fair game for any Tom, Dick or Harry over

R. H. Wethered
driving from the 4th tee at St Andrews during the 1936 Amateur Championship

Fox Photos

Bobby Jones on his return to America in 1926, after winning the British Open Championship for the first time

Fox Photos

Bobby Jones driving off from the 1st tee at St Andrews. The occasion was a return visit, in 1936, to the scene of his former triumphs. Watched by a gallery of some four thousand spectators, Bobby Jones played a round in which there were many glimpses of his old incomparable form

Fox Photos

Hector Thomson on the 10th at Troon, during his
match with Charles Yates in the semi-finals of the
Amateur Championship in 1938

Fox Photos

E. Martin-Smith (*left*) and J. de Forest, the winner and
runner-up of the Amateur Championship played at
Westward Ho! in 1931

Central Press Photos

Henry Cotton driving; Alf Padgham on the left

Topical Press

Henry Cotton driving from the 1st tee at Southport during the 1937
Ryder Cup match

Central Press Photos

At Royal Lytham and St Anne's, Henry Cotton sinks the winning putt in his match
against Norman von Nida in the final of the 1947 *News of the World* Tournament

Fox Photos

Densmore Shute, who won the Open Championship
in 1933 at St Andrews

Topical Press

Lawson Little playing his approach to the 1st at
St Andrews during the 1946 Open Championship

Central Press Photos

Charles Yates, a member of the 1938 Walker Cup
team, practising at St Andrews where the match
was played. In this year he also won the British
Amateur Championship

Keystone

Robert Sweeny
playing in the Grand Challenge Cup Competition
Royal St George's, Sandwich, in 1947

Sport and General

Arthur Havers in 1923, the year in which he won the
Open Championship at Troon

R. A. Whitcombe driving from the 6th tee at Sunningdale during the *Daily Mail* Professional Tournament
in 1948

Sport and General

Dick Burton driving from the 1st tee of the West Course in front of the club-house at Moor Park during the 'Silver King' Professional Tournament in 1950

Central Press Photos

Alf Padgham strays from the fairway on the 14th at Walton Heath into the heather which is so characteristic of that fine course

Central Press Photos

Walter Hagen. Open Champion, 1922, 1924, 1928, and 1929; US International Team v. Great Britain 1926; Ryder Cup team, 1927, 1933, and 1935

Topical Press

Central Press Photos

Sport and General

The 6th green at Rye during the Oxford and Cambridge Golfing Society's President's Putter Final in 1949. In this match P. B. Lucas, seen putting, beat R. H. Wethered

Sport and General

The President's Putter

Fox Photos

Fox Photos

John Beck, the British captain, and Francis Ouimet, the American captain, photographed with the Walker Cup at St Andrews in 1938. Francis Ouimet lives in golf history for his victory at the age of 20 in the American Open Championship of 1913, after a tie with Vardon and Ray who were then at their best. He has been elected captain of the Royal and Ancient, 1951–2

Graphic Photo Union

Charles Whitcombe (*right*), the British captain, congratulating the American captain, Ben Hogan, at the presentation of the Ryder Cup in 1949 at Ganton. Holding the cup is Lord Wardington. Hogan was non-playing captain of the US team, having but recently recovered from the motor accident in which he nearly lost his life. He is the only great American golfer who has never played in a British tournament

Norman von Nida during the 1947 *News of the World* Professional Tournament at Royal Lytham and St Anne's

Sport and General

Fred Daly driving from the 18th tee at Royal St George's while practising for the 1949 Open Championship

Planet News

R. J. White driving from the 4th tee at St Andrews during his match with F. Kamer in the 1947 Walker Cup match

Associated Press

S. M. McCready taking part in a match between the Walker Cup team and R. Oppenheimer's team at Maidenhead Golf Club in 1949. Watching him drive (*left*) is A. A. Duncan, runner-up in the 1939 Amateur Championship and winner of the Welsh Amateur Championship 1938 and 1949

Graphic Photo Union

James Bruen, the winner of the Amateur Championship at Birkdale in 1946

Associated Press

Henry Cotton with the Championship trophy
after winning the Open Championship for the
third time, at Muirfield in 1948

Central Press Photos

Henry Cotton putting on the 13th green at
Muirfield during the 1948 Open Championship

Planet News

Harry Bradshaw driving from the 14th tee at Sandwich during the final of the 1949 Open Championship. It was in this match that Bradshaw tied with Bobby Locke, losing the play off. It was Bradshaw's misfortune in finding his ball in a broken beer bottle (from which it took him two strokes to explode it) during the Championship which contributed to the subsequent change of the rule concerning movable objects

Associated Press

G. H. Micklem driving from the 4th tee at St Anne's during the 1948 *Daily Telegraph* Tournament which he won in partnership with C. H. Ward

Barratt's Photo Press

Louis T. Stanley, Esq

D. J. Rees. Winner of the *News of the World* Tournament, 1936, 1938, 1949, and 1950. Irish Open Champion, 1948. Member of Ryder Cup team, 1937, 1947, and 1949

P.A.—Reuter

Sam Snead at Ganton before the Ryder Cup match in 1949. He won the Open Championship in 1946

International News Photos

Willie Turnesa, who played in the Walker Cup in 1947, 1949, and 1951, at St Andrews before taking part in the 1950 Amateur Championship

Kent News Pictures

Frank Stranahan, Amateur Champion in 1948 and 1950, driving from the 4th tee during the 1947 Amateur Championship at Carnoustie

Sport and General

Bobby Locke
during a practice round at Troon before winning the Open Championship in 1950

Kent News Pictures

18 holes. One or two nearly beat him, but when he struggled through to the elbow room of the 36-hole final, there were those who could see Prestwick all over again. This was no disparagement to his opponent, the evergreen Dr. Tweddell, but it was the end of a long gruelling week. Tweddell was not as young as he was and was known to be none too well; he was bound to be heavily outdriven, and his putting could not last for ever.

Little won the first two holes and went steadily ahead to five up. All was going according to the book. However, Tweddell won back a couple and went in to lunch three down. If he could only get off to a good start this time, he might yet give the colossal crowd a run for their money. Nothing much happened, however, for eight holes and he was still three down. Then at the short ninth, with the tee beside the railway line, he holed a putt for a two. Then he won the eleventh and twelfth. All square! On the thirteenth, with the green ringed by many thousands of spectators, every one of them holding their breath in dead silence, Tweddell faced a 10-foot putt that would have put him one up. The ball faded at the very lip of the hole. Little, undaunted, won the fourteenth and fifteenth and saved himself with some wedge-like implement—of which I remember his carrying five in those days—and a long putt at the 16th. Back came Tweddell to win the 17th with a lovely pitch from the bunker—one down with one to play. The last hole at Lytham, a drive and a pitch finishing where all last holes should finish—under the club-house windows—was lined thick from tee to green. Standing on the balcony overlooking the green, I recollect making Tweddell's putt to save the match about 6 yards. How simple they look from above, where all paths seem to lead to the hole! He hit it well enough, but it just slipped by, and one of the greatest of all finals was over. To cap it, the winner returned to his own country and won the championship again, four in four years, turned professional, won the American Open, and remained as likeable as ever.

I trust not to have exhausted all the superlatives over Little's two finals, for the finish of the next one for sheer drama could hardly be matched. It was enacted, too, on the historic stage of golf, the last green at St. Andrews. The two protagonists were Hector Thomson, a quiet, slim young Scot in his early twenties, and incidentally a capital pianist, and a burly Australian, Jim Ferrier, whose curious swivelling movement due to an ailment in his left leg concealed a hitting method of the highest order. Scotland v. Australia, and at St Andrews! If the crowd at Lytham had been big, this was surely the biggest ever. Ferrier had been three up in the morning, only to drive over the wall—so easily done!—at the long 14th and give his opponent breathing space. Thomson recovered and we now see them coming into view with the vast crowd streaming on either side past the black railway sheds over which they have driven to the 17th, the Road hole. Thomson is two up now and there is nothing left for Ferrier but to go for the tiny diagonal green and hang the consequences. His second pitches on it and sticks—an heroic shot in the circumstances.

The crowds swarm up both sides of the flat green rectangle formed by the 1st and 18th fairways, ten deep on either side, leaving the players, their caddies and the referee small and forlorn figures on their own in the arena. Every window, ledge and roof has its occupants, and watchers cling precariously to the chimney-pots. The two drives are up the middle. Ferrier plays first, safely to the heart of the green. Can Thomson match it? I see the ball now, flying high and white against the blue sky. It pitches on the short edge of the green, bounces once, twice, and there is a great crescendo of roars and high-pitched feminine shrieks: 'It's in! It's in!'

It wasn't in, but it was in as nearly as mattered, perhaps 5 inches from the hole, and Ferrier with a wry smile walked across the green to shake the new champion by the hand. Golf may be a slow, pedestrian game, but, my word, it can be exciting at times!

It sometimes happens that at the end of a week's golf, having at first looked at the immense draw-sheet and marvelled that any man could aspire to survive long enough to see his name on the single line left for Saturday evening, one looks back and senses that it was 'So-and-so's championship all along'. Most people, I fancy, felt that way about Robert Sweeny's at Sandwich in 1937. True, he had reached the semi-final two years before and had long been known as a cosmopolitan golfer of a high order in London, Paris, Florida and New York, but this week he attained a stature that dominated the championship. Furthermore, he had the true classical style, which all of us can identify even if we cannot describe. It was a joy to see Sweeny hit the ball and a pleasure to see him win, though sad at the same time to see the gallant Lionel Munn lose. American by birth, Sweeny had spent some years at Oxford and had lived more on this side of the Atlantic than the other. We felt we could claim him as 'one of ours'.

Next year the Americans were back in force for the Walker Cup and therefore the championship, this time at Troon. There was a certain amount of fratricidal strife in the early stages and I remember thinking, as I watched Johnny Fischer, their champion of 1936, stymied out of his match on the 19th by Charles Yates, how cruel was the fate that brought him three thousand miles to lose in such a way by 11 o'clock on the Monday morning. At any rate, Yates reached the final, where his opponent was Cecil Ewing, a weighty Irishman with a compact, concise swing and a firm touch with his aluminium putter. Ewing put up a fine show in the final but, though he only lost on the 35th, he somehow never quite looked like winning. Golfers can do much good, or for that matter harm, as ambassadors. Jones and Hagen, each after a hesitant start, became great ambassadors in their day, but I doubt whether any American golfer to visit our shores was 'taken to' so quickly and so instinctively as Yates. His southern drawl, his friendliness to the world in general, his irrepressible good spirits, endeared him to everyone and, when at last we won the Walker Cup, it was he who on the steps of the Royal and Ancient led the crowd in a memorable rendering of 'A Wee Deoch and Doris'. We could do with any number of men like Yates in golf, and it was the game's loss when the banking business claimed him soon afterwards.

And so back to Hoylake for the last championship before the war, when the question was not so much 'Who will win?' as 'Will Bruen?' It is true that Bruen did, in the year following the war, win the championship, and the list of champions would not be complete without his name, but his heart by that time had gone out of the game and the effort took more out of him than a sensible man cares to continue giving to what is after all no more than a pastime. In 1939, however, there were no heights which he might not conceivably scale. In and before the Walker Cup trials he had played eight rounds of the Old Course at St Andrews, the worst four of which, when added together, would have won any open championship yet played there. His form had cast the Americans into obscurity and lifted the rest of the British team bodily from standards which hitherto would have 'got by'. In the Open of 1939, also at St Andrews, he had led the qualifying with rounds of 69 on both the Old and New Courses. He did not win, but he might well have done, and he was certainly the only amateur of whom this could be said since Jones.

So at Hoylake it looked like Bruen's championship in advance just as it had been Sweeny's in retrospect—but it was not to be. The man who beat him was Alex Kyle, a Scottish player long settled in Yorkshire, who had been one of the Walker Cup heroes of the year before. A tremendous match it was, with Kyle one up coming to the home hole. Here he laid his ball with a thump into the cross-bunker in front of the green, and well under the face at that. With Bruen safely on in two, a 19th hole seemed a certainty, and already, as Kyle descended to the bunker, the blue-jerseyed stalwarts who man the ropes at Hoylake were proceeding in advance to the first fairway. Their trouble was in vain. Kyle laid the ball stone dead and the match was over.

Kyle's opponent in the final was A. A. Duncan, a past Oxford captain, one of the shining lights of Welsh golf and now a regular soldier. Among the many merits of Duncan's golf was, and is, that he played with such speed and decision. Kyle, too, was no time-waster and the two of them produced a final that has left a most cheerful impression on all who saw it. With Hoylake stretched again to its uttermost, and with the crowds following alongside, not roped off as they are at St Andrews, they completed the first round in two hours and twenty minutes—a time which after the war, in a period not within my present province, was to seem incredible. Nor could one ask for better golf or a better match. After thirty-three holes they were still all square. Here Duncan slipped and a perfect four at the Royal, or thirty-fifth, gave Kyle a title he was not destined to defend for six long years.

INTERNATIONAL MATCHES

The international matches that we now accept as commonplace all grew up between the wars, even, though it seems hard to believe, the Walker and Ryder Cup matches against the United States. The old match between England and Scotland held traditionally on the Saturday before the championship gave way to the four-cornered affairs that are played today and, looking back on it, this seems only fair to Ireland and Wales. Every year, too, England plays against, and nearly always overwhelms, France, in a match which started in an atmosphere that was serious on the course and light-hearted off it and, having now become somewhat 'official', has lost a little of its first careless rapture.

In the Walker Cup, Britain has never been able to make much of a showing against the Americans on their own soil. Indeed, our first effort, at the National Links, Long Island, in 1922, when we secured four points out of the twelve, was our best. At successive 'inquests' many and ingenious reasons are habitually given for our lack of success. I confine myself to two of the less controversial, which I fear we shall never overcome. One is that our American friends have ten players to our one from whom to choose, and the other is that, while no reflection is cast on their amateur status according to the American definition, they do for the most part make a life-work of their golf.

At home our lot has also been disappointment, except on one glorious occasion which none who witnessed it are likely to forget. The scene is set on the historic stage of golf, the last green at St Andrews, the year is 1938, and the whole of the rectangle formed by the first and last fairways is lined ten deep with people behind the white posts. Once again every window, ledge, roof and chimney-pot is manned—the same setting as for Hector Thomson's extraordinary finish to the championship two years before. This time the figures in the centre are Cecil Ewing (Great Britain) and Ray Billows (USA), and everyone is under the impression that on their match depends the destination of the Walker Cup. With Ewing one up, each has reached the last green in two, when away in the distance is seen a small procession, some running ahead and waving their arms, coming in with Alex Kyle. The news flies fast that he has won—and so therefore have we. The crowd, perhaps ten thousand all told, swarms over the fairway and the green, leaving a little 30-ft. circle for the players to conclude what is now but a formality. Ewing wins and the cup is ours at last. No praise for this, alas, unique occurrence can be too great for the British captain, John Beck, who imbued into a miscellany of individuals of varying temperament, age, occupation and nationality a unity of spirit which proved invincible.

In the Ryder Cup the professionals had better fortune, and deserved it. They never, it is true, won in America, but it was not until 1937 that they were beaten at home. Incidentally, both the Ryder and Walker Cup matches were preceded by an unofficial match, and in each of these Tommy Armour, later to become one of the most successful of United States professionals, played for Britain, first as an amateur and then as a professional. To beat, as the British team did in 1933, an American side whose singles order read Sarazen, Dutra, Hagen, Wood, Runyan, Diegel, Shute and Horton Smith was a tremendous performance.

On the other hand it is, I hope, fair to say that the Ryder Cup matches have attracted more of what one may call newspaper interest and less true golfing fervour than their amateur counterpart. The need for finding a sponsor for the expense, usually in the shape of a municipality, led to the matches being played, up to 1937, at places where, though the club might do its best, the course was hardly worthy of a great occasion. People turned up in thousands and paid their half-crowns, but the attitude of too many was reflected by the comment of the lady at Southport who observed to her male escort: 'Never mind the golf; I have come to see t' Prince of Wales.' The match also lost public esteem, which reforms would enable it soon to win back, when the Americans took the field without the Open Champion of the United States, who was a full-time professional golfer—because he had not yet qualified for his union ticket.

At home the England *v.* Scotland match, which had begun in 1902, finished in 1931 with a scores of 14 victories to 9 in favour of Scotland. From then on it was 'all against all', but the result for many years was the same. I remember thinking that we in England would never beat the Scots at golf and that there was no reason why we ever should, a feeling with which any Oxford man will sympathize who recalls the thirteen successive victories of Cambridge in the boat race. However, the tide turned just before World War II and, aided by a selection committee in which the wide knowledge and enthusiasm of R. H. Oppenheimer, a past Oxford captain, played no small part, England won the 1938 match by a firm margin and, though they did not know it, were to remain unbeaten for the next twelve years.

OTHER TOURNAMENTS

And now, to conclude, I must mention—though without, I am afraid, doing them full justice—some of the other events in the steadily growing cavalcade of golf, between the wars. There were the national championships, of course, most of them originating in the twenties, and here I can only quote the names of some of those who made their mark in their own countries but never quite succeeded in winning the championship itself. In England one might put as outstanding Leonard Crawley, Stanley Lunt, J. Woollam, Harry Bentley and Frank Pennink. In Scotland, Jack McLean, E. D. Hamilton and Hamilton McInally. In Ireland, C. O. Hezlet and

J. Burke. In Wales, H. R. Howell, seven times champion between the wars, and of course A. A. Duncan.

The whole picture would require an encyclopaedia, so of the rest I will choose three events which it seems to me meant more to those who took part in them either as players, spectators, or followers in the newspapers, than any others. Of two it may be said that they were, and are, 'exclusive', a quality which it is the current fashion to hold in some suspicion. The first is the President's Putter at Rye, with which in January the season's golf may be said to open. No one who has not sampled it knows the charm of Rye in mid-winter. Sometimes we have been treated to snow and frost—for which shooting enthusiasts find compensation in duck-flighting in the neighbouring marshes—but more often we have been fortunate, occasionally to the unbelievable degree of playing in shirt-sleeves. In either case the remote charm of the links, which no amount of tinkering about in recent years has been able to diminish; the unpretentious little club-house, blown in by almost the last of the flying bombs and now restored in the same simple style; the traditional Rye dish of scrambled eggs and sausage; the winding road out from the town, clogged with holidaymakers with motor-cars and wireless in summer, but now ours alone; the warm comforts and good company in the Dormy House when the day's golf is done; all these make a pattern that men cherish lovingly in their minds. Above all, there lingers in my own memory the prospect of the little town perched on its hill some two or three miles away, with the golden weather-cock on the ancient church glinting in the pale sun of a winter's afternoon, a scene which almost unchanged has cheered the heart of the wayfarer across the marsh these last six hundred years.

As in the championship, so in the putter two names dominated the early years: Holderness and Wethered, with Tolley thrown in for good measure. Other winners were distinguished in their own spheres; Sir Harold Gillies, for instance, plastic surgeon and artist of no mean ability, and Bernard Darwin. I sometimes wonder whether any one man has had so prolonged and profound an influence on one sport as Darwin has on golf. He has, like others before him of course, been captain of the Royal and Ancient, chairman of the Rules of Golf Committee, a member of the Championship Committee and such like, but his writings, particularly in *The Times*, will always be his main contribution to the game. These have contrived, though I dare say not deliberately, to set a standard of approach to golf—a tone, if you like, for want of a better word—with which few games have been blessed. It was only after the second war, a period outside my province, that golf seriously became 'news', mainly through the financial angle of the professional tournaments, and that newspaper editors sent to write about it for the benefit of the masses, persons who pretended to neither knowledge of, nor affection for, the game. Even then, Darwin continued to set the standard. When the time comes for him to lay aside his pen, it will be said no doubt that he leaves a gap that cannot be filled. For once the cliché will be precisely true.

I must mention, too, the Halford-Hewitt tournament at Deal, if only because it is the biggest gathering of golfers in the year, not excluding the Open. Innumerable people have confided in me how they personally were responsible for the brainwave that induced the donor to present his cup for an 'Old Boys' tournament. Whatever may be the circumstances of its conception, let 'Hal', alas no longer with us, take the credit. As he was himself an Old Carthusian, it was perhaps fitting that, if any school was to dominate the tournament, it should be Charterhouse. From 1924 until the second world war, Charterhouse won seven times, Eton four, Harrow three, Rugby and Marlborough once. If the cheerful weekend golfers who made up the Carthusian team had any particular virtue to account for their success, I should suspect it to be the fact that none of the ten players in the side cared a brass farthing with whom they were partnered or whether they played top or bottom, but, as I had the pleasure of being a member of the team for the six years prior to the war—playing on every occasion in the bottom foursome with J. S. F. Morrison, in itself a notable experience—this is a subject on which I shall not enlarge. It is enough to say that of all the golfing tournaments in the game's history the Halford Hewitt has probably given the highest aggregate of pleasure.

Second perhaps would come the Worplesdon Foursomes, dominated this time by the figure of Joyce Wethered, who between 1921 and 1933 won seven times with six different partners and was on another occasion beaten in the final. Her prowess will have been dealt with elsewhere, and here the bare record must speak for itself. Worplesdon is to autumn what Rye is to winter. The golf is often first-class—how many men, I wonder, would back themselves on their own to do the scores they sometimes achieve with a woman partner?—but it is the scene that lingers in the mind, the sun blazing on the chestnut trees, the dahlias in the garden beside the 15th, the blaze of autumn colouring around the 10th green reflected in the pond in front of the tee. All these, and the friendliness of it all, make Worplesdon unique. They also, perhaps, make golf itself unique.

199

LEONARD CRAWLEY

1945-1950

A Fresh Start

NINETEEN FORTY-SIX was, as it were, a time of preparation for the great international matches against America in the following year and was also one when we were trying to find our feet again. Many of the leading amateurs of pre-war vintage still looked very good and on the whole our professionals scored well in tournaments. But the truth of the matter is we were all too prone to be impressed by figures and too blind to realize the stark facts that in neither our amateur or professional ranks were there any young players of promise ready to take the places of pre-war leaders when the time came.

Nevertheless there was some splendid golf played in the Amateur Championship which was held for the first time on the magnificent course of the Birkdale Club near Southport. Because there had been no championships since 1939, there was naturally widespread interest and a large entry. It was during this week that we had our first glimpse of Frank Stranahan, of Toledo, Ohio, whose considerable performances in America had commanded a good deal of attention. He looked to be a pretty good player but nothing like so sound or so impressive as he became two years later. There was also James Bruen from Cork whom we had not seen since before the war when as a boy of 18 he burst upon the golfing world and lead the British team in the Walker Cup match at St Andrews in 1938. He was now a fully grown man and one of great strength and great personality. His power with all clubs from a niblick upwards had to be seen to be believed, but though his splendid putting still remained he had lost some of that accuracy which had made him famous as a boy. He came over to England very short of practice and he had some hard struggles in the earlier rounds, particularly against that fine player from the Midlands, Charles Stowe, who was robbed of victory against him by a hopeless stymie on the home green, and then at last Bruen reached the final. Here he found as his opponent Robert Sweeny, one whom we might call an Anglo-American, having been educated in this country and having lived in England for many years. Sweeny is one of the finest swingers of the golf club one could wish to see and he had already won the championship in 1937. Oddly enough, he was dead out of form most of the week at Birkdale but, through sheer courage and determination, he kept himself going, winning many of his matches at the extra holes. By the time he reached the semi-final where he beat Gerald Micklem, a vastly improved player since the war who had already beaten Stranahan, Sweeny found his form and therefore entered the final with considerable confidence.

It was a curious match, as I remember, since it had two very distinct halves. In the morning Sweeny played beautifully and Bruen drove all over the place, but his immense powers of recovery saved him time after time, and Bruen actually led by two holes at lunch-time which, on the face of it, was an unjust advantage. In the afternoon Bruen found his finest form and there was no holding him. His colossal tee shots were followed by accurate iron shots, and his putting must have been heart-breaking to play against. In the end he won quite comfortably against an opponent who had done his noble best.

1946

When Sam Snead, Johnny Bulla and Lawson Little descended out of the skies from America only two days before the Open Championship began at St Andrews early in July, very few people thought that they had given themselves time enough to do justice to their long journey or to their ability. And yet, Snead won a notable victory by four shots, Bulla was second equal with Bobby Locke and our own players trailed behind. It was in many ways a thrilling championship and, as so often in the past, all sorts of people had a chance of winning with one round to go. Snead won primarily because he played best and, in the strong wind that prevailed throughout the championship, his stupendous driving helped him immeasurably. His pitching was also of a quality seldom surpassed, but it should be added that the rough faces on his pitching clubs, at that time permissible in American professional tournaments, might not have satisfied the impartial judges in this country.

With one round to play Snead, Bulla and Rees were tying at 215, with Cotton one stroke and Locke three strokes behind. There was now a strong head wind up the first hole and in this last eventful round the Swilcan Burn guarding the green played a tremendous part. Locke, who had been in the burn in the morning, got a great three in the afternoon, and Cotton, who followed him, put his second shot splosh in the burn. Rees hit a bad tee shot at the first hole, was over-ambitious with his second and suffered a similar fate, but worse still, he took seven to hole out and his chances vanished. Snead, who was out last of those with a chance of winning, sliced his drive nearly out of bounds and took five, and this for him was a bad start. Meanwhile Locke had gone out in 36 and was one under fours after 12 holes. But suddenly his wonderful putting touch deserted him and, after a pathetic exhibition on the greens, he finished in 76. Cotton's chances faded likewise as he took five at each of the first five holes, and a last round of 79 was bitterly disappointing. Bulla, having taken six at the Road hole, came to the last hole with a four to grab the lead from Locke. His putt for a three slipped 18 inches past the hole, and I shall never forget the groans of dismay when he missed the one back. Snead himself had also started lamentably and came very near to complete disaster when at the long fifth he crashed a brassey shot plumb into the whins to the right of the green, but he found his ball, got his five, and reached the turn in 40. He got a fine three at the 10th and a regulation three at the 11th, and now, with the wind at his back, he found his own majestic stride. A wonderful four at the long 14th (560 yards) made him, and with a well-played four at the Road hole all was over, and he won pulling up. Had he not found his ball in the whins at the fifth anything might have happened.

One further point of interest was that Snead, whose putting failures in America had already begun to cost him dearly at home, putted surely and confidently on the fast St Andrews greens throughout the championship. Though this magnificent golfer has swept all before him in recent years in the United States, the old putting bogy returns once a year and he has yet to win the Open Championship of America.

At the end of a rather depressing season, Henry Cotton won the *News of the World* Tournament (the Professional Match Play Championship) for the third time, beating James Adams of Wentworth by 8 up and 7 to play in the 36-hole final. Throughout the tournament the standard of play was universally high. In modern times there is nothing quite like a Cotton victory when the great man is at his best and destroys his opponents one by one. He always seems to play his best when the greens are green and therefore to his liking, and at any rate in round after round his play up to the pin and his putting inspired the utmost confidence in his supporters. His driving, too, was of that mechanical yet easy fluency and deadly accurate.

The one really exciting match was that between Cotton and Bobby Locke of South Africa. The two have always been great rivals and the atmosphere was tense. Cotton went to the 12th 3 up, but then Locke holed a chip shot of 40 yards and won the hole which he had looked like losing. He also won the 14th and excitement grew. Both made their mistakes and seemed unable to take their chances. Finally Cotton got a cast-iron 4 at the 18th and just got home.

1947

We had patiently to wait for 1947 when our trials of strength in the shape of the Walker Cup and Ryder Cup matches against the United States were due to be renewed. We were aware that there were very few new, young players ready to take their places in either our amateur or professional sides, and that they would be largely composed of members of the old guard. Their form, however, had been most encouraging during the two post-war seasons, and we were not quite prepared to believe all we had read and heard about the new and younger generation of American golfers.

The Walker Cup match was due to be played in America, but in view of post-war currency difficulties the United States Golf Association very generously agreed to send the American team to this country again, and the match was arranged to be played at St. Andrews early in May.

As in 1938, the selection committee organized extensive trial matches in various parts of the country with a final series at St. Andrews in which each match was played over 36 holes. Though this is a somewhat laborious process, it is, to my mind, far and away the best method of finding the best players for this great international match. Almost before the season had begun, the selectors heard the bad news that James Bruen, the holder of the Amateur Championship and one of the most brilliant golfers of his generation, would not be available owing to a serious illness. By general consent, the nine best amateurs were chosen, and John Beck, with his forceful character and ever cheerful personality, was appointed captain. The British team was as follows: J. B. Beck, J. B. Carr, C. Ewing, P. B. Lucas, G. H. Micklem, C. Stowe, R. J. White, J. C. Wilson and myself. Carr, a stupendous hitter and a brilliant if unorthodox player from Ireland; Micklem, the new English champion; R. J. White, of Birkdale; and J. C. Wilson, a grand golfer from the west of Scotland, were new-comers to Walker Cup golf. The whole side had played with great distinction in the trial matches and, whether I am right or whether I am wrong, I shall always think that it was one of the best Walker Cup sides ever picked to play for Great Britain.

Unfortunately the final trials were played within ten days of the Walker Cup match and in the short time available before facing the Americans, Beck had to get his foursome partnerships going. The British players were therefore compelled to play under pressure, and high pressure at that, for nearly a fortnight on end. We do not like excuses in this country any more than we like threats, but I do think that if the British side had had ten days' or a fortnight's rest between the trials and the Walker Cup match, they would not have faded into defeat in the very last round. Perhaps I may be a little biased since our very old and dear friend,

Francis Ouimet, the American captain, who had watched our trial matches, whispered in my ear one evening: 'Say, you boys will have had plenty of golf when this party's over.'

The foursomes produced some magnificent play by both sides and left us all square and all to play for in the singles next day. In the top match Bishop and Reigel of America just got the better of the Irishmen, Ewing and Carr, and the Americans won owing to their superiority on the putting greens where Ewing and Carr let one or two chances go begging. In the morning, both sides went round in 73, and the Americans, who just had the run of the green with them, led by one hole. Perhaps the match turned in the Americans' favour at the long 5th in the afternoon when Carr elected to play safe instead of going for the green with his second. He went too far and was bunkered, and so the hole was lost instead of won and counted two on a division. Only one down after 14 holes, the Irishmen took three putts at the 15th and were bunkered at the 16th, and we lost this critical and important match in which even a half would have been worth much fine gold.

Lucas and myself in the second match won a notable victory over Ward and Quick, two of the best golfers, and two of the toughest competitors that ever came to these islands from America. We started poorly, losing the first two holes, with Lucas distinctly jumpy and fretting like a highly bred racehorse before the Derby. He holed a fine putt of 9 feet for a win at the 5th, and thereafter he dominated the match with his magnificent iron play. We went into lunch five up, held on to the critical holes immediately after the interval and finally defeated our formidable opponents on the 30th green.

The two Scots, Kyle and Wilson, were a little disappointing in the third match, and poor Kyle was probably to blame. Kammer and Turnesa, the Americans, were two up after 18 holes and, generally speaking, deserved their lead. In the afternoon the Americans drew away steadily, and soon the match had to be written off. Very great credit was due to the last British pair, Stowe and White, who, after being one down to Stranahan and Chapman, went into lunch six up. Though the Americans were full of fight in the afternoon, Stowe and White never really allowed them to make any impression and they won comfortably in the end by four and three.

When at lunch-time next day the two sides were still level in the eight singles, everyone was full of hope, but there were three matches as good as over. Carr, playing brilliantly, was five up on the American champion, Bishop, who was thankful for lunch and a little rest. Reigel had been quite merciless with Micklem and was six up, and Turnesa, whose tremendous ability we had not yet learned to appreciate, held a similar lead over Ewing. This meant two to America and one to Great Britain. Of the other matches, I was three up on Ward, White was three up on Kammer, and Stowe two up on Stranahan. All three with a nice lead but none certain of victory for Great Britain. Lastly, Chapman was two up on Lucas, the hero of the foursomes, and Quick was one up on Wilson. These matches were still in the melting-pot. Since I was leading the British side, my match with Ward was perhaps the most important, particularly from the point of view of morale in these days when field telephones flash the news back from the front like wildfire. I hit a lovely pitch to the first green and ought to have been putting for three, but my ball plugged deep into the turf, and I lost a crucial hole which I might well have won. Incredible as it may seem, my tee shot to the second suffered a similar fate in the middle of the fairway, was hopelessly plugged, and within the twinkling of an eye my priceless lead of three holes had dwindled to one, against the best and most aggressive player in the American team. From the third hole onwards, Ward played like an inspired man and, with six threes in a row round the loop, he trampled on his bewildered opponent. As this bad news was flashed back to the club-house, it had a depressing effect on the rest of the British players. Wandering for one moment into the realms of 'if', it is reasonable to suppose that had the position been reversed, with Ward finding his ball plugged at each of the first two holes after lunch, it is in the highest degree probable that he would have been five down on the third tee, and a beaten man. The remainder of the British side would then have set out on their last round with the knowledge that another match was in the bag. As it was, the bad news spread and had its ill-effect on the rest of the team. Carr won most convincingly by five and three against Bishop, but Reigel and Turnesa soon disposed of Micklem and Ewing. Lucas hung on to Chapman for nine holes, but Chapman was still fresh and strong, and in the end drew away. Stranahan turned on the heat against Stowe and just got the better of him on the 35th green, and Quick defeated an exhausted Wilson far from home. The one bright spot from our point of view on this depressing afternoon was the magnificent golf played by R. J. White, who defeated Freddie Kammer on the 33rd green. Thus America regained the Walker Cup by eight matches to four. The result might have been very different if the British team had been allowed a fortnight's rest between the trial matches and the Walker Cup match.

The Amateur Championship was played at Carnoustie ten days later and the Americans as a team were badly drawn, a number of them having to commit fratricide in the early rounds. But, as the days went by, an all-American final seemed likely, for Turnesa in the top half of the draw and Chapman down below were both playing superb golf. Chapman had some anxious moments in his semi-final match against that polished Scottish golfer, Sam McKinlay, but he won on the 17th green. Turnesa won the other semi-final comfortably enough against J. G. Campbell, a useful Scottish player from Kilmalcolm, and so all was set for the American final we had feared. Next day our fears were soon drowned in our admiration for the magnificent golf played by these two young men from the

United States, and, almost more important still, they played all day in an atmosphere of camaraderie and in the most delightful spirit.

After some shocking weather which delayed the start of the final by an hour Chapman got off like a shot out of a gun with threes at the first, second and fifth holes. They were cruel thrusts, and he also won the long sixth in five to six to become four up. At the 9th he got a perfect four to be out in 34 and was five up on his adversary who, though looking rather shrivelled in the cold wind, appeared quite unconcerned. At the long 10th Turnesa's second shot jumped the burn and he got his four. Chapman, bunkered close to the hole, took six, and this proved to be the turning of the tide. On the long trek home a number of holes were out of range for Turnesa in two shots, but by means of his masterly pitching and putting, quite uncanny in their accuracy, he got his four time after time and Chapman did not. With an heroic four, Turnesa squared the match at the long 14th, and now it was Chapman who deserved the sympathy of the huge crowd. He had not wilted for one moment under this frightful ordeal, and to his eternal credit he was now able to put on the brakes and went into lunch all square.

In the afternoon both played golf with a solid, steady brilliancy and there were no more violent fluctuations. Chapman took the lead again with another great three at the second, but he lost the third through a monstrous stymie. Turnesa at last got his nose in front for the first time in the day at the 9th, where Chapman just failed to get his four. There followed five holes magnificently halved in four, four, four, three, four, and during this run Turnesa got down with a chip and a putt on at least three occasions. Another tiny slip by the brave Chapman at the 15th left him two down, and this was the beginning of the end. At the 16th Turnesa, after a bad tee shot, pitched back to within 8 feet of the hole, and then, with the confidence of Walter Hagen in his prime, knocked in his putt for the championship and so ended one of the greatest finals in the history of British golf.

The Open at Hoylake early in July was one of bewildering excitement from beginning to end, and up to the very last moment no one dared guess who was going to win. In the end Fred Daly, of Balmoral, Belfast, became the first Irishman ever to win the championship, and though his victory, well deserved as it was, confounded some of the critics, it set Daly going as one of the leading professionals in Britain for some time to come. Daly is not a great stylist, but he is a highly efficient golfer, and his pitching and putting are very fine.

His subsequent victories and performances in the principal events of the year give ample proof of his game and the toughness of his fibre.

The overseas challenge was not very formidable, Victor Ghezzi and Johnny Bulla, two professionals, and Frank Stranahan, a highly ambitious amateur, being the sole contenders from America.

1945-1950: *A Fresh Start: Leonard Crawley*

Henry Cotton, as usual, started favourite and, putting very well on the easy paced greens, had a first round of 69. But, there seemed to be something just wrong with both his game and his frame of mind as was proved by a second round of 78, and he never really got into his stride again. With one round to play, four players, of whom Daly was one, were tying for the lead, and several others were close on their heels. Daly, as I remember, was out early and therefore had his chance—if he could keep his form—to set up a target for others to shoot at. He went out in 38, hardly good enough as we thought, but he started for home three, three, four, three, four, and then came the critical short 13th where in the morning he had taken three putts. It was critical again, since he missed the green with his tee shot and only just extricated his second on to the putting surface. But he holed a vast putt of 20 yards for his three, and as I saw the ball disappear into the hole I remember thinking that this fortuitous blow might well make him champion. It gave him just that pep a tired man wants in a crisis and he played the next three terrifying holes magnificently, one after the other in four apiece. He took a tragic six at the 17th, ending with three terribly weak putts, and this left him with a four to tie with Horne who had finished in 294. He played a good second at the home hole and then holed out from fully 12 yards for a three. That has done it, we all shouted, and for once we were right. Before dealing with the final excitements of the day we must go back half an hour to pick up Horne. He had suddenly and unobtrusively come into the picture with a third round of 72 and he played magnificently in his last round. I watched him play the 16th hole, his second shot—one of superb quality played with a four wood—was ruled on the pin. It was either too straight by six inches or too short by a foot and he caught the corner of the bunker guarding the flag. Otherwise he would have been putting for a three, but as it was he took five. A poor tee shot at the 17th cost him another stroke and then his putt for three at the home hole sat impudently on the lip. It was undoubtedly the 16th that cost him the championship, and as so few people saw him finish even fewer realized how very close this magnificent striker of the ball came to victory. As Daly was finishing, the wind got up and all those behind with a chance of catching him were set more formidable, and in some cases, impossible tasks. Only one, the American Frank Stranahan, was able to rise to the occasion and right nobly did he set about the job. He wanted four, four, three to tie. Bunkered at the 16th, he got out and holed a grand putt for a four. He was on the 17th green in two, went boldly for his three and missed the one back. This was a major tragedy. Requiring a two to tie at the home hole, thousands of people standing round the last green watched him play his second with a number six iron and they gasped for breath as Stranahan's ball finished two inches short. Thus Daly won and he has since proved himself a most worthy champion.

And so to St Anne's for the *News of the World* Tournament (the Professional Match Play Championship). In the three days' play everything was dwarfed by the first round match between the holder Henry Cotton and Norman von Nida, the Australian. Nida had had a remarkable season, having carried off many of the richest prizes in the country. His admiration for Cotton's golf can only be described as colossal, and it is possible that on this great occasion, which an immense crowd turned up to follow, he allowed Cotton and the occasion to overwhelm him. It would be difficult to say whether Cotton is better in match or medal play, but there is no doubt whatever that in a big match he is a terrifying opponent. His golf was magnificent and when he turned four up on the Australian, the match was virtually over. In the quarter-finals Cotton was hunted to the last green by the carefree and gallant Smithers of Sunningdale, but Cotton just got through. This brought Cotton, who was the holder, and Fred Daly, the new Open Champion, together in the semi-final. It was another entertaining match, but Cotton was not quite at his best, hitting a number of brilliant shots interspersed with crooked ones. Daly on the other hand was playing beautifully, steady, accurate golf, and after the 6th hole he had the inside turn all the way. He also had the turn of the luck in the matter of stymies, and Cotton had to give in on the 16th green.

In the final Daly defeated that good Belgian golfer Flory Van Donck. In the morning round Van Donck putted superbly for the first six holes, but Daly hung on well and squared the match at the 12th. By lunch-time he led by a single hole, and then by means of magnificent golf he gradually drew away to win.

It was a victory in every way worthy of the Open Champion and one that put him on the same pedestal as the immortal James Braid who alone had won the Open and Match Play Championships in a single season.

Ryder Cup at Portland, Oregon
Early in October the British Ryder Cup team captained by Henry Cotton left for Portland, Oregon, for the first post-war international between the professionals of Great Britain and the United States. It would be fair to say that no one seriously thought we could win the match, but at the same time no one ever dreamt that our fellows would be almost annihilated. There was Cotton himself who knew all about American conditions, and every American professional has the highest respect for his game. There were also Dai Rees and C. H. Ward, who, after spending three months in America during the previous winter, had scored well in tournaments at home during the summer months. There was lastly Fred Daly, the absolute king of British professional golf.

It began to rain in Portland ten days before the British team arrived there and it never stopped for one moment until after they had departed. I shall never forget it.

The course was at no time fit for play and reminded one of some of the heavy clay courses around North London during the month of December in a year when it has rained without ceasing for six weeks.

No one can imagine the state of the fairways after some ten thousand spectators had paddled around watching the foursomes. Small ponds were intermingled with large areas of black mud, and there was the occasional and at once refreshing half acre of rich green grass. We lost all four foursomes, and Sam King of Sevenoaks won his single against Herman Keiser. Arthur Lees distinguished himself by holding the great Byron Nelson for 35 holes.

In view of the conditions the scoring was wonderful, and collectively the Americans beat par by many strokes. Our fellows did their best, and, as I thought at the time, could scarcely have done better. But informed American opinion was that they looked like a team of good club professionals struggling against the best tournament professionals in the world. It was, I think, a very fair estimate of the ability of the two sides.

1948

Few people who were at Sandwich for the Amateur Championship in 1948 will readily forget the magnificence and utter solidity of Frank Stranahan's golf. This was his third attempt in the Amateur Championship, and though he had played well here before, he had never looked like or come near to winning. Though still a distinctly 'made'-looking golfer, he had lost much of that 'golf by numbers appearance' that had characterized his play when we first got to know him. He also seemed to be armed at every point, and though he had never before been quite at home in match play, it was evident that his vast experience had done him good, and he took on all and sundry in a most impressive and at once victorious stride.

In the final Stranahan beat Charles Stowe by five up and four to play. It was not a great match, though it had its moments. Throughout the day a strong south-westerly wind accompanied by heavy showers of rain swept the course, and playing conditions were altogether as vile as any I can remember. Stowe was three down after nine holes and looked rather like being overwhelmed, but he came again with great spirit and dash and squared the match by lunch-time. It did not seem very serious when he lost the first two holes after lunch, but at the 22nd he took four dreadful little jerks to get down from a bank near the green and allowed Stranahan to win the hole in five. Though Stranahan made mistakes at each of the next two holes he got his par figures with ruthless efficiency and won them both. Stranahan was altogether too good and too strong for his adversary, and went on to win on the 32nd green.

P   209

Stowe was probably rather tired after his thrilling match in the semi-final against the holder, Willie Turnesa, on the previous day. This was as fine a game of golf as any ever I wish to see. As I remember, Stowe played brilliantly, got an early lead of three holes, but Turnesa, one of the finest match players that America has ever sent to this country, held on like grim death by means of wonderful recovery shots and quite miraculous putting. He was still three down with six to play and after a perfect tee shot at the 13th he could not make up his mind how to play his second. He changed his club at least half a dozen times and when he finally made up his mind one felt that he would have no confidence left with which to attack the shot, but he rose magnificently to the occasion and in the circumstances played one of the finest and bravest iron shots I ever saw, got his four and won the hole. Stowe went out of bounds at the Canal and so was now only one up. At the 15th Stowe hit two lovely shots into the heart of the green and Turnesa was heavily bunkered off his second shot. He pitched bravely to within 12 feet of the hole and then with infinite skill holed a most difficult putt across the slope in the centre of the green. At the 16th Turnesa got his three out of the bunker and was still one down. At the 17th Stowe was once again safely home in two and Turnesa was not. Turnesa nearly holed his frightfully difficult pitch and poor Stowe most humanly took three putts and all seemed lost. At the 18th Turnesa tacked from one side of the rough to the other and for the last time hit yet another pitch from heavy rough 6 feet from the hole. The gallant Stowe got a splendid four, and for once the demon that had inspired Turnesa's putter deserted him. As to which of these two heroes deserved most praise who shall say? It was the very devil of a game.

Henry Cotton won his third Open Championship at Muirfield in July 1948, and though there are many who insist that it was his greatest, I personally shall always remember his victory at Carnoustie as his most impressive. Then he was up against the finest professionals from America who shortly before had trounced the British Ryder Cup team at Southport. Nevertheless, Muirfield was vitally important to him because, though he had figured prominently in professional tournaments since the war and was still regarded as the best player in Britain, there was 'a kind of a feeling' that he was not quite so good as he used to be. A public figure such as Cotton has made himself is always apt to be conscious of what is being said about him, and Cotton, an acutely sensitive person in all business matters, must have realized that it was time he re-established himself or retired. In the Ryder Cup matches at Portland, Oregon, in the previous autumn he suffered two severe defeats, and this certainly did him no good. As has been his wont throughout his career, he trained himself most carefully for the Open and arrived at Muirfield at the peak of his form. He was also very confident about his chances, and I believe the one man he feared was Roberto de Vicenzo, a magnificent player from the Argentine who was on his first visit to this country. Cotton played well in his first round for a 71, and then in his second, when he was watched by His Majesty King George VI, he played like an inspired man and holed the course in 66. It was one of the very finest rounds of his career, and the ease and grace with which it was accomplished were most exhilarating to watch.

There were a number of critical moments during his third round which he started shortly after eight in the morning. It was blowing from the north-west and conditions were distinctly difficult. For a time his putting was a little shaky and he took 39 to the turn. When he started for home with two fives everything looked black and his overnight lead was rapidly disappearing. But with great determination he pulled himself together, and with a three at the 12th and a two at the 13th, he finished in 75. At lunch-time with a score of 212 he led King, Vicenzo, Rees and van Donck by three strokes.

During the third round Padgham suddenly began to burn up the course and at one time any score looked possible. But at each of the last five holes he dropped a stroke, the 18th being a tragedy for, left with a putt for a three from 12 feet, he took three more to get down. Cotton's last round was magnificent and, apart from three putts at the short 4th, only a series of superlatives can describe the splendour of his play. There was one small blemish at the last hole where he missed the green with a long, high pitch shot. He failed to get out of the bunker at the first attempt but made amends by holing a brave putt of 7 feet for his five and a total of 284 for the four rounds. No one else ever looked like catching him, but the holder, Fred Daly, played splendidly throughout the championship and finished second with 289. Of a number who finished one stroke behind Daly, de Vicenzo, who was distinctly handicapped without a word of English in his vocabulary, was the most impressive.

There was considerable disappointment that Henry Cotton did not enter for the *News of the World* Tournament (the Professional Match Play Championship) at Birkdale late in September, but Cotton is a man of many parts and his wide business interests had taken him thousands of miles away to the Argentine. As it turned out, the occasion proved a great triumph for Fred Daly, the holder, who by winning a second year in succession emulated the record set up by that wonderful player, the late Abe Mitchell. Again it is worthy of note that Daly within a period of fifteen months was first and second in the Open Championship and twice won the Match Play Championship. So far as I am aware, no other British golfer has ever come near to achieving such an astounding record. Daly is a very fine match player and where he seems to have an advantage over his contemporaries is his ability to start well from the very first tee shot whilst his opponents are taking

211

a hole or two to get into their stride.

In the final Daly beat L. B. Ayton—the present representative of a great golfing family from St Andrews—by four up and three to play. Although Daly never gave his young adversary a chance, he was not hitting the ball between tee and green with quite his usual accuracy, but his pitching and recovery shots were cruel to a degree. Daly also has a knack of holing a long and vital putt at the very moment it is wanted. Two holes, both in the second round, are a good example. At the 5th, Ayton, striving desperately to cut into Daly's lunch-time lead of three holes, was some 9 feet from the pin and Daly a good 10 yards away. Down went Daly's putt and Ayton very humanly missed his for the half. A good tee shot by Ayton at the short 7th, where Daly missed the green, was again rendered valueless, when Daly holed out from fully 15 yards for a three and a half. Ayton held on manfully and came out of the match with credit on his side against the undisputed match play champion of that period.

1949

The season of 1949 was long and exciting, and though in the end we had to bow to the supremacy of American golf, there were moments of ecstasy which we enjoyed to the full. The invaders from overseas were crushed in the Amateur Championship, and later on, after the first day's play in the Ryder Cup match at Ganton, our professionals, who had wrought noble deeds in the foursomes, appeared to have the enemy at their mercy. We must hurry straight to Portmarnock, near Dublin, where the Amateur Championship was held for the first time outside the British Isles. Since the amateur international matches were played at Portmarnock during the week before the championship began, all our best players were in form, and most of them with their minds intent on finding a place in the Walker Cup match due to be played in America later on in the year.

Of about a dozen American entries, there were three most formidable golfers. Frank Stranahan, the holder, was there to defend the title he had won at St George's the year before, and then there was Willie Turnesa for whom every amateur golfer on earth has a profound respect and who had won the championship at Carnoustie in 1947. There was also W. G. Campbell, a glorious player from Virginia, of whom at the time we knew very little.

Though old and wise hands have long since given up trying to forecast the result of the British Amateur Championship with its cut-throat 18-hole matches from Monday morning until Friday evening before the 36-hole final on Saturday, there were many who had a wholesome fear that Turnesa would play Stranahan in another all-American final. We knew S. M. McCready to be a good golfer, but no one in their wildest dreams ever imagined that he would win the champion-ship and, on his way to victory, put out both Stranahan and Turnesa. But he did so and throughout the championship he played a brand of golf and proved himself to have a temperament, of which every British heart was proud.

McCready was born in Belfast and has an eye for most games. He learned quite a lot about the game of golf when, as a flying instructor in the RAF, he spent some time in the Southern states of America. He is a big, strong man, with a fine free swing and is often a brilliant putter. At Portmarnock he was at the peak of his form and, apart from a brief and anxious period in the final, he played with the confidence of an innocent child. One never quite knows how any individual is going to stand up to the big occasion, especially the big occasion of which he has no previous experience. McCready played convincingly in the first few rounds of the championship, and his great chance came when he found Frank Stranahan waiting for him in the 6th round. To be brutally truthful, Stranahan never found his form at Portmarnock and his early opponents were content to let him win, but not so McCready. He was quite unconcerned with the enormous crowd that followed the match and, with Stranahan still far from his best, McCready took his chances in both hands and won very comfortably by four and three.

He had a desperate semi-final against K. G. Thom, a very good, strong, London golfer, and both played superbly. They were still all square after 18 holes and, but for a cruel thrust by McCready, Thom should have won at the 19th. McCready hit a wild slice from the tee and his ball lay in a dreadful spot. But he was able to hack it out somewhere in front of the green, and he courageously got his four and a half. After Thom had hit the hole with his putt for a three at the 20th, laying McCready a partial stymie, McCready with refreshing and almost insolent con-fidence stepped up and holed his putt of fully 15 feet for a three and victory.

In the other half of the draw Turnesa had had several close shaves on his way to the final. Everyone recognizes Turnesa as a killer, and even some of the best Americans cannot resist being killed by him. I would say, however, that he was emphatically lucky to beat E. B. Milward in the semi-final. It was in this match that Turnesa missed the prepared surface from the tee on no fewer than fifteen occasions during the 18 holes and yet he went round in 71 shots. Poor Milward hit the ball like an arrow all the way but could not get home.

And now for the great final next day. It began in heavenly weather and ended in a violent storm with lightning and thunder in the distant hills. McCready's first round of 70 was one of the finest ever played in the final of an amateur champion-ship, and he completely outclassed Turnesa all the way. Turnesa holed many brave putts in the course of the morning round, otherwise he would have been more than four down at lunch-time. After lunch McCready began to drive rather shakily, and Turnesa, inspired by his enemy's mistakes, squared the match at the

213

27th hole. When McCready lost the 29th to become one down, there was not a man, woman or child amongst the vast crowd who would have given tuppence for his chances. Though McCready won the 31st, Turnesa holed a cruel putt of 10 yards to regain the lead at the 32nd. Somehow this nasty jolt put new life into McCready, who played the next three holes like a hero. He won them all, and the championship was over. It was a great day for British golf.

Shortly after Portmarnock, all eyes were turned on Royal St George's, Sandwich, for the Open Championship and the return of Bobby Locke, the famous South African player. Locke, who first won the Open Championship of South Africa at the age of 17, came close to winning our Open Championship in 1939 and again in 1946; each time over the Old Course at St Andrews. Oddly enough it was his putter, one that has earned him a large fortune, that let him down both times, and some people began to wonder whether he would ever break through. There is something utterly tragic about a great player who fails to win golf's greatest prize, and therefore Locke's victory at Sandwich was extremely popular. He won from a good field after tying with Harry Bradshaw, the Irishman, with a total of 283 which equalled the record set up by Gene Sarazen at Prince's in 1932. He had not been to England since 1946, and had spent much of his time in America where he challenged the supremacy of the best contemporary American professionals. There were times at Sandwich when it looked as though Locke was going to win by the length of a street, but I suppose it was the very fact that he had never won before that brought about several major crises, each one of which went near to robbing him of victory. Locke and Bradshaw ran neck and neck from the first qualifying round until Locke holed out from 3 feet on the 72nd green to tie with the redoubtable Irishman.

In his first round Locke played wonderfully well for 13 holes and, when he stood on the 14th tee, his score was six under fours, but he sliced out of bounds, took seven, and what might have been a really great round was ruined by one bad shot. There was some splendid golf played on the first two days with Adams, Vicenzo and King in their finest form. At the end of two rounds Locke and Bradshaw lay together with a total of 145 and five strokes behind the leader Sam King. Bradshaw went out early on the last day and, long before many had started their third round, he was in with a superb 68. Locke was playing half an hour behind him and was also at his best, but a five at the 15th, where he was heavily bunkered in front of the green, kept him level with Bradshaw after three rounds. These two now led the field with a total of 213 with Vicenzo, Ward, King, Lees and Faulkner all on their tails. There were many who thought Bradshaw would not stand the pace in his fourth, but he went on just like a machine. It was not until he reached the Canal hole that he played his first bad shot of the day. He topped his second but his

1945-1950: *A Fresh Start: Leonard Crawley*

ball jumped the canal and we breathed again. A poor tee shot cost him one stroke at the 15th, but with a storming finish in three, four, four, he was round in 70 for a total of 283. Locke picked up one stroke on Bradshaw to the turn, which he reached in 32, but he threw it away again at the 10th when he missed the return putt for his four. He spent an anxious time in the cross-bunker guarding the 15th, but he got out and got his five. Left with three, four, four to tie, his tee shot to the short 16th finished on the left-hand side of the green, his first putt was very weak and he missed the next. How he pulled himself together at the 17th will always remain a miracle. A perfect drive was followed by a perfect iron shot which finished 10 feet from the pin, and down went the putt, and the fatal stroke that he had dropped ten minutes before was recovered. At the home hole he had to play a delicate little chip and a delicate little putt, each of which he judged to a nicety, and thus he tied.

Next day with only Bradshaw to worry about, he gave a magnificent exhibition of the modern golfer at his best, and Bradshaw trailed cheerfully after him.

Walker Cup

After McCready's great victory at Portmarnock and the magnificent form shown by more than a dozen British players in the Amateur Championship, the selectors had to deliberate for long hours over the final composition of the British Walker Cup team. They chose, and to my mind they chose quite rightly, the players who from the point of view of age and physical fitness were most likely to do best in the heat of an American summer. It was, I believe, a very fine side and one which might well have won the Walker Cup at home. But it was unfortunately an unlucky side. As they left the *Queen Elizabeth* on the jetty at New York, they plunged head first into the worst heat-wave of the last fifty years. Despite the kindness and most generous hospitality of their American hosts at Winged Foot, Marmaroneck, they cooked and stewed in the heat for a whole fortnight, and when the team faced the Americans nearly three weeks later, it was but a shadow of its former self.

Though the Americans won by the overwhelming margin of ten matches to two, I suppose the occasion will be best remembered for the magnificent golf played by and the personal triumph of Ronnie White. He won his single against W. Turnesa by four and three, and with J. B. Carr as his partner he won his foursomes against W. Turnesa and R. Billows by three and two. He had already made his reputation in the Walker Cup at St Andrews in 1947 when he accomplished a similar performance by winning both his matches, and many of the highest authorities in American golf today are of opinion that he is the soundest British amateur of the last thirty years. That, of course, is just a matter of opinion, but since he is blessed with the three greatest attributes of a golfer—style, physique and temperament—he is unquestionably a tremendous player.

Collectively the American team played about as well as was humanly possible, and though not disgraced, our poor fellows were no match for them.

Though the American victory in the Ryder Cup match at Ganton in September by seven matches to five was a distinct disappointment, the match was one of the most thrilling ever played between British and American professionals, and, of the tens of thousands who paid to see the play, everyone had his money's worth. On the day before the match Ben Hogan, the American captain, asked for an inspection of clubs, and this time several British players, notably Richard Burton, had to file the faces of their iron clubs before being passed. Neither side was quite at full strength since Hogan had not fully recovered from his shattering motor accident. Byron Nelson, having practically given up competitive golf, was no longer eligible under United States PGA rules, and Cary Middlecoff, the American Open Champion, was not a full-blown member of the PGA.

On our side, for some reason best known to himself, Cotton declined to play, and no British side without him is ever complete. During the two days' play the golf by both sides was of a wonderfully high standard and the scoring terrific. Often in the past both amateur and professional sides have failed dismally in the foursomes against American opponents, but this time our players excelled themselves, and never for one moment during the first day had we any doubts about holding our own. Rather was it a question of by how many matches were we going to lead. It was not that the Americans played ill, but almost without exception the British side played unbeatable golf. Adams was the hero of the top match in which he and Faulkner beat Harrison and Palmer on the 35th green. Faulkner was inclined to start shakily, but Adams took complete charge of him and soon had him going at his best. In the second match F. Daly and a good young golfer, Kenneth Bousfield, proved far too good for Hamilton and Alexander. Daly and Bousfield got an early lead of three holes, but were pulled back to all square by the 14th, and they finished the round two up. They were three up at the end of 30 holes and then Bousfield, playing a wonderful pitch from a nasty bare lie at the 32nd, prevented the two Americans from raising their heads. Ward and King, whom I thought were our strongest couple, were in fact the only British pair to lose, but Demaret and Heafner were indescribably brilliant all day. To finish off their opponents they did the last eight holes in three, four, four, three, three, four, three, four, and no one could stand against that. In the last match R. Burton and A. Lees won a great victory against S. Snead and L. Mangrum, a partnership which on paper looked quite unbeatable by any combination on earth. They had a terrific struggle in the morning with never more than a hole between them. Burton holed out splendidly at the 27th and 28th holes and Lees rubbed it in at the 29th by holing a vast putt of nearly 20 yards. The British couple were now two up but the Americans came again winning the 30th and 32nd holes with splendid threes. Finally, at the home hole, Snead drove into the trees and we just got home by one up.

We always consider that a lead of one on the foursomes is a winning lead, and therefore with a lead of two matches we had every right to look forward to the morrow with sober confidence and almost certain victory. It would be impossible to over-praise the golf played by the American professionals next day. One and all, they were magnificent. I shall always consider that the giant, E. J. Harrison, was the villain of the piece since he was leading the American team against Faulkner. He actually did five of the first six holes in three strokes apiece, and this sort of news does not take long to get around. It seemed to inspire the rest of the American side and there was absolutely no holding them. Mercifully for us, both Adams, who beat Palmer by two and one, and Rees, who beat Hamilton by six and four, were infected with the same devastating germ of brilliance. I suppose the best match of all was that between Mangrum and Daly who, around in 65 and 66 apiece in the morning, continued with the same terrific figures in the afternoon, until Mangrum suddenly decided that he had had enough and 'shot' three, three, two, four, three at the gallant Daly and thus killed him stone dead. As to how many threes and twos they did between them during the day, I tremble to think. It was a match the like of which had never been seen before. All admitted that the Americans won on their merits, but nevertheless defeat after the first day's excitement was a bitter pill to swallow.

And so to Walton Heath for the *News of the World* Tournament (the Professional Match Play Championship) a few days later. This is always one of the most interesting professional tournaments of the year, and I suppose principally because most of us enjoy watching the cut and thrust of match play better than the more cold-blooded and acid test with a card and pencil. In addition most of the victorious American Ryder Cup team took part, and a natural curiosity amongst southerners wanting to see for themselves what the new generation of American professionals had got which our fellows had not, made the tournament even more exciting than usual. The course was very dry, some of the fairways being of a rather treacherous character and many of the greens were too hard to pitch on. From the very outset the American professionals showed their dislike of the conditions, as was borne out by Jimmy Demaret's observation that he felt he was playing ping-pong and not golf. One was a little surprised that few of them were ready to accept what they found instead of getting on with the problem before them and which, after all, was the same for everybody. With the exception of Mangrum and Palmer, all of

217

them had been eliminated after four rounds, and most people expected that one or other of these two fine players would win. But Cotton, who though he had been unable to see his way to playing for his country the week before, was in his finest form and up in their half of the draw. In the 5th and 6th rounds he beat Palmer by two holes and Mangrum by four and two, and throughout the day he gave further proof that he was still one of the world's finest players. His control with all his clubs over the fast and rather bumpy ground was masterly, and his figures were quite unbeatable. Because of his self-imposed absence from the Ryder Cup side it was impossible to say that he had struck a great blow for British golf. On the other hand, the day was a great personal triumph for him.

Down in the bottom half of the draw D. J. Rees, one of the heroes of the Ryder Cup match, was still in his finest form and brushing his opponents aside one after the other, arrived to meet Cotton in the final without ever being very hard pressed.

The next day was as full of thrills as any that I can remember on a golf course. Well as he played, Cotton found himself on the defensive in the morning, and actually went into lunch four down. Both were a little shaky at the first two holes after the interval and then quite suddenly Cotton got into his stride again and was only one down with nine to play. He probably lost the match at the 32nd hole. Rees was bunkered from the tee, and a five was all he could hope for. After a gorgeous tee shot, Cotton badly cut his second into heavy rough to the right of the green. To make matters worse his ball lay nearly unplayable, and he lost this critical hole which he ought in fact to have won. With a lead of two holes and victory in sight, Rees's putting suddenly became jerky, and for once he seemed almost frightened of winning. He held on to a priceless lead of one hole, but how near he came to losing it on the 36th green only those who saw Cotton's ball stay on the lip can tell.

1950

There was a record entry for the Amateur Championship at St Andrews in May 1950. This entry was swelled by a large and distinguished company of American golfers, a number of whom were on their first visit to the headquarters of the golfing world. The week will be remembered for many reasons. We must give pride of place to Frank Stranahan of America who won for the second time. We must pay due respect to the astonishing performance of Cyril Tolley who at the age of 53 won a bronze medal by reaching the semi-final exactly thirty years after he had won his first gold medal. Lastly, it is quite possible that in ten years to come golfers may look back upon this championship as the one which brought the question of slow play both here and in America to a head. For some time both the Royal and Ancient Club and the United States Golf Association have been doing their utmost to hurry up the slow coaches, but so far their efforts have been unsuccessful. It happened that one of the worst offenders was drawn at the top of the list, and since he reached the closing stages of the championship, he set the pace for the field day after day.

We may count ourselves as having been unlucky that P. B. Lucas, R. J. White, C. Stowe, James Bruen and K. G. Thom, all of whom had played in the Walker Cup at Winged Foot the year before, were for business reasons unable to play. It is conceivable at any rate that any one of them might have stopped Stranahan or Richard Chapman, the two Americans, on their way to the final, but I am not trying to suggest that an American victory would have been prevented by their presence in the field. Indeed the Americans were so well drawn up and down the long list that even before the championship began one could not help feeling that an American victory was in the highest degree probable.

The championship was a great triumph for Frank Stranahan in more ways than one. When he first came to this country he was very young, short of experience and a little truculent about our customs, and he did not leave a very favourable impression. He was also appallingly slow and many of us were after his blood. When he left St Andrews with the cup he was acknowledged by all as a great amateur golfer. He was an emphatically popular figure with old and young, and it must also be recorded that throughout the championship he played quickly and with the utmost courtesy for all his opponents.

As to his golf, one can only say that it was magnificent, alike in power and accuracy, and he never at any time looked like losing a match. A little favoured by the draw, he had several easy matches, and after he had defeated a very good golfer, W. L. Goodloe from Georgia, he looked set for victory. Again, perhaps he was a little lucky to find Cyril Tolley in the semi-final, a tired man after his brilliant and exhausting match with J. B. Carr over 20 holes in the morning. It was not that Tolley played badly against him, and indeed for a man of his age he played uncommonly well. All he lacked was the old vigour and strength of his youth to sustain him.

In the other semi-final there was a terrific struggle between Richard Chapman, an old friend from America who had been runner up to Turnesa two years before, and James McHale, another first-class American player. It was the general opinion that McHale was the better golfer of the two, and I personally think that the general opinion was right. But, as so often happens in an 18-hole match, one hole, and that quite early on, made all the difference. McHale was playing magnificently and was one up going to the fourth. Two fine shots left him putting for a three, whilst Chapman had had difficulty in reaching the green in three. But

219

Chapman holed a vast putt of some 30 yards for his four and McHale, a little shaken, took three from nowhere. Chapman now got his tail up and, playing magnificently, won on the 18th green.

Next day the final was played in cold, showery and thoroughly unpleasant weather, and the first round took nearly four hours. In the afternoon Stranahan, hitting the ball like an arrow through the difficult cross-winds, was altogether too good and too strong for his stout-hearted opponent, and he won on the 30th green.

Even though most of us felt that Harry Bradshaw was unlucky not to win at Royal St George's in 1949 I never heard anyone say that Bobby Locke, the ultimate winner, was other than a most worthy champion. At any rate he went to Troon in 1950 one of the strongest favourites ever to start in the Open Championship. He won in the end from Roberto de Vicenzo by two shots, and his total of 279 was four strokes better than the previous record held jointly by Gene Sarazen, Henry Cotton, Locke and Bradshaw.

Old Troon is by modern standards a little short for a championship course, but it has stood the test of time, and even the best players today have a wholesome fear and great respect for it. It is perhaps too dependent on prevailing winds from a westerly direction to keep it in the front rank of championship courses, and it so happens that a dead calm prevailed throughout the Open of 1950. Therefore, the scoring was low, but nevertheless the order of Locke one, Vicenzo two, Daly and Rees three equal is overwhelming proof that it is still a most worthy battleground.

During the practice rounds when the normal winds were blowing, Locke and his principal opponents were of opinion that a score of 288 would be good enough, and when the calm came during the week of the championship, every one of them had to readjust his ideas. The fairways were running fast and the greens, of a lovely texture, had been well watered and would hold a well-played second shot. Locke, determined to make his task as easy as possible, drove, with a brassey or a spoon throughout the championship and was only twice off the fairway in 72 holes. His iron play and particularly his short iron play was wonderfully accurate, and as ever his putting was of his own high standard. His four rounds 69, 72, 70 and 68 were wonderfully consistent, and it was his great courage in his second round during a period of disaster that ultimately won him the championship. It was in this round that he took six at the short 5th after a bad tee shot had finished outside the bunkers guarding the green. His ball lay some 20 yards from the hole, he fluffed it into a bunker in front of his nose, took two more to get out and then two putts to get down. Such a disaster would have broken the heart of any ordinary mortal and it shook Bobby to the core for a few holes. He bravely got his four out of sand at the 7th and his final crisis came at the 8th, the famous 'postage stamp'. Here he hooked his tee shot to the left of the green; he exploded right across the green with his second into another deep and terrifying bunker, and, at the risk of repeating the whole performance, he went straight for the pin with his third and holed the putt for four. The operation took a good quarter of an hour to complete, and, as I watched it all going on from a distant sandhill, I could not help imagining the despair that was rending his mind. He had to finish without further mistakes and he did so with Olympian calm.

Next day he was at his best and after a morning round of 70 he found himself leading the field with de Vicenzo and Rees. In the first two rounds Rees had been playing brilliantly. But once again a certain natural impatience in his temperament cost him dearly, and a lead that might have been never materialized. Vicenzo, playing far from well but putting like a demon, had a 70 in his fourth round, and Locke behind him heard that he had finished in 281. Thus, with some seven holes to play, Locke knew exactly what he had to do. It is on such occasions that the real greatness of a golfer comes out, and facing the situation before him, Locke seemed to know instinctively which were the putts that had to be holed. He did miss one of 4 feet at the 12th, but he at once corrected this mistake with a fine putt for a two at the 14th. Though he missed the green with his tee shot at the 17th, he chipped dead and got his three. Requiring a five to beat Vicenzo at the home hole the vast crowd surged down the ropes on either side of the fairway. He got the easiest of fours and then he knew that he had set poor Rees, struggling manfully behind him, more than he could do. Vardon, Braid, Taylor, Jones and Hagen had all won championships in successive years, and of the present generation there is no one more worthy to join their distinguished company than Bobby Locke.

At Carnoustie in September Dai Rees won the Professional Match Play Championship for the second year in succession and for the fourth time in his career. This was a real triumph and came at the end of a season in which he established himself quite clearly as the best British professional of the year.

The great course at Carnoustie was playing very long and the greens were, as ever, quite perfect. The weather, too, was blustery, rather wet, and cold. In these conditions the best player always has a better chance of winning. It was unfortunate that those from overseas, notably Bobby Locke, who had played through most of the season, were absent, and Rees had everything very much his own way. In the final he beat Frank Jowle, a good Yorkshire player, with considerable ease and it was never a very exciting match. Rees, playing extraordinarily well, won on his merits. Jowle should be heard of again for he is young and strong. In the semi-final he beat Henry Cotton, who was making his first appearance of the season in a first-class tournament and rather naturally was never quite at his best.

ENID WILSON

Women's Golf

THE origins of golf being shrouded in antiquity, it is not surprising that the first women players are unknown to us. We do know, however, that Mary Queen of Scots was playing golf and pell-mell in the fields at Seton shortly after the death of her husband, Darnley. Also, in old prints and paintings of the Dutch 'kolven' we see young ladies disporting themselves at what is generally considered to be one of the earliest sources of golf, and if this is so we may assume that women have enjoyed the game from the time it began.

It is in the records of one of the oldest golf clubs that we find the first mention of a competition arranged by the menfolk for the women to play for prizes, the Minutes of the Musselburgh Club on December 14, 1810, being enlivened by the following:

> The Club resolve to present by Subscription a new Creel and Shawl to the best female golfer who plays on the annual occasion on 1st Jan. next, old style (12th Jan. new), to be intimated to the Fish Ladies by the Officer of the Club.
> Two of the best Barcelona silk handkerchiefs to be added to the above premium of the Creel.
>
> Alex. G. Hunter. C.

Unfortunately, the name of the winner and the manner in which she accomplished her victory are lost to posterity, and a further fifty years elapse before we come to any consistent records of women's golf.

Some of the earliest of these are provided by the *St Andrews Gazette and Fifeshire News*, which by August 31, 1872, considered the activities of the ladies on the links of sufficient interest to form the subject of a second leader, from which the following is a brief extract:

> . . . The Ladies' Golf Club is an institution that was born in the soil of St Andrews links and made its struggle for existence there a few years ago. . . .

222

Its remarkable success has led to the introduction and culture of golf as a female recreation in England and elsewhere. . . . Of course, the yielding of the club assumes a mild form under the sway of the gentler sex and has never as yet extended beyond the simple stroke of the putting green. . . .

They evidently received every encouragement at St Andrews, as in addition to the reports of their regular monthly and annual meetings, we find frequent accounts of competitions for prizes presented by members of the men's club. On these occasions it seems that everyone set out to enjoy themselves, and on one of them we find the 'gentler sex' embarking on a sort of golf marathon: 'All players who scored above 52 in the first round were thrown out. Those under this continued to play; and round after round was played, the number of competitors becoming less every round until the players became equal to the number of prizes. A final round was then played for a decision.' From this ordeal, six of the forty-two starters emerged triumphant to receive their prizes from a Dr. Macdonald, who was one of those who took a great interest in the club from its inauguration and for many years gave prizes annually for competitions.

The Ladies' Golf Club at St Andrews was formed in 1867, and by 1886 there were five hundred members. By 1872, the St Andrews Ladies' Spring and Autumn Meetings were regular events, at which they competed for a gold medal and the Douglas Prize; by 1879, a silver cross had been added as second prize. During the early days of these meetings, the most persistent and regular winners were Miss F. Hume M'Leod, Miss A. Boothby, Miss Mary and Miss May Lamb, and Miss Douglas.

At about the same time that the women in Scotland were forming their club at St Andrews, there was a similar move afoot in the south-west of England at Westward Ho! Five years later, there were women's clubs at Musselburgh and Wimbledon. Carnoustie, Bath and Yarmouth had their lady pioneers, too, and the remoteness of these places from one another suggests that the urge for women to play golf was pretty general throughout Scotland and England.

Whether it was that the Scots were more severe in keeping women off their links, or that the Englishwomen had greater powers of persistence than their cousins in the north, we do not know; but all the records suggest that once the game was known south of the Border, the women went ahead rapidly, and Englishwomen were the prime movers in the formation of what is now the premier women's golfing organization in the world.

In 1893, Miss Isette Pearson, who would have been a pioneer and outstanding leader in any field to which she turned her hand, with the aid of Mr Laidlaw Purves and other members of the Wimbledon Club, was instrumental in calling a meeting in London on April 19 which was really the beginning of the Ladies' Golf Union.

Wimbledon were supported by Ashdown Forest, Barnes, East Sheen, Great Harrowden, Great Yarmouth, Lytham and St Anne's, Minchinhampton, North Berwick, North Warwickshire, Portrush, Belfast, St Andrews, Southdown and Brighton. The meeting decided that an annual golf championship should be held, the winner to receive a gold medal and to be styled Lady Champion for the year. Lytham and St Anne's had already thought of something on these lines and had advertised a challenge cup valued at £50 for competition annually over their links. This was amicably settled by the Ladies' Golf Union agreeing to hold the first championship over the Lytham and St Anne's course. Subscribers towards the championship cup were forthcoming from the clubs who were in at the birth of the Ladies' Golf Union. All entries for the initial championship were subjected to the approval of the Lytham and St Anne's Club, and any disputes were to be settled by the Council of that Club. On June 13, 1893, thirty-eight ladies were vying for the cup, and after three days' golf, the winner was Lady Margaret Scott. The play was over the Ladies' Course of nine holes, and the winner was a model of steadiness because her scores were always between 40 and 42. There were entries from Ireland and France, but none, unfortunately, from Scotland.

Lady Margaret Scott defeated Miss Isette Pearson in the final, and thus came together two women whose names will be legendary as long as women play golf. They met again in the final the following year, 1894, at Littlestone, and although Miss Pearson was the honorary secretary and backbone of the newly formed Ladies' Golf Union, she had found time to improve her game—not sufficiently, however, to prevent any change in the ultimate result, as Lady Margaret Scott was again the winner from a field of sixty-three. This second championship marked a venture, which was the employment of the men's course, though from shortened tees.

Meanwhile, there were stirrings across the sea, and the Irish women launched their native championship at Carnalea, Miss Mulligan being the winner. This probably had something to do with the migration of the Ladies' Golf Union, who visited the Royal Portrush Club for their championship meeting in 1895. There was an auction selling sweep before the championship began and Lady Margaret Scott, the hot favourite, went for £30. Her purchaser must have felt rather rash when she was four down at the turn in the semi-finals to Mrs Ryder Richardson; but the holder of the championship won six holes of the homeward half, and the next day she went on to win for the third year in succession. After the final, there was an informal international match between England and Ireland with six players a side, the scoring being by holes, and England the winner by thirty-four holes to nil.

The championship at Portrush was remarkable for the début of two of the

Hezlet sisters and Miss Rhona Adair, who watched Lady Margaret Scott with astonishment, interest and determination. So, with the passing of one giantess, three others were born. Portrush was the last appearance in competitive golf of Lady Margaret Scott, who retired unbeaten and never again took part in any serious contest. She was, by the unanimous consent of all the critics of those days, the most graceful swinger of her time. Lady Margaret must have been exceptionally supple, because we have pictures of her swinging with the club almost past the ball—at the bottom of her downswing—a horrible sight to modern teachers. With this tremendous backswing, her left heel hardly moved from the ground, and this is all the more remarkable when we consider the fashions of the '90s, which demanded tight lacing and wasp waists.

Before going any further, it might be interesting to pause for a moment or two and consider the fashions that were prevalent when women first began to play golf. The dress was formal and distinctive, and the leading ladies were strictly conventional in observing the correct turnout. Red coats, with the club facings, and buttons of gilt bearing the club crest were popular, and each course had a uniform. Those which did not approve of the conspicuous red had jackets of a more sombre hue, which were embellished by multi-coloured pipings to denote their origin. Medals were worn on the left breast of the jacket in military style. Deep starched collars formed plinths, around the bases of which club ties were correctly draped. Also popular with the ladies were broad webbing or leather belts with monstrous buckles, which bore the club insignia or their owners' monograms. Voluminous cloth or tweed skirts draped the first women golfers from their waists downwards, and remained the accepted fashion until the game was interrupted at the outbreak of the 1914–1918 war. Thick boots with a few metal tackets in them were concealed beneath the draperies. On their heads, the ladies wore what must have been the most unmanageable portion of their dress, stiff boaters, with braids of club colours around the crowns. How they were kept in position was a secret known only to those who wore them.

In England, golf became fashionable, and there were soon reports of it in the society journals. The earlier meetings—and, for that matter, the championships, during their first few years, until the large entries removed the intimacy—were run on the lines of a large house or garden party. After the day's golf, it was the custom to entertain and be entertained with musical evenings in which everybody took part.

To revert to the actual play: 1895 was the first year that a Scottish entry, that of Miss Sybil Wigham, was received for the Ladies' Championship, and she returned the lowest score in the Open Meeting held by the Royal Portrush Club prior to the commencement of the championship. During this same year, Ranelagh was revisited by the ladies, and Mr. Pearson presented a trophy for inter-club competition which has since become one of the most famous golfing cups.

Also in 1895 the Ladies' Golf Union published the first of a long line of annual handbooks, and contained within the pages of this volume was a system of handicapping which was not given a serious trial for many months. Such was the beginning of a world-wide system for which the Ladies' Golf Union is famed and envied.

Before going on to 1897, the birth of the Yorkshire Ladies' Championship in 1896 must be mentioned, as this was the first of the Women's County Championships.

The most remarkable aspect of the Ladies' Championship in 1897 was the unfurling of the Ladies' Golf Union flag in Scottish air for the first time. Gullane was the venue, and it attracted over one hundred entrants. The final was distinguished by a match between two sisters, Miss E. C. Orr winning from Miss Orr; and a third member of this family reached the last eight. This was the only time the Orrs left North Berwick, and was their first and last venture in big golf. At this meeting, it was possible for the serious-minded to make a comparison between English and Scottish swings, and the opinion was that Scottish swings were quicker and shorter.

Another event which has not failed to make its presence felt in the most distinguished company was heralded in 1897 and has gone happily on its way ever since then: this was the Midland Ladies' Championship, accelerated, maybe, by the advent of the Yorkshire, but in effect serving a larger area.

On we go, to the second visit of the Ladies' Golf Union to Ireland, Newcastle, Co. Down, in 1899. The Irish ladies held their championship over the same course during the week before the Ladies' Golf Union held their event, and at 17 years of age Miss May Hezlet achieved the double, winning the Irish and the Ladies' Championship within a space of eight days. This was the commencement of a tremendous career which gave her three wins in the Ladies' Championship and five in the Irish by 1908, and so ensured her immortal fame in the record book. Fifty-one years after her initial success in the Ladies' Championship she returned to watch this event held over the Newcastle course, but regrettably few of the competitors were aware of their distinguished spectator, although they must all have been familiar with her wonderful record.

To continue the story of women's golf, we must return to Newcastle, Co. Down, in 1899, and observe that a second 'informal' international took place there between England and Ireland with ten players a side, the result being counted by holes. England won by thirty-seven holes to eighteen.

So we begin the twentieth century, with the game of golf well established in Britain, with the English at the helm of their Ladies' Golf Union, and the best players in Ireland.

Miss Adair was the next of the great Irishwomen to come to the fore, and she exactly copied what Miss Hezlet had done the previous year by winning first her native title and then the Ladies' Championship. In all, her bag was not quite the equal of Miss Hezlet's—two British and four Irish, all achieved between 1900 and 1904.

The first year of the twentieth century saw yet another innovation—one that had far-reaching results—by the Ladies' Golf Union. This was the introduction of county golf on an official basis. Fourteen counties formed clubs; there were ten players in each team, and every county played all the others in a home and an away match. This has been the nursery of the best of Britain's golf, and though there have been changes in the composition of the teams and the areas in which they play (the present limit being seven a side and only four or so teams forming a divisional area), these restrictions have come about through necessity, as it would not be possible in modern times for every county team to challenge all the others annually.

In 1900, Surrey won the County Championship; and they have had a far more imposing list of successes than any other county in the event.

The Ladies' Golf Union took their championship to Wales—their first visit to the principality—in 1901, and at Aberdovey, England and Ireland renewed their friendly rivalry with another informal international, which was decided by matches instead of holes. Ireland won this time, and the direct result of this contest was a gift from Mr. T. H. Miller, who presented the Ladies' Golf Union with a beautiful shield, which is now competed for by England, Scotland, Ireland and Wales. The 'Home Internationals' then became the prelude to every British Championship. Another international trophy was presented to the Ladies' Golf Union in 1901, for score play in the big two-day meeting of the Ranelagh Club.

The Scottish Ladies' Golfing Association was formed in 1903, and the Welsh Ladies' Golf Union in 1905, both mainly for the purpose of holding their native championships and fostering their players until such time as they could hold their own with all comers in the British.

By this time we had achieved all the major events and meetings, and they are run on much the same lines today, with slight modifications brought about by the intervals caused by the two wars.

A match which has great historical interest took place at Cromer in 1905, when the British Championship had gone there and attracted an entry of American women who were a sufficiently large party to make up a team. They met an English side—though why it achieved this caption, with an Irish and Scottish content larger than the home representation, it would not be wise to inquire. The galaxy of women stars who took part in this friendly contest make it worth while recording the results in full:

227

AMERICA			ENGLAND		
Miss Georgina Bishop	..	1	Miss Lottie Dod	.. ..	0
Miss Margaret Curtis	..	0	Miss May Hezlet	.. ..	1
Miss M. B. Adams	..	0	Miss Molly Graham	..	1
Miss Harriet Curtis	..	0	Miss Elinor Nevile	..	1
Miss Lockwood	.. ..	0	Miss F. Hezlet	.. ..	1
Miss Frances Griscom	..	0	Miss Alexa Glover	..	1
Mrs. Martin	.. ..	0	Miss Dorothy Campbell	..	1
		1			6

The last player in the 'English' side, Miss Dorothy Campbell, was successful in the Scottish native event that same year, and with her arrival we must note that she has a special niche of her own in the hall of golfing fame. She won the Scottish three times, the British twice, and then left to live in America, where she won the National twice, and the Canadian Open three times. To her went the distinction of being the first player to win the British and the American events in the same year. When Miss Campbell departed to America and married and settled down there, the first world war was close at hand; and when the game was resumed, after a break of six years, only the older generation remembered that Mrs Hurd had been Miss Campbell, and the greatest of the Scotties.

In 1908, the Ladies' Golf Union visited St Andrews, and the British event was held on the hallowed turf of the Royal and Ancient Club. This was a proud and unforgettable meeting for the women who had worked so assiduously for the establishment of their game, and who now felt that it had achieved status in receiving recognition by and the assent of the Ruling Body. If awe was felt by any of the competitors, this must have turned to curiosity quite quickly because of the debut of Miss Cecil Leitch, a young lady of 17, who struck the ball with a crispness and ferocity that was a revelation to all who saw her reach the semi-final at her first appearance in the British. The fact that Miss Whigam, at Westward Ho!, had hit two consecutive drives of 234 and 216 yards with a gutty ball eight years previously was completely forgotten by those who marvelled at Miss Leitch. The impact of her game and her tremendous personality have had a more far-reaching effect on women's golf than those of any other player. Like a meteor, she swept across the sky at St Andrews; and then had to wait six years before she took up her rightful position in the sporting universe. In the early summer of 1914, the British, English native, and French Open Championships fell into her hand like over-ripe cherries; but, alas, the achievement, and the enjoyment that it merited, were swept away by the Great War.

The reason why Miss Cecil Leitch required so much time to gain her first British Championship was due to the presence of several great players who did not reach

228

her degree of eminence but whose skill helped to temper the Silloth girl's game and gave her incentive to work for improvement.

Miss Ravenscroft won the British in 1912 and the American National in 1913. Her friend, Miss Dodd, had the distinction of holding the British and Canadian Open titles in 1913.

The Ladies' Golf Union, which had gone happily from strength to strength, was in 1910 involved in an issue concerning county golf, and feeling ran so high that county golf was completely upset, no team was fully representative, and an opposition show called the National Alliance came into being. The National Alliance and the LGU waged a cat-and-dog warfare until 1914, when the rebels capitulated and returned to the fold. The Alliance was no more, and the English Ladies' Championship which it had started in 1912 was handed over to the LGU.

After Miss Isette Pearson married Mr T. H. Miller in 1911 she still retained her secretaryship of the LGU, and her official work for women's golf continued until her retirement in 1921. As Mrs Miller, she gave a shield for the winners of the County Finals held before the English Championships, similar to the one given earlier by her husband for the Home Internationals. The work she began is being carried on in a manner of which she would approve.

It would be foolish for anyone who did not experience the atmosphere of those early golfing days to be anything other than factual when discussing them. The leisurely *tempo* of an age when road transport depended on the horse, and there were husbands who would not allow their wives to go to golf fixtures if doing so necessitated travelling by train, seems to belong to another world. Nor can we understand the ordeal which each advancement and expansion into the sporting world cost and meant to the women who dared to venture. They did this with bold spirit, asking in return only that the quality of their golf might improve and that the numbers who could join in might multiply.

Much depends on the angle from which anything is presented to the public by the official pens which are detailed to describe it. Women's golf has been exceptionally lucky because Miss M. E. Stringer and Miss E. E. Helme have done more for the publicity of the game than anyone other than the officials of the LGU could possibly imagine. Their influence has been, and is, profound; their knowledge great; and their contributions to the game, in founding associations and instigating minor championships, inestimable. Miss Stringer's friendship with Miss Isette Pearson began in the early '90s, and Miss Helme's association with the Surrey county team commenced in 1906. No mention of the pre-1914-1918 war days, when the foundations of women's golf were dug out and then so well and truly laid, could omit Miss Pearson and her allies and helpmates, Miss Stringer and Miss Helme. Without their labours, Lady Margaret Scott, Miss May Hezlet and her two sisters, Miss Rhona Adair, Miss Dorothy Campbell and Miss Cecil Leitch would not have had the opportunities to show the world their outstanding skill, and many thousands of women would not have enjoyed the facilities of golf.

The charm and simplicity of those early days and the pleasure of them can be recaptured, perhaps, in a remark by Mrs. Cuthell, who, in answer to a pertinent question regarding the changes in championship golf since her day (when she was Rhona Adair) and the rather slow and studied progress of the golf in the 1950 British which she was watching, replied: 'I hit the ball as hard as the Good Lord would let me. And kept on hitting it!' This spirit of joyful adventure has tended to decline with the departing pioneer spirit, although we have reminders of it when we have visitors from the Empire and British possessions, who followed the lead of the home country even in women's golf until the dark clouds of 1914 brought about a cessation of play. The four years of warfare brought in their train innumerable changes; but they did not extinguish the desire and need for women's sport.

Some mention must now be made of the equipment which the early women golfers used. During the period which we have been examining in detail, there was one radical change: this was in the evolution of the construction of the ball from the solid rubber 'gutty' to the 'rubber-core'. The rubber-cored ball was much nicer to hit and travelled better, but although the effect of this was profound, it came gradually. When it was first on the market it was expensive and easily damaged, and although the ladies preferred it to the solid 'gutty', they did not change over to it immediately because they could not afford such a luxury. No doubt, when the early difficulties had been overcome and the ball was more serviceable, it did make the game more attractive to women. But there was no question of the revolution being instantaneous and complete; it came over a matter of several years, during which time the leading lady golfers used both types of ball.

The clubs they used had thick grips, different shaped heads of varying fashions, and, of course, hickory shafts. The women used thinner and whippier shafts than their menfolk, and the breaking of a favourite hickory shaft was a tragedy which could be remedied by the outlay of five shillings for a replacement. There was no particular catering for women's equipment, and although the leading women players must have had their likes and fancies as to the types of clubs they preferred, it would seem that they relied quite considerably on the 'left-overs' and 'cut-down' clubs of their men. During the quarter century prior to the 1914–1918 war, the shape of the wooden club head varied from an over-sized pear to the short, stubby 'bulldog', not much larger than the ball. The blade of the iron varied, too, in a similar manner, and as it was not made of rustless metal, it could be worn away by constant cleaning.

The women were content with fewer clubs than are deemed necessary today. They could get on perfectly happily with four or five, and even the most exalted performers did not have more than seven or eight clubs in their bags. They were, in fact, completely kitted out for rather less than the cost of one modern steel-shafted iron, and were modest and economical in their requirements because the fashion had never been otherwise. One accessory they had which is rarely seen nowadays was the india-rubber tee, which consisted of a strip of rubber moulded to hold the ball at one end and a bob weight, to keep the whole contraption from straying, at the other. This was before celluloid pegs, or even wooden ones, had been evolved. Thus equipped, and with three good golf balls in respectable condition, our grandmothers were ready to undertake all the serious competitions in one season.

When hostilities ceased in Europe, the women soon set about restoring their golfing calendar to its former shape. Everything was ready for the British to be resumed in 1919, at Burnham in Somerset, but a strike of the railwaymen upset this and it was not until the following year that Miss Leitch was called upon to defend the title. In the meantime, she had met Mrs. Temple Dobell, *née* Ravenscroft, in the final of the English at St Anne's, and beaten her in no uncertain manner. The pre-war queen had no intention of being usurped; she was clearly the best player of her own generation, and the likelihood of anyone new and inexperienced beating her was unthinkable. A contemporary of Miss Leitch, Miss Janet Jackson, who had come to the fore in 1913, resumed her monopoly in Irish golf; she won the Irishwomen's Championship six times in all, twice before the war, and four times afterwards. Mrs J. B. Watson was unbeaten for three years when the Scottish event was resumed. But neither of these two outstanding golfers added the British to their spoils because Miss Leitch and Mrs Dobell kept them at bay.

Before we reach the season of 1920, mention must be made of the Girls' Open Golf Championship, which should have begun in 1914 but was deferred until the autumn of 1919. This was Miss Stringer's child; and a right lusty one it was, too. Held always at Stoke Poges, a delightful park course, it was a social success from the start, and it is no exaggeration to say that practically all the leading women golfers who came to the fore between the two wars were competitors in the GOGC; while to win it was a short cut to a national championship, or the British. What happened in the nursery at Stoke Poges had a distinct bearing on subsequent events.

However, this is anticipating, and the British at Newcastle, Co, Down, in the spring of 1920 comes into place here. This was the first championship held by the LGU at which Mrs Miller (*née* Isette Pearson) had not been present, and although the entry was not a large one, it contained several distinguished golfers from overseas. Miss Marion Hollins, Mrs Vanderbeck and Miss Sherwood from America, and Miss Ada Mackenzie and Miss Florence Harvey from Canada. They were all out by the fourth round, but their form was impressive in conditions which must have seemed strange and distinctly adverse to them.

Miss Leitch was never in danger of relinquishing her hold on the title, and only a month later she was at Sheringham with every prospect of winning the English native championship for the third time in succession. The prelude to the English was a qualifying round, 18-hole medal, and no one took any heed of the occupant of 25th place in that test. As the week wore on, Miss Leitch made her way to the final, only once being in any danger at all, and extracting herself with fireworks when cornered. Her opponent in the final was the young lady who had occupied 25th place in the qualifying test: a tall, pallid, Surrey player, who had come to Sheringham for the purpose of acting as companion to Miss Molly Griffiths and with certainly no thoughts of setting Sheringham and the whole of the golfing world on fire.

Thus, modestly, arrived Miss Joyce Wethered; though as she progressed she left in her wake a series of opponents who were full of praise for her golf—praise that was very quickly turned to awe. Miss Leitch dominated the first round of the final and went into lunch with a comfortable lead of four holes, which was increased to six by Miss Wethered making mistakes at the first two holes in the afternoon. Six up and sixteen to play in Miss Leitch's favour was the sort of thing that her followers hoped for and expected; and she herself had every reason to believe that she was virtually home against a player with no championship experience other than that acquired during the week. Then Miss Wethered, playing with the utmost calmness, as though she was oblivious of the state of the game and the stake that depended upon it, delivered a volley of threes—invincible stuff, which must have taken Miss Leitch by surprise. The champion found herself one down with four holes to play; and it was Miss Wethered who won by two and one.

Referring to this match afterwards, Miss Wethered, when she had left the arena of championships for good, suggested that she would not have won at Sheringham had the ground not been baked to brick-like consistency. This shortened the course so much that Miss Leitch found her most telling shot, the punch with an iron to the holeside, denied her. Another observation of Miss Wethered's about her first championship was that she found herself launched in championship golf before she had even thought about it. Those who were not at Sheringham could not be blamed for thinking that perhaps Miss Leitch had toppled to a flash-in-the-pan sort of golfer, and this trend of opinion was encouraged when Miss Leitch beat Miss Molly Griffiths in the final of the French Open Championship later on that year.

In the meantime, American eyes were being cast on our British Championship; and the cream of their players came over to Turnberry in 1921: Miss Alexa Sterling, thrice holder of their National; Miss Hollins, who won the National from Alexa later on that year; Miss E. Cummings, Miss Elkins and Miss Fowns. With them came Miss Ada Mackenzie, the Canadian. By the third round they had disappeared. Miss Leitch saw to the going of the two most redoubtable—Miss Alexa Sterling in the first round, and Miss Hollins in the next. The Leitch-Sterling encounter was the last match in the first round, and any hopes that the American's supporters may have had were extinguished by vile weather which drenched the players and buffeted Miss Sterling's swing to pieces.

This particular game was the forerunner of several historic encounters between reigning British and American champions. Miss Leitch estimated that the gallery was several thousands, who, undeterred by the sheets of rain and strong wind, followed the fortunes of the British champion against the American on what must have been the worst day on which Miss Sterling had ever played competitive golf. Miss Hollins very nearly played the part of avenger in the next round, being one up on Miss Leitch with two holes to go, but she then generously threw both holes away and allowed the holder to escape. Miss Leitch was in a similar predicament in the semi-final against Miss Janet Jackson; but then she took the last two holes with glorious iron approaches.

Her opponent in the final was Miss Joyce Wethered, who had come through the other half with little difficulty apart from a desperate 19-hole affray in the first round with Miss Gladys Bastin. Here was proof that more than luck had given Miss Wethered the English title at Sheringham; but she was not yet ready to relieve Miss Leitch of the British crown. At Turnberry, Miss Leitch won the title for the third time in succession. She was seven up at the half-way stage of the final, and eventually triumphed by four and three over her rival. A month later they met in yet another final, the French Open at Fontainebleau, and the result was the same. No further battles were possible between these two that season.

Miss Leitch went off to Canada, where she won the Canadian Open, in the process defeating Miss Alexa Sterling in the semi-final. All she needed now was the American National, and this seemed likely to go into the bag when she qualified easily for the match-play stages and won her first round game on the eleventh green. However, she was stopped in the second round by Mrs. F. C. Letts, Junior, of Chicago, who beat her by a hole after being down all the way to the fifteenth. Rock-steady, short and straight, and a marvellous putter, the Chicagoan was quite unmoved by her temerity in hanging on to the British champion, and rolled in a long putt to beat her on the eighteenth. After this, Mrs Letts, although winner of many important American events, was always introduced to golfing strangers as 'the player who had beaten Miss Leitch'.

Miss Wethered stalked unmolested through the English, improving enormously with every championship she played in, and it was patently obvious by now that so far as British golf was concerned, she and Miss Leitch were in a class alone. Both of them were vulnerable, but they could call on powers of recovery and strokes that were denied their rivals. In the quality of greatness both had liberal portions—and in courage and fighting ability, too. But in everything else they were as opposite as the poles are apart.

Miss Leitch, immensely vital, strong and energetic and physically tough, was distinguished-looking in any company in which she chose to walk. She was a natural leader, who took command of the game of golf on the first tee as instinctively as she drew breath. Her swing was not pretty to watch; it was incredibly flat compared with modern teaching. She used the palm grip with her right hand very much under the shaft, and this, and her straight left arm, always stiff like a ramrod, gave her exceptional control and power over her iron shots. This style was her own instinctive method of attacking a golf ball from early childhood onwards. She and her sisters learned their golf at Silloth, where their father had laid out a nine-hole course, and for a long time an old cleek and a gutty ball were her only equipment. Lured from obscurity by the thrill of playing in the British Championship at St Andrews, Cecil and her sister Edith, daughters of a Fifeshire man, went to try their luck on the Royal and Ancient course in May 1908, and inside a week had become national figures. The limelight never dimmed from that début. Most of it was Cecil's, but her sister Edith, when she had become Mrs Guedalla, won the English Championship nineteen years later, and so achieved her own right to fame. Cecil captivated the sporting world because of the downright and forceful manner in which she hit the ball. Miss May Hezlet and Miss Rhona Adair had commenced their successes at an equally early age; but although they must have hit hard to have gone so far as they did, the power of their strokes was concealed in full and flowing swings, and they did not use their iron clubs with the same crispness as the Silloth girl. Miss Leitch revealed to her sex that there were distinct possibilities of their being able to reproduce the artistry of the irons, which had hitherto been the prerogative of the best men golfers. This, then, was her gift to the game, which in turn rewarded her with the highest honours.

Miss Wethered, tall and thin, shy and unobtrusive, became a student of the game largely because of the enthusiasm of her brother, Mr. Roger Wethered. When he was Captain of Golf at Oxford, she met and played with his friends, was drawn into their arguments, and must have theorized on the perfection of style and the composition of the swing in a manner which no other woman had ever done before. Playing with the leading amateurs developed her game quickly and made her impervious to superior power. From a quiet house or a secluded part of an hotel, she would come to the first tee, smile charmingly at her opponent when they met at the commencement of their game, and then, almost as though in a trance, become a golfing machine. She never obtruded her personality, and those who played her had the impression that they, the crowd and the state of the game had ceased to exist in her mind and that her entire faculties were being focused on swinging to perfection and holing the ball in the fewest number of strokes. The match concluded, Miss Wethered would vanish and be seen no more until the starter called her name for the next round. Her seeming remoteness from all the stress and strain that troubles ordinary people who go to championship meetings bewildered her opponents; her indifference to what they did became positively nightmarish to them, and made her task very much easier. This cloak of inhumanity was not created to frighten the enemy; it served to conceal an intense concentration, and to conserve its owner's physical strength. Miss Wethered was fragile in appearance, and there was nothing of the Amazon about her. Strength and stamina she must have had to withstand the physical and mental effort of a week's championship golf; but perhaps, knowing that her resources were not over-abundant, she evolved the most economical method to suit her physique and by shutting out everything of an extraneous nature avoided the strain which others found so sapping and destructive, although this strain was not unknown to her in the later stages of her more memorable battles with Miss Leitch and Miss Collett. Miss Leitch brought power into women's golf; Miss Wethered brought power combined with perfection of style and a hitherto unknown degree of accuracy. After the first surprise encounter at Sheringham, any meeting between these two players became an event of national importance, and the publicity which was accorded to it naturally caught and held the attention of an ever-increasing number of women golfers.

The inevitable came to pass in 1922: Miss Leitch and Miss Wethered were in opposite halves of the British Championship held at Prince's, Sandwich, and once again they met in the final. On this occasion the roles were reversed, Miss Wethered remaining inflexible and Miss Leitch recovering brilliantly, and the younger player had the lead at lunch-time—only one hole, but a hole of the value of diamonds in a match of that calibre. In the second round Miss Leitch's powers of recovery were still needed—and they deserted her. So Miss Wethered won easily.

To mention that Miss Wethered annexed the English for the third time in succession that year is, by comparison, almost prosaic; and we will dwell for a moment on the fact that she entered for the English each year between 1920 and 1924, and was never beaten.

The next season was rather an anticlimax. Miss Leitch was kept out of the game by arm trouble, and Miss Wethered, who by now had become almost a legend of invincibility, was deprived of the British by Mrs Allan Macbeth. Her conqueror, formerly Miss Dodd of pre-war championship fame, administered the beating in the semi-final, and then succumbed to Miss Doris Chambers.

The following year, Miss Wethered and Miss Leitch met in the fifth round of the British at Royal Portrush. The initiative having gone to the younger player, she retained it, and having dealt summarily with her deadliest rival, Miss Wethered gobbled up the rest of her adversaries as a matter of course and so found herself holder of the British for the second time in three years.

So absorbed had we become in the affairs of our two great ones that we took little heed of what was happening on the other side of the Herring Pond, and the progress of Miss Glenna Collett, who in 1924 swept the board in America and held every title of importance, apart from the National which she had held previously, meant little to us until she arrived here in the spring of 1925, to challenge Miss Wethered for the British, which was held at Troon. In no time we had a very real respect for her, and the meeting between these two was an epic of the third round. In this match, Miss Wethered was greater than she had ever been before, and although Miss Collett produced golf that would have eliminated anyone else with ease, she lost on the fifteenth, the score against her being level fours.

The onlookers, aroused to frenzy by this display, were given time to cool off, and then they were pulverized by the duel at the end of the week between Miss Wethered and Miss Leitch, a scintillating battle of varying fortunes and of magnificent golf, which was level after thirty-six holes. The tragedy was that the game had to continue until there was a decider; and this went to Miss Wethered at the thirty-seventh. She went round, morning and afternoon, in 75. All square after the first round, dormy two in the second, only to see her lead snatched away; and then, with the tension at its height, and all Scotland witnessing the ordeal, she had her four—and victory. The two heroines must have found the excitement of the crowd infectious. They would not have been human had they not reacted to the tension; but what must have made the day a dreadful ordeal for them was the crowd who ran, stampeded, and made the players' progress from tee to green a continual anxiety and constant evasion of hurtling bodies. Only the most determined and gallant stewarding saved Miss Wethered and Miss Leitch from being trampled underfoot.

This may have contributed to Miss Wethered's decision to retire from championship golf. She was then twenty-four, and having won the British title three times and the English title five, felt that she had earned a less active role. So she quitted the stage; although, as it turned out, not for good.

Miss Collett brought to our notice that women's golf in the United States was making giant strides, and that any invasion party she might lead would constitute a menace to the British. She came to Harlech in 1926, and then went home again when the General Strike caused the championship to be postponed for a month. The honours went to Miss Cecil Leitch—her fourth British—and aptly gave her a championship in each of the home countries. This was the last of her major titles, which also included the English twice, French Open five times, Canadian Open once and every medal event of consequence during her fifteen years of competitive golf.

Women's Golf: Enid Wilson

So occupied were we at the thought of the American threat, that our eyes were turned westward when they should have been in the other direction. We had been given a fair warning in 1924 that France had a player of great potentialities when Mlle. Simone de la Chaume captured the Girls' Championship at Stoke Poges. A year later, she won the French title and began a monopoly which lasted six seasons in this event. In 1926 she was Open Champion of France, and only needed the British to set the seal on her greatness. When she went to Newcastle, Co Down, in 1927 she immediately captivated everybody by her charm, and the championship by the excellence of her golf. The only other matter of importance at Newcastle was that the combined ages of the four medallists totalled less than the years enjoyed by Mr Hugh Kelly, who refereed the final.

The presiding imp of championship draws played a very scurvy trick when the names came out of the hat for the British at Hunstanton in 1928. He paired Mlle. de la Chaume and Miss Glenna Collett together in the first round. The holder was beaten, and the door wide open for an American success; but the weather blew hard, wet completed the ruination of the American swings, and to our surprise we again had a Frenchwoman for our champion—Mlle. Manette le Blan, tall, strong and capable, and one of the youthful medallists of the previous year.

The lure of St Andrews was too strong for Miss Wethered, who came out of her self-imposed retirement when the British was held there in 1929. It also attracted Miss Glenna Collett, and several other prominent Americans. Miss Wethered, with characteristic honesty, denied that her motives in entering were patriotic ones to keep the invaders away. The historic associations of the Old Course were more than she could resist. Only her intimate friends were aware of the quality of her golf, and the rest of the world had to wait patiently until her arrival in Scotland to see if any changes had taken place during the past four years. About Miss Collett there were no uncertainties; we knew she was at her zenith and that she was easily the best and most powerful woman golfer on the other side of the Atlantic. She was fully acquainted with our courses and climate, and we were not a little afraid that she would achieve her ambition and carry off our cup. With Miss Wethered and Miss Collett in opposite halves of the draw, the concern of the entire golfing community was centred on the final to come. Had anyone upset the apple-cart and prevented the drama from taking place, they would never have been forgiven—especially in the light of what followed. The earlier rounds were training canters to build up form for the vital combat. Certainly nothing else was talked of at St Andrews that week. The opinion prevailed that 'she' would win; and yet, with all the implicit faith we had, there was a little gnawing worm of anxiety. Miss Wethered arrived at St Andrews with no idea of the impending strain; but as the week wore on, she must have been fully aware of the hopes

237

which she carried, and on the morning of the final the tension of this terrific meeting must have been very real to her.

The weather had wavered during the earlier part of the championship, and then relented, so that when the enormous crowd gathered to witness the *pièce de résistance*, the sun was shining from a cloudless sky. This lovely morning must have helped Miss Collett. In the previous rounds, the American had not quite produced the golf of which we knew she was capable. Now, with everything at stake, she rose to the occasion, and without a vestige of a mistake she reached the turn in 34. Such golf was almost unbelievable, and Miss Wethered, who had played neither very well nor very ill, was five down. Up to the twelfth, Miss Collett was a woman inspired, beyond mortal reach. And then, with a putt to become six up, certainly no more difficult and not as long as some which she had holed with ease that morning, she missed. The spell was broken, and she became human once more. This was what Miss Wethered must have hoped and waited for, and slowly but surely she took command of the game and won back three of the six holes that remained before lunch.

A thoroughly scared and chastened crowd went to find nourishment and fortification for what the afternoon might have in store. The consensus of opinion was that Miss Wethered had passed the storm and would sail home with moderate comfort. The Elders of St Andrews must also have been shaken by the best ball of the two distinguished ladies, which was 71. Nothing to equal this had been produced in a women's final before.

After lunch, Miss Collett's lead evaporated. The position at the twenty-seventh was Miss Wethered four up. She had taken 73 strokes for the homeward half of the first round and the outward half of the second one. All seemed secure, and then back came Miss Collett with two birdie threes, to make a fight and show that she still had shots left in her locker. Crisis loomed large on the thirty-third hole for Miss Wethered, who looked likely to lose it and be only one up with three to play; however, a six-yard putt rescued her, and provided the vitally-needed half. The match concluded at the Road hole. Miss Wethered had achieved her ambition of winning the British at St Andrews, and the fulfilment of the wish had come to pass with superlative golf. Miss Collett never capitulated, never ceased from fighting, every inch of those thirty-five holes. What a glorious game it was!

Every generation swears that its sporting heroes and heroines are better than any before or since, and one spectator at least will always be happy in the belief that nothing could surpass the final of the British in 1929. Superb skill, artistry, sportsmanship and drama for an entire day! These qualities, and the classic setting in which they were framed, make this the finest moment in British women's golf.

*   *   *

238

Steel shafts were taking the place of hickory. Their lightness was a distinct advantage to women players, and during the '30s the transformation came steadily and surely. The younger school, nurtured for the most part by the Girls' Open Golf Championship, now began to hang around the threshold.

The spring of 1930 was remarkable for the largest invasion of American players we had ever welcomed. They interested us immensely by bringing with them huge quantities of clubs and balls—the latter for practice purposes—which were carted about the countryside in the most awe-inspiring and voluminous leather caddie bags. Not only was the prodigality of their equipment something to marvel at, but the way in which they applied themselves to the game was completely novel. They made each stroke with a care and deliberation which suggested that the whole world might be affected by its outcome. Part of the deliberation was taken up by a practice swing or two; a handkerchief was produced to determine the strength and direction of the wind, and the line of a putt was perused with microscopic intensity—this was all part and parcel of their normal progression round the links. But before and after playing round the course, they spent a considerable time practising, hitting away shot after shot, seemingly never to tire or to be bored by their drill.

Another novelty was their brightly-coloured clothing. We were tempted to scoff—and, like so many scoffers, soon followed suit.

Miss Collett had arranged with the holder of the English title, Miss Molly Gourlay, to take her party to Sunningdale and spend a day there before going to Formby for the British. Miss Gourlay invited several of her friends to come and play at Sunningdale with the Americans, and what had begun in all innocence as a carefree outing was suddenly pounced upon and transformed into an informal international. The British side won by eight points to six, and the lesson was lost upon us. We were probably more concerned with the championship at Formby and preoccupied with the thought of Miss Collett, Miss Van Wie, Miss Hicks and several others who were bound to give a lot of trouble. They did; but by hammering away, we pulled them down one by one until only Miss Collett remained, the championship virtually in her grasp. Her opponent in the final was Miss Diana Fishwick, who had twice won the Girls' Championship and had begun to make a name for herself in the senior events. Miss Fishwick, a slender youngster, just nineteen, was the possessor of a temperament which would not permit of any thought of fright. She met Miss Collett with the coolness of a veteran, and beat her.

The outstanding event of 1931 was the presentation by Monsieur André Vagliano of a silver challenge trophy to be competed for annually by teams from Britain and France. Three foursomes and six singles were the order of play, and in the first match, at Oxhey, France were only allowed to take half a point. Miss

Wethered was the leader of the British side and Madame Lacoste (*née* Chaume) leader of the French. This was the first occasion on which the Ladies' Golf Union had sponsored a fully representative British team.

Next in the international field were Miss H. and Miss M. Curtis, of Boston, Mass, who presented a cup for biennial competition between teams from the USA and Great Britain, with the proviso and hope that other countries would join in later. The first match in this series was held in Britain at Wentworth in May 1932. Both America and Britain were at full strength, and three foursomes and six singles decided the issue. So confident were we of the outcome of the match that we were casual in our preparations. The Americans were at Wentworth a week before the match and their captain, Miss Marion Hollins, experimented with the foursomes pairings—a form of golf rarely played in America—with such thoroughness that when the great day came, Britain, with couples who knew one another by repute but had never teamed before, lost all three foursomes. The shock of this debacle, which left too much to be retrieved, led to their downfall in the singles, as they then needed to gain five singles to win and four to draw. The result was: America $5\frac{1}{2}$ points, Great Britain $3\frac{1}{2}$ points.

That was the blackest day in our golf to date. No one could be blamed for the beating we got. We chose our side. They knew the day, and were left to their own devices, whether they practised at Wentworth, elsewhere or not at all. At tea-time on the day prior to the match, when the captains exchanged their order of play, we did not even have the sense to retain the three foursomes pairings which had won against France at Oxhey. The most aggravating part of the whole business is that since we began these international contests with the Americans by stepping off on the wrong foot, we have never been in sight of recovering from our initial error. The away matches have never lured us into false hopes; the home ones we should contrive to win. But a draw at Gleneagles in 1936 is the best we have done to date.

Whilst dwelling on these internationals, it must also be recorded that teams which have gone to America for the Curtis Cup matches have also played a fully representative Canadian side, usually on the way home. These matches we have won, Canada having nothing like the golfing resources of the USA.

In 1933 the South African Ladies' Golf Union asked their parent body, the LGU, to send a team of girl golfers to tour the Union. The purpose of this was to stimulate interest in women's golf within the Union, and to give their players an idea of the standard prevailing in the Mother Country. Miss Doris Chambers captained the British side during their tour, which was a great success. Two years later, in response to invitations from the Australian and·New Zealand Ladies' Golfing Unions, an officially sponsored British team, with Mrs. Philip Hodson non-playing captain-manager, sailed away to undertake a most extensive pro-

Miss F. Hezlet, the runner-up in the 1909 Ladies'
Championship at Birkdale

Sport and General

Miss Dorothy Campbell, the winner of the 1909
Ladies' Championship at Birkdale

Sport and General

Miss Rhona Adair, the winner of the Ladies'
Championship in 1900 at Westward Ho!, and in
1903 at Royal Portrush

Miss Cecil Leitch in 1908

Sport and General

Miss Cecil Leitch in 1920, the year in
which she won the Ladies' Championship at Newcastle, Co Down

Central Press Photos

Miss Gladys Ravenscroft (Mrs. Temple Dobell), the winner of the Ladies' Championship in 1912 at Turnberry

Central Press Photos

Mrs. Allan Macbeth (Muriel Dodd) playing in the Ladies' Championship at Burnham-on-Sea in 1923

Topical Press

Miss Joyce Wethered holding the Ladies' Championship cup after winning the Championship at Troon in 1925

Central Press Photos

Lady Heathcoat-Amory (Joyce Wethered) in 1938. Among those watching her driving from the tee are Miss Pam Barton, Miss Enid Wilson, Mme René Lacoste (Simone de la Chaume) and Henry Cotton

Sport and General

Mme René Lacoste (Simone de la Chaume) in 1933. She was the winner of the Ladies' Championship at Newcastle, Co Down, in 1927

Central Press Photos

Miss Lally Vagliano defending her Girls' Open Championship title in 1938 at Stoke Poges. As the Vicomtesse de Saint Sauveur she returned to win the Ladies' Championship at Newcastle, Co Down, in 1950

Fox Photos

Miss Enid Wilson driving from the 2nd tee at Ranelagh during the 1937 Ladies' Autumn Foursomes. Watching is her opponent, Mrs. Andrew Holm

Topical Press

Miss Glenna Collett, runner-up in the Ladies' Championship at St Andrews in 1929 and Formby in 1930

Topical Press

Mrs George Zaharias driving from the 3rd tee in the 4th round of the Ladies' Championship at Gullane in 1947, which she won

Sport and General

Miss Louise Suggs driving from the 15th tee during the Ladies' Championship at Royal Lytham and St Anne's in 1948, which she won

Sport and General

Miss Gloria D. Minoprio, who used only one club. In 1934 she was also the first lady to appear in a championship match wearing trousers

Central Press Photos

Miss Pam Barton, the winner of the Ladies' Championship in 1936 and 1939 and the runner-up in 1934 and 1935

Central Press Photos

Mrs. Andrew Holm (*left*) receiving the congratulations of the runner-up, Mrs E. C. Beddows, on winning the Scottish Ladies' Championship in 1950 at St Andrews. This was the fifth time that Mrs Holm had won the trophy. She won the Ladies' Championship in 1934. Mrs. Beddows (formerly Mrs J. B. Watson) was Scottish Champion in 1920, 1921, 1922, and 1929, and represented Scotland in home international matches nineteen times between 1913 and 1950

G. M. Cowie, St Andrews

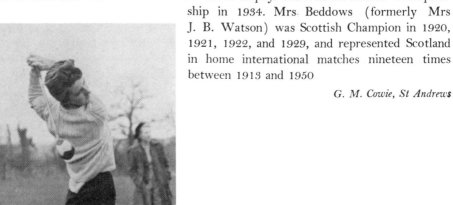

Miss Frances Stephens, Ladies' Champion of 1949, driving from the 6th tee during the Women's Challenge Cup Competition at Roehampton in 1950

Central Press Photos

gramme, which was completed to the satisfaction of all concerned, Mrs. J. B. Walker winning the Australian championship, and Miss Jessie Valentine the New Zealand title.

We were visited by a touring team of South Africans in 1938, and although we have every reason to believe that they enjoyed themselves, we were perhaps not so kind as we might have been during their matches. Their standard was the equivalent of one of our better county sides, and with different climatic conditions and strange varieties of grass on our courses, the odds were heavily against them.

To conclude the saga of international golf up to the autumn of 1939: we lost to America at home in 1932; drew at home in 1936; and lost away in 1934 and 1938. We reaped a small measure of consolation by beating France each year, except in the fourth match, at Chantilly in 1934, when they forced a draw.

From 1930 until the outbreak of the second world war, the British Ladies' Championship was farmed by youth. Miss Collett became Mrs Vare, and after that we felt her heart was in her home and not entirely set on our trophy. The Americans came in force in 1932, but our youngsters would not let them have the British; and though they kept on trying quite hard, we never let it go. The narrator of this chronicle had her hour*, and was followed in 1934 by Mrs Andrew Holm, who took the trophy to Scotland, where it had not been since 1911. Mrs Holm won again in 1938, and thereby joined the small select band who have been successful in the British more than once. Tall and slender—reminiscent of Miss Wethered in build and pretty well her equal in power, but without her deadly accuracy—Mrs. Holm is still one of our leading golfers, and certainly one of the most stylish we have ever seen.

The next champion was of an entirely different build. Miss Wanda Morgan, although short and stocky, developed tremendous power, and she had three victories in the English as well as her British title. After her came a thoroughly tenacious young lady who was twice finalist in the British before she broke through in 1936. This was Miss Pamela Barton, who then went off to America and won their National title in the autumn of the same year. Miss Barton won the British again in 1939 and tried to repeat the double, but was not lucky the second time. She had by no means reached her peak as a player when the war came and golf ceased.

It is rather ironical to relate that Miss Jessie Anderson, who won the British in 1937 and the French Open in 1936, had to wait until the following year before she added the Scottish title to her bag. 'Wee Jessie', despite her lack of height and weight, is one of the finest iron players ever seen in the women's championships.

This brings us to the moment when players and promoters dispersed to other

* Miss Enid Wilson won the championship in 1931, 2, and 3.—[ED.].

tasks, in the more serious game of warfare. They did take a few brief breathers in charity matches at the beginning of the war; but then our needs became urgent, and the time and inclination existed no longer. Golf club-houses became the head-quarters of units in the Services or the base of their local Home Guard. The War Agricultural Committee requisitioned portions of inland courses in order to grow vital food, and the seaside links were, many of them, incorporated in the coastal defence schemes. Women golfers were to be found in every section of the Services and war industry, driving MT, ferrying aeroplanes, coping with evacuees, censorship, telephones, canteens, and the whole gamut of strange tasks which war provides.

Women's golf suffered a most grievous loss when the British champion, Miss Pam Barton, serving as a Flight Officer in the Women's Auxiliary Air Force, was killed at the Station where she was in charge of the airwomen, and was buried with military honours at Manston.

When hostilities ceased, the women were too worn out to make any mad rush back to golf, or any other game. Those who might have wanted to were tied by domestic chores, business and the lack of petrol for their cars to take them to and from their clubs.

The British was resumed when the Ladies' Golf Union went to Hunstanton in the summer of 1946. The idea was chiefly to get started and to have a gossip with old friends, and no one had an inkling as to what the golf would be like. Mrs. Hetherington was the winner, and she had a really exciting final with Miss P. Garvey. Mrs. Hetherington was Jean McClure from Wanstead, and she won the British when she was on her honeymoon. Miss Garvey won the Irish when it was resumed in 1946; the two following years, and again in 1950.

We were visited the next season by an American, Mrs. George Zaharias, formerly an Olympic athlete, and record-maker in jumping and javelin throwing. Before her arrival we had heard incredible stories about her athletic prowess, and we knew that she had spent a season or two carrying off most of the leading feminine golfing tournaments in America. We were given to understand that her length was phenomenal, and that any hope there might be of holding her would be around the greens. Mrs. Zaharias arrived at Gullane, the venue of the British, and we learned that she had at one time or another tackled most of the American Walker Cup team level and beaten them. Nor, it seemed, did she require anything more than a wedge for her second shots to reach all the greens at Gullane. This is being recounted with respect by one who saw the 'Babe' (Mrs Zaharias was given this nickname as an Olympic prodigy and it has stuck) reach the Long hole home at Gullane—some 540 yards with the green on a hill—with a drive and a four iron, which pitched over the putting surface: there was no wind behind, and the fairway was soft and slow. She consistently produced this vast length from the tee, followed by astounding recoveries from the rough and sound putting, and nothing we had could live against such length. Miss Stephens and Mrs. Sheppard took the siege gun farther than the others, and Miss Gordon held on for the first round of the final. When the American Wonder met Miss Jean Donald from North Berwick in the semi-final, the whole of Edinburgh watched. And the enormous crowd was greatly to the liking of our visitor.

Mrs. Zaharias had hardly stepped off the gang-plank of the liner that took her and the British trophy to New York when she signed a multi-thousand dollar contract, and automatically became professionalized. Her game and her personality were the talk of all the women's clubs in Britain that season. The secret of her power lay in the muscles and sinews trained in the Olympiads, which enabled her to hit harder and faster than any other woman golfer has ever done before. Her style was not one that any other woman could copy with profit. Her game was based on hitting the ball into the hole. There have never been any half measures about anything that Mrs Zaharias has done; nor were there any half shots about her golf. Such force leaves no room for finesse.

America won the British the following year at Royal Lytham and St Anne's, when Miss Louise Suggs, an entirely different sort of player from Mrs Zaharias, beat Miss Jean Donald by one hole on what must have been the wettest day on which the women's final has ever taken place. Accuracy and superb putting enabled her to add the British to the American title which she had won the previous autumn. Like Mrs Zaharias, Miss Suggs turned professional immediately on her return to the United States.

Then came England's turn, and Miss Frances Stephens won the British at Harlech in 1949. An infinitely painstaking golfer, Miss Stephens won the French Open and every British event for which she entered that season. She did not bother to defend her English title in the autumn, and instead went to America in search of higher game, which was denied her. But she had the satisfaction of finishing high up in their Open—a 72-hole medal tournament—in a field that comprised leading amateurs and professionals.

There is one more British to relate: the 1950 Championship at Royal Newcastle, Co Down, won by the Vicomtesse de St Sauveur on the same course and twenty-three years after the success of her friend and compatriot, Mlle. de la Chaume. Her powerful game to the greens was backed up with beautiful putting, and she was in every respect a most worthy winner.

International women's golf since the war has picked up all the former threads. The Home Internationals were resumed in 1947, and so were the matches against France, only, at the request of the Ladies' Golf Union, they are now held bi-ennially. The Curtis Cup matches were recommenced, the first one at Birkdale in 1948, where we could only take $2\frac{1}{2}$ points to the Americans' $6\frac{1}{2}$. Nor could we hope for much better, our youngsters being out-generalled by the Americans' extraordinary ability to deliver par golf on the right day. One new fixture, a match against Belgium, now adorns the calendar, the first official match being played at Waterloo in 1949.

The 1950 season has been made more memorable by the visit of a team sponsored by the Australian Ladies' Golf Union. Their captain-manager, Miss L. Wray, brought with her six charming players who are all first-rate golfers and put up a fine show in the British. Miss Judith Percy reached the semi-final, and this is the first time a championship medal has been won by an Australian golfer. In their international matches, they beat Ireland and Wales, lost by one game to Scotland and, after a tremendous struggle on a day when conditions were far from encouraging, halved their match with England.

* * *

British women's golf is still trying to make up for the war years, and the restrictions and economies which are still imposed make the task a hard one.

Pre-war players are still holding their own: Mrs. Critchley (*née* Diana Fishwick), the English champion and captain of the Curtis Cup team which will travel to America this autumn, is capable of beating anyone. Mrs. Valentine (*née* Jessie Anderson) reached the final of the British this year and showed that she could wield her irons with the same skill as fifteen years ago. Mrs. Holm won the Scottish this year for the fifth time, to beat Mrs. Watson's record. Mrs. Watson, now Mrs. Beddows, the veteran champion, is still in the Scottish side thirty-seven years after her first appearance, and at the age of 62 reached the final of the Scottish Championship this year.

Of the newcomers, Miss Stephens is the steadiest; Miss Donald, twice winner of the Scottish, the most powerful and courageous; and Miss Garvey the most stylish.

To bring this record right up to date, it is necessary to include the result of the Curtis Cup match at Buffalo on September 4 and 5. In this match, for the first time, and at the request of the LGU, the games were played over 36 holes instead of 18. We sent our strongest team, and the result makes melancholy reading, for we only managed to win one of the three foursomes, and halve one of the six singles. Miss Stephens was the heroine of the British side, for with Miss Price she combined successfully against Miss Sigel and Miss Kirk, and in the top single, she forced Mrs. Mark Porter, the American champion, to share a drawn game, which was one of the best encounters of the Curtis Cup match.

The inference from this result is that we still have some way to go before we can equal the standard of our pre-war golf, and we have considerable lee-way to make up before we shall be able to hold our own with the Americans in these contests.

We are not without hope, and we are not without talent. The major meetings have all been restored, with the exception of the *Eve Bystander* whose big four-some tournaments run on handicap, which used to attract anything up to five hundred entrants, are still lacking from the calendar. The county fixtures, the associations and the societies are all back in circulation, and all that we need now is the time to encourage and foster our players.

Youth is not coming to the fore in the strength of the 1925-1939 era; but we have young players of distinct promise, including Miss Pam Davies, the holder of the Girls' Championship, Miss M. Glidewell, Miss E. Young and Miss M. Paterson.

There is every indication that women's golf has taken a firm foothold throughout the Commonwealth and the Colonies, and that the Unions there are looking towards Britain and the Ladies' Golf Union for leadership and example.

CLOSING WORD

by *LORD BRABAZON OF TARA*

The Future of the Game

IF IT WERE true that history repeats itself, then you should, for this chapter on the future of golf, read again the historical section. It would be a great economy in space and work. But unless hydrogen bombs eliminate all human beings and the existing race of gorillas start evolving afresh, I do not suppose we shall again play golf to a stick instead of into a hole, as did once the Dutch. The substitution of a hole for a stick, with the diabolical consequence of holing out, brought the new control of speed of the ball into the game, a very real and important thing and a very great improvement, introducing a new technique of skill.

We don't know exactly what the early balls were made of, but no doubt they were something on the lines of the real tennis balls that have been used for years and which have never changed. They would not be bad, but not very good. Anyhow, we do know that the feather ball must have been an improvement on them, otherwise it would never have come in. The introduction of the gutta-percha ball was a very real move forward and there is no doubt that modern golf starts with its arrival.

Just as an example of how good a ball it really was when hit hard, the great Ted Blackwell is reputed to have driven from the last tee at St. Andrews and to have hit the club-house steps. I have no doubt there was a gale behind and the ground was hard, but still it is a colossal shot. The gutty ball is a very good ball to play with but its chief merit is in putting, when you can hit it hard and very true. But it is a very brutal type of ball off other clubs. In the days of the old wooden clubs they had to be spliced on to withstand the strain, such was the shock. A modern steel-shafted club, socketed at its head, would never stand the shock of a hard drive on the heel with a gutty ball. Whether the game of golf would have achieved its present popularity all over the world had the ball remained the gutty ball I am not prepared to say. There are some people who claim that this great 'golf stream', as it was so humorously described once by Sir Hamilton Grant, is due to the introduction of the rubber-cored ball, while others say that golf would have advanced just as well with the gutty ball. But, frankly, I think the rubber-cored ball has introduced great ease into the game. If you hit it on the heel or toe it still goes somewhere, whereas the old gutty ball hardly moved at all, which was very disheartening to the bad player.

The story of the introduction of the rubber-cored ball is not without interest, because the idea of stretching elastic over a solid core, or later, as has become the practice, over a small liquid core, was really an entirely new invention. And here there is a lesson to be learned, because if the inventors of the Haskell ball had put down as their claim that it was a very good golf ball to play golf with, and it went farther than anything else, they would have won their patent. But in patent law you have got to make good your claims, and whoever put the claim down made the most absurd statements. He said that because this ball had an elastic interior and a hard exterior if you hit it gently it would not be very elastic, but if you hit it hard it would be elastic. Professor Boys, the great physicist, was employed to show that this claim was not true, and obviously it was not. He introduced the most elaborate apparatus to show exactly what were the results of various shots, hard and soft; and when the matter was brought up to the House of Lords before Lord Justice Spencer Moulton, he declared that this particular claim could not be justified and uttered these remarkable words: 'Professor Boys' experiments have not been answered and are unanswerable. The patent fails.' Let that be a lesson to anybody making an invention, never to claim anything they cannot substantiate. But, frankly, I think we were all very lucky that such a wonderful invention was not established as a patent. Now in the various balls that we have known since the introduction of the Haskell Patent there have been many different types; all sorts of sizes and shapes and all sorts of weights have been seen. There is, of course, no doubt that the rubber-cored ball from the point of view of distance, and in a general way as a golf ball, is superior to anything else we have ever seen, and the great superiority of it was shown when Sandy Herd won the championship at Sandwich with a rubber-cored ball, being, I believe, the only competitor in that championship to use the rubber-core. The Royal and Ancient eventually took charge of the situation and laid down a very salutary and wonderful rule, the rule was that the ball should not weigh more than 1.62 ounces and should not be smaller than 1.62 inches. That is our ball today. The point is, will it remain so? What will be the ball of the future? The Americans have kept the weight the same as ours, it must not be more than 1.62 ounces, but they have increased the diameter to 1.68 inches. This sounds a very small difference, but I can assure you the difference in appearance is very big and undoubtedly the ball sits up better than the English ball on the fairway of any course.

Now the difference of these two sizes, bearing in mind that they are the same weight, means that the specific weight of the English ball is higher than that of the American. In other words the ratio of weight to diameter is bigger in the English ball than in the American, and with that one would assume, and it is indeed true,

247

that a ball of such a type as the English would bore through the wind better than the lighter ball for its size. Frankly, in a calm, I don't think there's a very great difference although theoretically there should be, but certainly in a wind the English ball pays. The curious thing is, however, that the Americans are quite satisfied with their American ball and the British are quite satisfied to play with the smaller type of ball in this country, and there is no great movement on either side to make a change, although it must be obvious that if golf is to be played as a universal game all over the world then the rule, and consequently the ball, should be the same.

The point which one must remember, however, is that in America it is prohibited to play with the English ball, but in England it is not prohibited to play with the American ball. I have referred to the fact that purely from the point of boring through the air in a wind the English ball is slightly superior. Here I would like to put on record a point in favour of the American ball. Not only does it, of course, sit up better to be hit and look rather more attractive to hit at, but on the green there is no doubt that it putts better than the English ball, and this would bear out theory, because obviously if you have a big ball it is less susceptible to variations or slight inequalities on the green than a ball of very small diameter, and here it might be of interest to readers to record some results from experiments I have indulged in myself to test this. I made an automatic hitter of a putt, a rather heavy tripod with a swinging pendulum, which one could adjust, not only from the point of view of swing-back, so as to get the striking of the ball absolutely the same every time, but also for direction by means of an aimer with micrometer setting. Having installed this tripod machine firmly on the green you could direct the ball to a definite position, absolutely, and you could rely on a repetition not only of the stroke in strength but in direction, with unfailing regularity. Now we know that in our own game if you could always hole a six-foot putt that would be very good putting, so I started with a six-foot putt and tried to see what was the percentage of failures at six feet both with the English and American ball. It may startle you, especially you good putters, to be told that at six feet, both with the American ball and the English ball, you can stay there all day and every single one will go in, without exception, for the whole afternoon. Never mind what the slope of green is, once you have set your machine right, the ball will go in; every time. The second experiment was at twelve feet. That is quite a respectable putt, and the experiments with the English ball showed that twenty out of twenty-one would go in, but with the American ball twenty-four out of twenty-five went in. My experiments were extensive and I can assure you that those results are correct. It is interesting to notice, although I am quite prepared to be contradicted in this, that what goes wrong in a putt occurs in the first eighteen inches of its movement.

248

The Future of the Game

You must remember that in a putt the ball has got to acquire its rotational speed through friction along the ground. In other words it gets its rotation by virtue of the friction over the first eighteen inches of its travel. It is here that inequalities occur. If, during this frictional time, some slight inequality hits the ball, then it starts wrong and will miss the hole. There is a lot yet to be studied in this matter. If you hit the ball with a slight loft the ball will go through the air over the first few inches with back spin, then on hitting the ground it has got to change its direction from backward to forward spin. If you hit it with a vertical putter then it will get its rotational speed all along its first foot of sliding. There is something to be said for reverse loft on clubs—that would be equivalent to hitting the ball slightly down, which many good putters say is a very good way of hitting the ball—but there again it depends on the inconsistencies of the green.

I mention these tests to impress, on all aspirants to great skill, what end of the game should be given most attention.

At present you find most people concentrating on the long game, whereas if we could all hole six-foot putts and put twenty-four out of twenty-five in the hole from twelve feet, what remarkable players we should be.

It can be done, but it requires very concentrated attention, but if we are ever again to aspire to the higher honours in golf, then future practice should be on the short game rather than perpetually banging the ball a mile with wooden clubs under the impression that that is the way to perfection.

What has happened, however, and what people object to in the modern ball is that the manufacturers have made it too good, and it has consistently over many years gone farther and farther, with the result that golf courses all over the world have necessarily become longer and longer. After all golf is a game at which we want to play shots, not just go for a walk. The point arises therefore how are we going to limit this ball in length and what is to be the ball of the future? The Americans have done some very curious experiments in which they have laid it down, although I do not quite see yet how it can be implemented, that a ball that is struck with a velocity of 140 feet per second shall not over the first ten feet of its flight exceed 250 feet per second. The trouble about all these definitions and limitations is that they are very hard to check before or during a game. After all, with our old rule, 1.62 as to weight and size, you can weigh it and you can test it by a gauge. It is all over in a second and you know whether the ball is all right. But with the American system I cannot see how you can on the tee, for instance, decide whether the ball is right or wrong, unless it has been stamped with some official mark. But you don't want marks on balls—you put quite enough of them on yourself.

Now it is of course a trite platitude to say that if you hit a ball harder it will go farther, but there are limits to this. The trouble about the modern golf ball is that

249

the very hard hitter gets an enormous increase in length over the ordinary hitter, and this in scientific language means that the coefficient of restitution is maintained very consistently right up in the hard-hitting end. What we want is a ball that is quite efficient in moderate hitting, such as the ordinary golfer indulges in, but which falls off in efficiency when hit extremely hard. The ordinary golfer today who, say, hits the ball two hundred yards, if he is playing a first-class pro, won't be outdriven by fifty yards, he will be outdriven by a hundred and fifty yards. If we could diminish the efficiency on the hard hitting side then we could arrange a ball that would only outdrive the ordinary driver by, say, fifty to sixty yards. It is a physical problem which is not in any way insoluble, but like all these things which have to be applied to a golf ball it is so very difficult to make something which can be tested and known before you go on to a golf course. I don't think the average golfer wants a ball which goes a shorter distance than he hits it now, all he objects to is the colossal distance a ball goes when hit extremely hard. After all, the game is a game of skill, it is not a game of brute force; there is no doubt that extreme long-hitting is spoiling the game. If you take the record of Sam Snead, when he won the championship at St Andrews he never played wood with his second at any time. Well, that is really reducing golf courses to an absurdity, nothing else. There must come a time, of course, when the Americans and ourselves get together over this ball, and as they are working along the same lines as ourselves on this matter, I have no doubt that some general policy can be agreed. As I say, the method of proving the ball is always going to be a difficulty; economy is of course a point which I am going to deal with later on. But I would in this connection, as to the length of the ball, try to impress upon everybody that the general expense of keeping a course of 7,000 yards is one thing, but the cost of one of over 7,000 yards is a very material additional expense for the average golf club.

This continual lengthening of courses is a thing that clubs object to very much. Consequently you have got to consider in the future what is going to be done about it. First of all, I believe it was a mistake to do away with the cross bunker. It is a very funny psychological thing that if anybody drives into a cross bunker they always think it is rather bad luck, whereas if they hit over a green all they say is that they have misjudged the distance. It would seem to me that it is a highly desirable thing to introduce the cross bunker again and make people play definitely controlled shots, and it would compel them to play a long second shot, instead of playing the second shot with the number seven or eight iron, which the very long driver generally does today. It would introduce that wooden club second shot which was one of the charms of the early game. If we could get that back, I think that would be an advantage. The cross bunker, certainly, would in some cases introduce this.

250

The Future of the Game

As we have now passed into the design of golf courses it is interesting to speculate how they should develop in the future. Of course, long driving, I admit, has its advantages, and indeed it should have advantages, but if you are going to drive very long and get advantage you should also drive very straight, and consequently the fairway should tighten up at the end of a very long drive so that it must be very straight to get its advantage. I notice that some of the Americans at Walton Heath said that it was unfair because very long drives had to be straight since the fairways were narrow at the end. Frankly, I hope this unfairness will increase very much because I think that it is right and progressive, nor indeed would it penalize our American friends, because of all people in the world they are particularly long and particularly straight. But to have golf courses opening out at the end of a drive, so that you can shut your eyes and hit in any direction as hard as you can, is not the game as it should be played.

There should, in my opinion, always be a few yards of semi-rough between the fairway and the quite unplayable heather or bushes, because it is ridiculous that between the fairway and, say, bushes there should be no half-way house. As to bunkers—here let it be understood that the bunker is a hazard and should be deep. This idea of getting into flat bunkers where, if you are short in the bunker lying well, you can take a brassey, is not one that should be encouraged. Once you are in a bunker you should be compelled to lose a shot. Then we come to penalties beyond the green. Here I think that the general consensus of opinion is that there is no very great vice in going over a green, and if you do do such a thing you should not meet dire trouble and impenetrable rough and bunkers from which you can scarcely recover. After all, if you are short, you usually do not suffer from any penalty except the penalty of being short. By committing a mistake not so bad as being short, to be up and a little over, should not gather to yourself dire trouble. I notice in the very modern courses (and, I should say, in the future it is a thing to be encouraged) there is a tendency not to have what are called gathering greens—that is, greens where the general contour of the ground will gather a ball into the middle if it is not quite straight but a little off the line. I think these are thoroughly vicious types of greens. A green should really be rather hump-backed, not exaggeratedly so, but on the whole hump-backed so that the straight shot carries on straight, but a bad shot is encouraged to go off the line by the general shape of the green. Here we get, in consequence, the true good second shot being rewarded and the one which is not so good slightly penalized. That I think is a thoroughly satisfactory move, and I hope that it will be encouraged in the future design of golf courses.

Now we come to length of holes. I quite agree that the length of holes is dependent upon the efficiency of the ball and how hard people hit it, but, as you look through your career of golf, the only real pleasure is the two-shot hole. If you try

251

to recall the three-shot holes which are really good ones all through the golf courses that you have played in your career, you will not remember many more than three good ones. I recall one very well, which has disappeared; that was the seventeenth at Prince's, Sandwich. And I consider the long hole 'in' at St Andrews one of the most remarkable of all three-shot holes. But they are very rare, and usually three-shot holes on most courses are of the most insipid and ludicrous type. They consist of a drive, a full brassey and a chip, which is not a very interesting form of golf—in fact, it is the sort of dull golf that women play when playing from the back tees on men's courses.

Here I must mention something which I think really is long overdue on some of our courses, and that is a different position for tees in summer and winter. If a hole is a good two-shot hole in the summer, then it must be a bad hole in the winter, if the tee is kept in the same place. Back tees which should be used in the summer should be out of commission altogether in the winter; otherwise what was a very good two-shot hole in the summer becomes for most players a miserable three-shotter in the winter.

I always think there is a future in an altogether new system of tees. After all, we don't want tee boxes today; we don't use sand, everybody uses pegs, so that tee boxes could be sunk. And on a windy course it would be a wise thing, I always think, in order to keep the holes at their right length, to have a sort of wind-vane which would indicate according to the direction of the wind and its velocity what numbered tee you should use throughout your round. If the wind showed you that three was the number, then you would select number three tee right throughout the round and in this way you would keep the holes good holes from the point of view of two-shotters throughout the round.

I noticed in America a very good plan being adopted in most designs of new courses. This is that the ninth hole finishes at the club-house and you start again your second nine from there. This has many advantages, chief of which is that you can get more people starting in a shorter time than any other way. Especially in England is it an advantage where in the winter there is so little time to play. It is absurd to waste so much time waiting on the first tee when by having the tenth hole near the club-house, you could get off on the second nine quite easily. There is another point also, and that is that about the sixteenth hole; one should be somewhere near the club-house again; nothing is more ridiculous than that when anybody is beaten three and two or round about that figure, they should have to walk miles home instead of being fairly near the club-house.

I think it should be remembered that golf started by the side of the sea; it was played on a type of country called 'links', which is the link between the sea and the land, and today most of our great golf courses are links, but you cannot have links anywhere else but by the seaside. Golf courses inland, however good, can never be 'links'. I think for this reason that trees are not a desirable hazard. After all, let us have all our troubles in two dimensions; that is, on the ground. We want no hazards in the air, such as enormous trees or enormous branches sticking out on our correct path. The only obstacle we should have up in the air and off the ground is the wind, and that is quite sufficient. We do not want any other obstacles. No one, of course, will say anything else but that golf courses and their general condition have improved enormously. And here I would like to draw attention to the fact that in most courses the Green Committee—and, in fact, the Greenkeeper— is practically an amateur. The Greenkeeper generally acquires a certain knowledge, but the Green Committee really has no technical knowledge at all. Here I think it high time that the full uses of the great Green Research Committee at Bingley should be used up and down the country to improve course upkeep and general condition. It is not beyond the bounds of possibility in the future that commercial firms with all their technical knowledge and experience will take charge of courses. They would be under the general direction of the Green Committee as to policy, but the day-to-day work would be done by contract.

I don't think it would be right not to say a word about club-houses—their position, construction, etc., in the future courses to be built. I am not in any way trying to criticize the interior of the golf club-house, as to its food or amenities or anything like that. I am only talking about its position. Now, there are two splendid examples of badly and well-placed club-houses—the first one is St George's, down at Sandwich. Here, for some unearthly reason, the club-house is nowhere near the course. You cannot see the first tee; you cannot hear anybody strike off, nor can you, without the greatest difficulty, see the finish of a match on the eighteenth green. In fact the club-house might as well be at Canterbury twenty miles away for all the intimate connection it has with the game of golf played on that links.

Now let us pass to St Andrews and see what a superbly situated club-house there is there. You can stand in that wonderful sitting-room and see people tee off within ten yards of you; it is a source of constant amusement being there and seeing people strike. From the great window you can see them play the second stroke and practically the whole of the first hole, although it is a good way away. And as you glance to the left you can see people finishing the course, coming up to the eighteenth hole. I cannot think of anything more pleasant or anything that keeps you more in touch with the game than a club-house situated like that. Of course there are other attractions about the great St Andrews club-house, but one of its greatest attractions is its situation, and I hope that that will be considered very, very seriously by everybody making a new course.

And now a word about handicapping. I think here again, in the future, we have got to have some agreed system of handicapping. I notice a funny thing coming into handicapping, and that is that people imagine that the scratch score of a course should be a very low one, on the curious basis that if you have a very low one you will produce better golfers! I have never followed the logic of this, because, frankly, the good golfer reckons his score on the basis of fours, one or two shots over fours or under fours as the case may be. He really is not relating his play to a scratch score at all. It is pure nonsense to make the scratch score of a course very, very low, and the only reason it is made low is to avoid people having plus handicaps. What does it matter whether they have plus handicaps or not? After all, a golf course is for the moderate player. A moderate player does not like stroke competitions at all; he likes bogey competitions, or the more modern Stapleford competition, and here if you tighten up the course too much and make all difficult 430-yard holes bogey four, what sort of pleasure does the moderate golfer get out of it? If it is a bogey five hole and he has a stroke, he has a chance not only of halving the hole but possibly of winning it, but when it is a tight four, even with his stroke, the only possibility he has is of halving the hole against bogey; and if he hasn't got a stroke, he hasn't got the smallest chance of halving it with the ridiculous scratch four.

The great Unions of this country have tried to make a standard score, but here I think they have got into a state of mind in which they want to make all scratch scores too difficult. The idea of making par golf and bogey golf the same is, I think, a pity and thoroughly undesirable, from the point of view of the general amusement of the ordinary golfer. Do not let us forget now and at all times that the game of golf is supported not by the scratch and professionals but by the ordinary moderate golfer of a handicap of about eight to twelve. He is the backbone of the game and his enjoyment must be considered. His enjoyment must be considered more than anybody else's in such a thing as the definition of scratch scores.

No one, I think, will deny that the tools that we use to propel the balls in the various directions that we do, have improved, and probably the most important improvement was the introduction of the steel shaft. Here there is no doubt that the absence of twist in the shaft does not exaggerate some of our bad shots. For instance, a slice with an old hickory shaft will continue as a slice right round its flight, but with a steel shaft the slice will very often start and then not continue. The reason for this is that the head is not left behind the shaft. In a hickory shaft, if you hold the grip and then try to rotate the head you get quite a big movement, but in the steel shaft there is no movement allowable in this way at all. That is no doubt a definite advantage. If there is a disadvantage, it is that in the iron shot, if you hit a particularly sweet shot, it is inclined to go much farther than you expect, and will go a good deal farther than a moderately hit shot; and this was not so apparent, I think, with the hickory shafts. There, if you hit a good one or one not quite so good, the distance was more or less the same, but with a steel shaft, the very accurately, beautifully hit ball does go an extra distance which is sometimes quite alarming.

I am not going to get despondent about golf just because we cannot win the Walker Cup very often. Golf is still a game; you cannot expect people to devote their lives to it. I find in America that some of the amateurs have what is called a patron. The competitor is the perpetual guest of the patron. He tours the country with him, staying at the very best hotels, and devotes the whole of his life to playing golf. Now he may be technically an amateur, but his is a professional's job. Anybody who is devoting the whole of his life to golf is taking the thing up, in my opinion, professionally, even if he doesn't make money out of it. We have had as some of our adversaries in the Walker Cup men who are ex-professionals. Well, that is quite a fantastic idea. Of course, anybody would give up being a professional if he could live a life of luxury with a patron. Not earning actual money by your golf, but really having a delightful time and all the money you want by virtue of the patronage given to you, is a new idea, but it is not at all our idea of amateur golf.

As to our professionals, they must now rate their skill on the basis of level terms with the best in America, and I think a race of young professionals is growing up that will do that in this country. In fact, in the last Ryder Cup we were, perhaps unfortunately, beaten, but still the Americans are very, very good scorers. In America they think of competition, in terms of the Press, and competitive professional golf appeals to the public only if they can do courses in the very lowest scores. I don't think there is much in that. You can always design a course so that it is very easy—the thing is to tighten courses up so that the best player wins, not the man who just shuts his eyes and drives a long ball in any direction and then uses a number eight iron and pops the ball on the green, and holes a long putt. Scores are becoming fantastically low. I call to mind a round—four rounds—by Jim Courrier. The rounds were 69, 67, 68, and 69 and he was only fifth with that. Courses for professionals want very much tightening up, especially for the long driver. If he is a long driver, he at least must go straight to get the advantage of the long drive; otherwise he should be in such rough as to be incommoded very seriously. The concentration that they have indulged in in America on the short game, however, the approach with the wedge and the tremendously accurate putting, is something which the English professional will have to give attention to, at least if he is to rival his American cousins.

As to the Rules of Golf differing in America and here; the differences are quite small and they are tending to disappear, so that we are getting nearer together, and I do hope that in the next few years we shall be able to get one code under which we both can operate. I think we have made mistakes in the past—for instance

255

the barring of the Schenectady putter was quite a silly thing. After all, if you go to America today you won't find everybody with Schenectady putters, showing that they are not the enormous advantage that we thought they were just because Travis won our Championship. If you remember we instantly barred it because he putted so well! He would have putted just as well with anything else. The Americans are not very logical, however, over this club, for the reason that they allow the shaft to come in at the middle of the club for a putter, but do not allow it so to do for any other club! There is practically nothing of major importance in the way the Rules differ today—there is a slight variation about the stymie rule about which debates are always interesting, but the size of the ball is, of course, the thing we must get some agreement on. The present situation is rather ridiculous in that we can play with the American ball and our own here, whereas the American can only play with the American ball and not with ours, when playing in America. Nothing is more important than to keep the game international and to get the Rules pretty well standard throughout the world.

Many clubs are now allowing young people in at reduced prices and putting the price up when they get to a more advanced age. There is a good deal to be said for this. Anything to start the young man playing golf. But I believe the trouble is that so many golf clubs will not cater for the girls—for the women; and after all, if you are a young married man and you want to play golf, it is not a very pleasant thing to go down to some golf club where women are looked upon as almost a weed or an excrescence which is not required anywhere near the place. Many clubs have that outlook on life, and if women are not going to be welcome at golf clubs, they are not going to allow their men to go there. And you've got to remember this, that the arbiter in the home as to how a man spends his leisure is, very largely, the woman; and if she is not going to be made welcome at a golf club, and if she is not going to be allowed to play at a golf club, or if there is not going to be accommodation for them to eat and be merry and social, she is not going to allow her young man there. It is high time that many of the old people in charge of some of the old golf clubs realized that the club has got to be a social thing with women there, so that everybody can find amusement. If you take that attitude, then you will find that many people will come. Even if the women cannot play, so long as they are welcome to be there to lunch and to sit about or to take part in some form of occupation—even a very tiny women's course, or putting green, or tennis courts, or something to amuse them—they will go there; and once you can get a lot of people, then you are on the way to prosperity for your club. But if you look upon the whole thing as something which is only for men as it was twenty years ago, then your club is as good as dead.

There is one bright spot about the future of golf, and that is the spread of the artisan movement. Of course I know that golf started in Scotland where there are numerous courses; where, for a few pence almost, you can play a round; and certainly many people have risen to great eminence in the golfing world by virtue of using these municipal courses upon which anybody can play for a very small amount of money.

Well, now, in the south we have never provided many public courses. There are a few but not nearly enough, but what has happened is that many clubs have an artisan side, and allow artisans to play at stated times. Now here is a very great movement. It is a movement which I think will restore golf to its pristine glory in this country, so that everybody takes an interest in it, and I believe that some of our great players will rise from the artisan ranks. They are as keen as anybody, they start young, they are not worried by the expense, they haven't got high subscriptions, and they carry their own clubs. These are noble people, doing great work, and I can well see in the future a Walker Cup team being composed largely of artisans. The whole movement is well looked after by an organization—there are over 200 clubs in this country of the artisan type and it is, from the point of view of the future, one of the most healthy and invigorating signs that this game is being taken up so enthusiastically by so many more people than was possible when everyone had to be a member of a club. Mark you, I think it is a very important thing that those people who are starting young should be trained to hit the ball more or less in the right way. I am not saying one should be an advocate of the closed face or the open face, but that every player should have the basic idea of the swing and the proper grip. These things should be inculcated into the youth right at the very beginning; otherwise the most astonishing stances and grips are adopted, and once they are adopted they are very difficult to get out of.

I have seen myself, in winter sports, many years ago when nobody knew how to ski, people trying to learn by themselves with the most disastrous results, but now, as soon as you arrive in a winter sports place, you join a sort of school with an instructor, and, before three days have passed, at least you know more or less the basic actions which are expected of you, and everybody has improved enormously. That is the sort of thing we want in golf today, and some of the professionals are doing it—giving a sort of class free for young people. That is really very good service. Cox, of Poole, I think it is, has done very noble work in this regard. Because, really, once they have started; once they have got the idea; once they know they can hit a long ball and they are tickled with the whole game, they are then the slaves of the game; but if they are allowed to start in their own way, missing the ball and hitting it in every direction, and not getting a long ball and generally getting discouraged, well, then they go in for something else. One wants to get them young and make them enthusiastic young. That is the way to get a new race of golfers.

s

257

We now come to what I consider far and away the most important part of an article on the future of golf, and that is the expense.

In the old days caddies cost five shillings a round at the most; golf balls could be bought for two shillings; and most clubs could be bought easily for from six and eightpence to about twelve shillings. Subscriptions to golf clubs were very moderate, from five to eight guineas. Under such conditions golf was not really such a very expensive game if one did not lose too many balls or break too many clubs, in temper. But what is the situation today? Let us visualize a young man thinking that he is going to take up golf as a pastime. He first of all has to get elected to a club and maybe pay an entrance fee. He has to face up to about fifteen guineas a year subscription. And then before he starts, what is his outlay? He has to get a bag and a set of clubs, and in these days a bag and a set of clubs will cost him up to sixty pounds. Then every day, if he plays two rounds, as he will if he is a young man, he will find himself faced with a caddy fee of ten shillings a round— a pound a day—and he will lose many balls, all of which cost three and ninepence. It is not a very pleasing prospect for anybody beginning, and indeed I am perfectly certain that as you look at golf clubs today, you will notice that most of the members are middle-aged and that young people are not taking the game up because it is too expensive. And with the difficulties of transport to various golf courses and the high price of petrol and the scarcity of cars, all these things are having the most baneful effect on the general prosperity of golf clubs. There are, of course, various things that can and have been done—for instance, now we are allowed only fourteen clubs. Frankly, I believe fourteen is still too many because they make a very big load, whereas if we were to limit the number to eight, nobody would be unduly handicapped if they had to carry their own clubs around. With fourteen they are very seriously handicapped. There has now, of course, come in the trolley, an apparatus upon which you put your bag of golf clubs and pull it. These trolleys originated in America and I had the privilege of taking the first one around St Andrews, which caused some consternation among the caddies, but still the idea has grown and grown, and now you will scarcely find a golf club without these things to hire for about two shillings a day. Provided the course is fairly flat and the paths are not too narrow, and the bridges are broad enough to carry the trolley, they are the most admirable things. And do not forget that to pull a thing is much less effort than to carry it, as can be very easily demonstrated by the fact that there is little work required in pushing a big trunk to the station on a trolley, whereas to carry it on your back would be extremely exhausting. That certainly is one point. Another point I very much disapprove of in the present day is having all these matched clubs. When you say a five should be like the six and the six like the seven, I agree there should be a similarity, but nobody is going to convince me that a number one iron and a number eight iron bear any relationship to each other.

258

The fact that they are all paired introduces the most needless expense, because if you want to change your clubs nowadays you have to expend about forty pounds in changing the whole lot of irons, whereas in the old days you could pick up odd clubs at every pro's shop. Whether you liked them or not, it was not a very serious expense, because if you did not like them, they went into the hall or gun-room. But now if you want to change your clubs, it is a major operation involving almost a visit to the bank manager. Nor do I think the golf professional has benefited by this new device of the paired club, because whereas in the old days, as I have already said, one always bought an odd club here and there, now one never thinks of buying even an odd wooden club because wooden clubs are now sold four together at the most enormous expense of about three pounds or three pounds ten a club. Three and ninepence for a ball is really the most exorbitant price. I know it is not the manufacturers' fault or the professionals' fault—a lot of it is due to this awful purchase tax, but there it is, one has got to face up to the situation as it exists.

All these things will no doubt come right, and, frankly, I insist on being an optimist over this game, because it is a game which gives you pleasure if you're bad and it gives pleasure if you're good; it gives you pleasure if you're young and it is the only game which you can still play passably well even when you are over sixty. It is, *par excellence*, the most magnificent game for getting two players, whatever their prowess, level by a system of handicapping. You can handicap the greatest player in the world with a beginner by allotting him a certain number of strokes. There are very few games where you can get a very fine player and a beginner together to have a thrilling game, by virtue of handicapping. That is one of the charms of the game. In most other games the very good player does not even get any amusement by playing somebody who is very bad.

Golf has so many virtues: it is not too strenuous; it is healthy; it can be played, anyhow in our climate, practically the whole year round. It has so many advantages over all other games that it must endure and prosper, and consequently I am an optimist over its future. It was started, I know, in Scotland. We owe all Scotsmen thanks for their great invention, which is spreading throughout the world and will spread more and more, knitting the world together.

Afterword
by
Robert Green

The French have a word for it—eight of them, in fact: Plus ca change, plus c'est la meme chose. *The frequency with which the phenomenon occurs—"It's* deja vu *all over again," as Yogi Berra put it—was brought home to me several times while reading "A History of Golf in Britain". How often that the happenings and developments of today are redolent of those of yesteryear!*

In the opening chapter, Bernard Darwin, the world's first great golf writer, refers to the golf boom of the '80s. He meant the 1880s, but could have meant the 1980s had he been writing now. He mentions the lurking detectives employed to guard Arthur Balfour, then the Irish Secretary, during his rounds of golf in Dublin. If Balfour's contemporary counterpart in Margaret Thatcher's government were to take time off for golf, the same security blanket would have to be thrown around him. Henry Cotton observed forty years ago how "modern" golf courses have tended to over-emphasize the importance of putting; how the rough at the U. S. Open was too penal; and how a "cold chisel and hammer were employed to deepen the face grooves on "standard markings" on iron clubs. Who said Karsten Solheim was a genuine innovator?

Further on in this fascinating review of the pre-1950 golf scene, Darwin recalls the remarks of one Robert Chambers in 1858 after he had been detained longer on the links than he would have liked because of the remarkably slow play of his opponent: "Give me a novel and a camp stool, and I'll let the old chap do what he likes." Those were almost the precise words used by Jose Maria Olazabal about Nick Faldo at the 1990 British PGA Championship. Later we find Henry Longhurst lamenting that "the love of the dollar has sapped the crusading spirit in the great American professionals of today". That's the same sort of sentiment we presently hear from Jack Nicklaus. In making a few common-sense comments regarding the relentless endeavors of the manufacturers to construct a golf ball that goes even farther than its predecessors, Longhurst wrote that "we have successfully lengthened the thirty-odd thousand holes of golf in Britain to fit unsought 'improvements' in one ball instead of fitting one ball to thirty thousand holes." Longhurst's analogy remains an apposite for the issue which today is regularly and inelegantly described as the "obsoleting" of golf courses.

Of course, "A History of Golf in Britain" also demonstrates that we have made progress, albeit sometimes in the wrong direction. Within these pages we learn:

 • *How a hundred years ago it was* de rigeur *to wear a jacket while playing golf.*

 • *How a hundred years ago fourball matches were hardly played at all, with or without a jacket.*

 • *How a hundred years ago even the best professionals, such as Harry Vardon and J. H. Taylor, had to double as greenkeepers.*

 • *How ninety years ago even the likes of Taylor were hitting 3-irons only about a hundred and fifty yards.*

 • *How sixty years ago Jose Jurado may have lost the chance to force a playoff in the Open championship at Carnoustie, because, there being no scoreboards, he played for a 5 on the seventy-second hole and not for the 4 he needed to tie for the top.*

● How fifty years ago the first eighteen holes in the Amateur championship at Hoylake were completed in two hours and twenty minutes.

If you're going to have a conducted tour of the championships past, who better to guide you than Darwin and Longhurst, two men who would perhaps detest the fact that posthumously they are more famous than most of those whose exploits they bring to life with such vibrancy, clarity, distinction and humor! Darwin puts into perspective the deeds of Young Tom Morris by citing how an expert witness told him when asked to compare him with Vardon, "I can't imagine anyone playing better than Tommy did." Darwin describes the final day of the 1914 Open at Prestwick, the year that Vardon and Taylor were vying to win a sixth Open championship and were drawn together. Vardon prevailed, and the crowds were so colossal that a Scottish miner, asked to make room for the players, complained, "Players be ———d! I've come to see."

Longhurst reminds us that in 1957 Charlie Whitcombe was prematurely acclaimed Open champion by the press because it seemed that no one could catch him in the appalling weather that was battering Carnoustie. Somehow, Henry Cotton did. We also have Longhurst's marvellously graphic portrayal of the briefly great American amateur, Lawson Little: "He was a beefy, broad-shouldered young fellow, strong as an ox, with a shut-faced method of driving that led one to fancy he might have done well in a slaughterhouse."

And there is Lord Brabazon of Tara on the future of the game, an essay that includes a timeless suggestion that should be noted by everyone who is concerned about the continuing welfare of golf: "Do not let us forget now and at all times that the game of golf is supported not by the scratch and professionals but by the ordinary moderate golfer of a handicap of about eight to twelve. He is the backbone of the game and his enjoyment must be considered . . . considered more than anybody else's."

Robert Green